T0255978

Fundamentals of Software Culture

Zheng Qin · Huidi Zhang · Xin Qin
Kaiping Xu · Kouemo Ngayo Anatoli Dimitrov
Guolong Wang · Wenhui Yu

Fundamentals of Software Culture

ZHEJIANG UNIVERSITY PRESS
浙江大学出版社

Springer

Zheng Qin
School of Software
Tsinghua University
Beijing, China

Kouemo Ngayo Anatoli Dimitrov
School of Software
Tsinghua University
Beijing, China

Huidi Zhang
School of Software
Tsinghua University
Beijing, China

Guolong Wang
School of Software
Tsinghua University
Beijing, China

Xin Qin
School of Information Science
  and Technology
Shanghai University of Science
  and Technology
Shanghai, China

Wenhui Yu
School of Software
Tsinghua University
Beijing, China

Kaiping Xu
School of Software
Tsinghua University
Beijing, China

ISBN 978-981-13-4483-1   ISBN 978-981-13-0701-0   (eBook)
https://doi.org/10.1007/978-981-13-0701-0

Jointly published with Zhejiang University Press, Hangzhou, China

Printed on acid-free paper

This Springer imprint is published by the registered company Springer Nature Singapore Pte Ltd.
The registered company address is: 152 Beach Road, #21-01/04 Gateway East, Singapore 189721, Singapore

Preface

In human history, after the fast-paced development of science during industrial civilization era, we have been through three important scientific revolutions, each of which brought about abundant fruits and new products. These new achievements accelerated our civilizing process. It is easy to conclude from the past thousands of years' history that by interacting and interfering with each other, science and culture manifest a power driving the wheels of history to the future.

Culture is, in the words of E. B. Tylor, "that complex whole which includes knowledge, belief, art, morals, law, custom and any other capabilities and habits acquired by man as a member of society." Cambridge English Dictionary states that culture is, "the way of life, especially the general customs and beliefs, of a particular group of people at a given time." Terror Management Theory posits that culture is a series of activities and worldviews that provide humans with the illusion of being individuals of value in a world meaning-raising themselves above the merely physical aspects of existence, in order to deny the animal insignificance and death that Homo Sapiens became aware of when they acquired a larger brain. As a defining aspect of what it means to be a human, culture is a central concept in anthropology, encompassing the range of phenomena that get transmitted through social learning in human societies. In Chinese, culture is a word consisted of two characters, *Wen* and *Hua*. *Wen* indicates images and textures with crossing colors while *Hua* means changes and reforms. The earliest literature recording *Wen* and *Hua* put together and used as one word was Zhouyi Bagua: Look at the stars, and see the changes taking place; look at the people, and see the world. What we refer to culture today is usually knowledge and experience accumulated during the evolution of man.

As an emerging industry, software industry developed rapidly in the past decade, under the background of global information technology. People's life is undertaking tremendous changes not only in their working and living but also in the pattern of thinking. The integration of software into civil life fostered a new cultural form, which evolves with the development of software. We name this culture, the culture of software.

Some people regard culture as a uniting bond and spirit of a nation. The five thousand years' experience in China indicates that politics and economics inseparably associated with culture enhance social productivity and promote social progress. To stand out among all countries when scientific innovations are taking place globally, we mainly need to learn from the transforming new culture.

This book takes credit from the view of science and technology development. It analyzed scientific innovations and the social areas promoted following the growth of technology. And according to the fact that information helps to build human cultural form, we proposed the concept and researching method of software culture. The aim of writing this book is to strengthen the connection between software and culture, to replenish knowledge system in the subject of software engineering, and to establish a new area of study that is the culture of software.

Starting from our first calculation and going through the entire history of the growth of computer and software, we introduce categories and utilizations of software. Knowledge relevant to software culture is being revealed before the readers' very eyes, with full representative cases. Constituted of four chapters respectively talking about the history of compute, development of software, classification and software culture, and software applications and software culture, this book is valuable in the studying of software culture.

In order to help readers understand the software culture more comprehensively, this book discusses software culture from three perspectives including historical perspective (the first and second chapter), the range of software (the second chapter), and software applications (the fourth chapter). As we all known, different histories produce different cultures, thus, the first two chapters lay the history foundation of the whole book. Then, the third chapter discusses the width of software culture on the aspect of software classification. Finally, from the perspective of applications, the influence of software culture on society is discussed in fourth chapter.

This book shall be used as a guidebook for university courses or as a reference book for researchers and other learners. As the first domestic book involves software culture, the author tries his best to provide a systematic and accurate work for readers. Considering the limits of resources and human power, we might have committed mistakes in the book. We would be glad if readers help us correct the mistakes.

Beijing, China   Zheng Qin
Beijing, China   Huidi Zhang
Shanghai, China   Xin Qin
Beijing, China   Kaiping Xu
Beijing, China   Kouemo Ngayo Anatoli Dimitrov
Beijing, China   Guolong Wang
Beijing, China   Wenhui Yu
March 2017

Acknowledgements

Professor Qin Zheng determined and finalized the specific content and overall structure. Zhang Huidi and Qin Xin did the final editing. Zhang Huidi wrote the first chapter, Qin Xin the second chapter, Xu Kaiping and Wang Guolong, the third chapter, and Qin Xin and Yu Wenhui, the fourth chapter. Zhang Huidi and Kouemo Ngayo Anatoli Dimitrov proofread the full text.

We would like to thank the people for their help and support for the successful publication of the book. We are thankful for Liu Jianzhong, Zhu Haolong, and Wang Qiaoqi of Shanghai University of Science and Technology who took part in writing the first chapter, and particularly thankful for the contribution of JianZhong Liu. Our thanks also go to Zhao Xuhong of Central China Normal University who took part in writing the first two sections of the second chapter. Thanks equally go to Jing Qiaonan of NanKai University and Zhou Wenhao of Guangdong University of Foreign Studies who participated in writing the fourth chapter.

Besides, thanks also go to Huang Kai of Tsinghua University for proofreading the first chapter, to Wang Binxu and Zhao Yanan of Tsinghua University for proofreading the second chapter, to Li Jingwei, Ye Shuxiong of Tsinghua University for proofreading the third chapter, and to Hu Shaohan, Xu Tao and Liu Jiqing of Tsinghua University for proofreading the fourth chapter.

We acknowledge the support of Springer and Zhejiang University Press showed towards the publishing of the book and also express thanks to the editors for their hard work. The excellent job of these people, their endeavor, and collaborative spirit were the measureless driving force in the process of writing the book.

Contents

Chapter 1
The History of Computing

Abstract Diving back as early as the fourth-century BC, China had been using a prototype of abacus called counting boards. With regard to the current dominance of China as a major contributor to Science and Technology, it is obvious that computing has played a key role in this palmy rise. Nowadays, computing runs throughout the entire of our society, from the granular microscopic level of image processing applied in facial recognition to a bigger macro-standing such as port management automation. Computation has been driving all angles through the whole of our civilization since the apparition of the abacus. Computers have proven to be the best and the pillar of the most top inventions of mankind. They reflected the desire of humans to faster perform heavier and cumbersome computations. Later came the requisition for precision and accuracy of evaluations and as a consequence, computing bolstered up from mechanical and manual where they were engaged in printing manuscripts to digital and finally quantum computers which accommodate humanity in bringing to fruition teleportation and lighting data conveyance from earth to satellites in space. Here and now, computers have grown so powerful and versatile that they impersonate every single corner in our syndicates, hence people call up on I/O peripheral devices and media channels such as joysticks and wireless channels respectively to communicate with them and ease the communication exchange. In the chapter below, we shall sequentially recall how these events made history and shaped our future.

1.1 From History to Culture

Philosopher Karl Marx argues that what distinguish human beings from animals are tools, the product of human's intelligence, experience, and creativity [1]. The evolutionary history of tools is the evolutionary history of human civilization. As the most important tool nowadays, computer, is absolutely a sign of culture. And software, the approaches to control computer, is the crystallization of human wisdom. In this chapter, we will introduce computer, the stage of software, from its history to culture.

© Springer Nature Singapore Pte Ltd. and Zhejiang University Press 2018
Z. Qin et al., *Fundamentals of Software Culture*,
https://doi.org/10.1007/978-981-13-0701-0_1

Our future lies in our past. If we were to explore the development of an object, the best way would be to learn from its history.

The term "Computer Software" has only been around for a few decades. During these years, computer software has evolved from hardware-dependent instructions to code which is portable and platform-independent, and in recent years we have seen the boom in web apps in many public fields and markets. To date, software has gone through many iterations. The underlying factors in the rapid development of computer software are the experience gained in the decades of using computers and the knowledge and methods acquired in centuries of developing computational skills as well as the evolution of humanity itself. We have been able to achieve rapid progress in software development and transformation, which contributes to the formation of the culture of computers and computer software.

If we were to dive deeper into the characteristics and progressions of software in its various ages, further understand the origins of software and software culture, we would need to discuss the history involved. The reason being we would have to trace back to the roots of the history of computation to understand the bond between computers and humanity.

You would probably see history as either boring and tedious or fascinating and educational. But no matter which one it is, let us start our journey down the line of history of computing and computers, and explore the reasons behind the needs of humanity for computers.

This chapter divides the ages of computers based on the most popular method used by scholars worldwide and will attempt to demonstrate it clearly to the reader.

1.2 From Fingers to Computers

Computers have played a significant role in the continued development of human civilization.

From the early ages of wisdom, computation has been a major issue for the society. When it comes to recording events, the growth of production, the development of commerce or the advancements in science and technology, computational power has always been a requirement for these developments to take place. We have evolved from using fingers for counting, using a bargaining chip or an abacus, and have strived to improve the speed, range, and accuracy of our calculations.

It is these efforts to improve our computational power that led us to the birth of computers.

1.2.1   Early Calculation Tools

It is probable that no one will exactly know when humanity first encountered computational problems. Archaeological findings suggest that humans have already used carvings on bones and stone during the Paleolithic age to represent some calculation. As civilization progressed, the calculations needed in the daily lives of people gradually increased in range and complexity. This need forced humans to find more efficient and accurate ways of conducting calculations.

And of course, counting fingers would be the first method of calculation.

Since our fingers are relatively flexible and easy to use, the method of counting fingers is highly influential. Our binary system of counting numbers may have originated from using our ten fingers to count. Even today as we are developing more and more sophisticated computers, using fingers represent pure numbers have assisted people in exchanging numbers. In ancient China, there even existed a practice in which people used fingers to bargain. In those ages, people wore long and loose clothes with spacious sleeves. When bargaining, people would either pull up their overalls or extend their right hand out of their sleeves and would bargain inside sleeves or overalls. During this process, holding the index finger would mean one, both the index finger and middle finger would represent two, if the ring finger gets added, then it would express the number three, and adding the pinky would mean five. For numbers above five, holding the thumb and the pinky would mean six, while holding the thumb, index finger and middle finger would mean seven, the thumb and index finger extended would convey eight, the index finger curved into a hook would stand for the number nine. Therefore, in a bargaining process, one side would be giving finger gestures while the other end would say whether or not to agree on this price. This approach allows the buyer and seller to communicate in a covert fashion to protect their interests. This method was suitable under those circumstances, and also became a cultural feature and had gradually been handed down to this date.

Despite having apparent advantages, counting fingers are also deeply flawed, with a narrow range of calculation and subjected to volatility, meaning the results of the calculation cannot stay preserved for long. It gradually phased out due to its flaws and people began to explore other methods of calculation.

The intelligence of humans has enabled us to use other forms of calculation, such as rope counting and bargaining disks. They have made the calculation for people convenient, and in this collection of calculation tools, the abacus would probably be most familiar with us.

1.2.1.1   The Abacus

The abacus is a traditional Chinese calculating tool and the oldest one that still exists today. It got developed from counting rods and was once the most widely used calculation device worldwide.

There have been many claims about the origins of the abacus [2]. One of which dates the birth of the abacus to 600 B.C. During the final years of Eastern Han Dynasty, the book Shu Shu Ji Yi by the mathematician Xu Yue recorded fourteen ways of calculation, where the 13 ways "Zhu Suan" means the method of calculation of using an abacus. Northern Zhou Dynasty mathematician Zhen Luan noted "the board is divided into three parts, each containing five beads, the top bead has a different color than the lower four beads. The dot with the different color represents five while the other four represents one." Therefore, it suggested that the abacus existed in the Han Dynasty, taking a different form than those found in modern days. But its representation of five using the top bead is identical to the modern abacus. Some historians believe the name of the abacus "Suan Pan" first appeared in the book Jing Xiu Xian Sheng Wen Ji (The Collections of Mr. Jing Xiu) written by scholar Liu Yin in the Yuan Dynasty. The name "Suan Pan" has also appeared in Yuan Qu Xuan (Selected Yuan Dynasty Songs), in the anonymous Pang Ju Shi Wu Fang Lai Sheng Zhai, in which the line went "Being idle, I put my age on the abacus." The Jiu Gui Chu Fa (Nine normalized division) of the abacus equally got found in Cheng Chu Bian Tong Suan Bao written by Yang Hui in 1274 and Suan Xue Qi Meng by Zhu Shi Jie in 1299. The book Jiu Zhang Xiang Zhu Bi Lei Suan Fa Da Quan written by Wu Jing contains a detailed description of the usage of the abacus. The painting Qing Ming Shang He Tu by Northern Song artist Zhang Ze Duan also provides a drawing of an abacus. Apparently, the use of the abacus was widespread during or before Northern Song Dynasty.

In the tenth century, the abacus found in Northern Song Dynasty is not that much different from the ones we use today. Elaborate or simple, they still play a significant role in people's lives, while some have become antiques and still are an integral component of Chinese culture.

With the popularity of the abacus, some common ways of its usage got compiled into rhymes for easy understanding which have been passed down generation to generation. Other books such as Suan Fa Tong Zong have introduced ways of using the abacus to multiply, divide, even to evaluate the square root and cubic root of numbers. During the 1960s, when China was developing its atomic bombs, the leader of the research team Deng Jia Xian used the abacus and hand-tuned computers to evaluate the equations for the bomb, which took them nearly a year to accomplish but laid the foundations for their continued research. If we assume that the abacus is a computer, and the rhymes for using the abacus to perform computing are simple algorithms, then a group of people using the abacus to calculate would be the term "Distributed Computing." They used oral language to convey information and arrived at the result collaboratively, improving the efficiency of using the abacus when compared with using it independently.

In fact, China was not the only one with computational tools such as abacuses. Civilizations around the globe have developed various tools to aid computation. Some were to use fine sand and draw computational components on the surface, called the sandbox type abacus. Some had lines drawn on a board and used the stones to perform computing, called the panel type abacus. Although they vary in form, their underlying principle is similar. These basic calculation tools have once been widely used to simplify computation and helped human civilization progress further. Even now some of these tools are still used as a common way of calculation.

1.2.1.2   Slide Rule

The Slide Rule was once a very popular computational tool apart from the abacus.

The Slide Rule originated in Europe in the sixteenth century [3]. During the Renaissance, the European countries made considerable progress in science and arts. After the Scottish mathematician John Napier introduced logarithms in his book *The Construction of the Wonderful Canon of Logarithms* [4], people realized the importance of logarithms in mathematical research. The Slide Rule got found through this opportunity.

The Slide Rule, most often the logarithmic slide rule, consists of three inter-locked marked rulers and a sliding window, called a cursor. From its introduction in the seventeenth century, it has been the most widely used computational tool and dominated scientific and engineering computations for three centuries. We cannot underrate its contribution towards the development of human society.

The slide rule was introduced between 1620 and 1630, after the publication of the concept of the logarithm. In 1620, The English mathematician Edmund Gunter marked logarithms with a ruler, so he and his colleagues could look up logarithms conveniently. Gunter put the numbers proportionally in a line thus the numbers are denser on the left and more spaced on the right. With this ruler, we multiply two numbers by measuring the length of the logarithm of the first number by a compass, then marking the amount of the two logarithms added. The number pointed to by the compass will be the logarithm of the product of the two numbers.

Using the basis of this ruler, at approximately 1622, the Anglican priest William Oughtred put two wooden logarithm rulers together and created the first Slide Rule. A few years later he invented the circular slide rule.

Oughtred's invention made it possible for people to drop the logarithm table or even not knowing what a logarithm was to conduct multiplication by just moving the slide rule. The slide rule was easy to use and carry around and alleviated people from the numbers.

As the utilization of the slide rule grew popular, people made several changes and improvements to it. In 1814, Peter Roget, while delivering his speech to the Royal Society, introduced the double logarithmic slide rule, allowing for solving the power or root of fractions easily. In 1850, the French artillery lieutenant Amédée Mannheim chose four most commonly used logarithm rulers and added a cursor, forming a newer logarithm slide rule. In just a few years, this variation of the slide rule gradually became frequent with engineers, surveyor-cartographers, chemists, and astronomers.

The manufacturers of the slide rules added more and more symbols and markings so that calculation could be even more convenient, and they introduced slide rules for specific subjects. For instance, the slide rules for chemists had molecular weights while the slide rules for shipbuilding engineers had water pressure formulas, and the slide rules for designers of the atomic bombs had the nuclear decay constant inscribed.

As time went by, the slide rule became paramount. It participated in the construction of the Empire State Building and the Hoover Dam, the design of the suspensions of the Golden Gate Bridge, the automobile hydraulic transmission, the transistor radios and the Boeing 707 airliner. Countless engineers used these simple tools to create engineering marvels.

But after the invention and improvement of the steam engine, our society progressed into the first industrial revolution; they introduced numerous inventions of machinery origin got introduced, and the slide rule got gradually replaced with other machinery and got gradually phased out of daily use. During this period, it was trendy to try to use machine power to replace manual labor. It is also right with computational tools. People began to invent automatons which could handle different functions.

1.2.2 The Mechanical Age

Human society progressed into the mechanical age after the first industrial revolution. In this period people started to search for ways of letting machines replace manual labor to improve the quality of living. It was also during this epoch that many acute builders sensed the possibility of using gears, plates, wheels, shafts, bolts and levers, and other mechanical parts to construct the machine capable of conducting mathematical operations, thus forming a mechanical calculator.

During this period, many powerful tools got introduced, from the first Pascal calculators to the Thomas quad operation calculator. Mechanical calculators became smaller, more robust and convenient, and gradually able to solve addition, subtraction, multiplication, and division, and even getting the square root of a number.

The invention of hand-operated calculators combined machinery and calculation.

1.2.2.1 Manual Calculators

The first Manual Calculator was introduced by the French philosopher and mathematician Blaise Pascal in Paris, 1642 [5]. But the first truly mechanical calculator, the adder Pascaline, was the predecessor of hand-operated calculators. It could do addition and subtraction. Pascal invented the machine to help his father with the calculation of taxes. With the help of missionaries, several hand-operated calculators got made during the Kangxi period in Qing Dynasty.

But before explaining the workings behind the hand-operated calculator, let us take a look at Pascal's personal experience. He was born in a French mathematician's family in 1623. His mother passed away when he was three and was brought up by his father who was a tax official. He expressed interest in science and research very early in his life.

Young Pascal got revered by his father. He watched as his father calculated taxes with difficulty and hoped to make a machine relieve his father of the tedious manual labor. So at the age of 19, he invented the first mechanical calculator in history, which was an adder. This adder had six wheels which represented one, ten, hundred, thousand, ten thousand, and hundred thousand. He would only have to turn the wheel clockwise to conduct addition while turning the wheel in the opposite direction would perform subtraction. The fundamentals of this machine are similar to that of a mechanical watch and got recognized as the precursor of computers.

1.2.2.2   Hand Computer

Odhner's hand computer uses a variable number of gear teeth to replace Leibniz's stepped shaft [6]. Its basic principle is to use the specific transmission ratio of the gear transmission group as a calculation unit for numerical calculation. In the above process, there is no central gear between the wheel and base gear and the number is engraved directly on the tooth number of the gear, then the set number is displayed in the shell window. The mechanical calculation of hand computer is similar to that of abacus theory, only the former is more complicated in structure and is devoid of human participation in computation. The data input is the initial position of preset gear. We obtain the result after a certain number of turns in gear by turning crank according to the relationship between formula configuration transmission ratio and transmission.

In general, hand computer can only do four operations, several squares, cubic number, square and cubic. It is necessary to have a table look up when trigonometric and type in the logarithmic. The process becomes extremely complicated once brackets appear in the calculation. It is needful to use a pencil to record the times in a clockwise and anticlockwise turn. And it has been employed in the research and development of China's first atomic bomb, as mentioned in the previous chapter of the book.

Later, Odhner made bulk-production of his hand computer in the Russian language. After, he prompted numerous foreign companies to follow the suit and conduct mass production by similar structure and principle, of which the most famous is German Cloth Dragon Siwei, who started to put into production from 1892 and had its annual output reached up to 2 million units in 1912.

In the first or 30 years of the twentieth century, hand computer has become the primary human computing device. In fact, as early as the 1880s, a variety of mechanical computer machines employed a keyboard to set numbers. When doing division operation, keyboard computer needs to pay attention to signal bell, which will ring and add the extra deduction once the number of divisors minus outnumbers the set one. In 1905, Gamen, a German who adopted the "leverage principle" in computers with keyboards that have specified number, which reduced computer operation noise and made it unnecessary to pay attention to bell rings when doing division. This computer gained popularity gradually, becoming a mechanical computer with extensive use.

In 1936, Dutch Philips made a binary hand-operated mechanical computer, which got widely utilized for a relatively long time due to its simple structure and convenient operation.

Hand computer is a mechanical computer that uses hand-cranking as its power, which is rather high when paid by the hour. After the emergence of cheap and sharp computers, hand computer withdrew from the stage of history naturally.

Then there is Charles Babbage's analytical machine, which offers the value of a given function calculation via machinery. It can be called as the world's first computer prototype and enjoys a high praise by future generations to date.

1.2.2.3 Analytical Engine

Charles Babbage, born a son of a wealthy banker in Tottenham southwest of England in 1792, later inherited a rich heritage that was all put into scientific research [7].

Babbage showed immense mathematical talent when little. After being admitted to the University of Cambridge, he even found that he had more knowledge of algebra than his teacher. He chose to stay at the university after graduation. The 24-year-old young man got honored by being hired as a math professor of Cambridge "Lukasin lecture." He could have blazed a smooth way filled with success if he had chosen to continue research in the field of mathematical theory. Nevertheless, the unprecedented prodigy chose another rough road that is dangerous and difficult to grade up.

They say that one day when Babbage was with Herschel, the famous astronomer, they found numerous mistakes while remarking on astronomical tables of two departments. Babbage stunned when faced with these mathematical tables riddled with errors, which is the trigger why he thought of developing computer. In his biography—*Passages from the Life of a Philosopher* [8], Babbage talked about one thing that happened in around 1812. "One night, while I went wandering in some Analysis in the Society office of Cambridge University and looked at a logarithm table opened in front of me, a member came in and shouted the moment he saw me, "hey! Did you dream something?" I pointed to the logarithm table and said, "I think that these tables might be able to be used by machines to calculate!"

Babbage's first goal was to make a "difference engine" in the year when he had just turned 20. He got his inspiration from the jacquard loom invented by the French Jaccard. The design of difference engine shows the advantage of program control, which can deal with the calculation process of various functions automatically by the will of the designer. The then industrial technology was so poor that anything, ranging from design drawings to parts processing, should be done by oneself. Fortunately, Babbage loved and knew machining well since he was little. That explains why he was good at every piece of machining. In 1822, Babbage gained his first success after ten years of trying. The machine, made on his own, takes brass as its accessories and steam as its driving force. Also, it enjoys an operational accuracy of six decimals and can calculate several function tables immediately. Later practical application proves that the machine is very suitable for the establishment of mathematical tables in navigation and astronomy.

The joy of success inspired Babbage to write a letter to the Royal Society at that same, asking the government to fund him to build the second significant difference extension with an operational accuracy of 20 decimal. The British government, who saw Babbage's research as profitable, unexpectedly signed the first contract with the scientists. Hence, the Ministry of Finance generously offered 17,000 pounds fund for the large difference engine. Babbage spent 13,000 pounds himself to make up for the shortage of research and development funding.

Babbage's ideal analytical engine should be as follows: First of all, he designed a "storage" with gear for analytical engine, a gear which can keep ten numbers, a total of 1000 numbers with 50 digits. The second part of the analytical engine is the so-called "operation room," the fundamental principle of which is identical with Pascal's reel, but Babbage improved the device, making the calculation of 50 digits plus 50 digits be able to finish in one reel. Also, Babbage also designed a mechanism for data in and out and components to transport data between "memory pool" and "operation room," and even thought about how to make the machine process operate in line with a conditional jump. More than a century later, the structure of modern computer is almost pirated version of Babbage analytical engine, only with the main components of the modern one has been replaced by large-scale integrated circuit. That said, Babbage is well-deserved to be the first person in computer system design.

However, it is no smooth road to put one's idea into reality. There are appropriately 25,000 components in the second differential engine, with the error of principal components less than 1/1000 per inch. It is no simple thing to create such a high precision machinery, even if to adopt nowadays' processing equipment and technology. Babbage entrusted the differential engine to the manufacturing plant of Joseph Clement, the most famous mechanical engineer in British, but the progress of works is very slow. Another 10-year ticked by, but he was still worried about those machines that were unable to operate. And more than half of the integral components were left unfinished. Those colleagues who participated in the trial can no longer hang in there. Hence, they left him one after another. Babbage alone struggled through even when the British government announced to cut off all subsidize for him in 1842. Friends of the scientific community regarded him as bizarre and authority of the Royal Academy such as famous astronomers Eyrie and so on all claimed his differential engine as "worthless." Despite all these, he never gave up.

Someone brought warmth to him on his way of struggling alone. Ada Lovelace Countess, who has been firmly supporting him by offering him money and assistance, later was widely considered to be the first programmer in the world. The punch card program designed by she was used to calculate Bernoulli sequence. We will mention her in the subsequent chapters.

Unfortunately, it did not end up well. The pioneer who had devoted his whole life to computer business died in 1871, with his analytical engine unfinished. However, he left the descendants in computer world a precious legacy that includes 30 different design alternatives, around 2100 assembly drawings and 50,000 parts diagrams and fighting spirit to be self-improvement in adversity and perseverance in the pursuit of ideal. Although Babbage's invention got downplayed at that time, the concept of the then computer that he put forward, i.e., that a computer is a machine operated under external program command, is the prototype of modern computer architecture.

Ten years after Babbage died, the American statistician Herman Hollerith invented the Tabulating Machine. Both the Tabulating Machine and the Analytical Engine got based on the punched card, and the tabulating machine got successfully applied to the census. On this basis, Herman Hollerith set up his company, which is the predecessor of IBM's.

1.2.2.4 Herman Hollerith's Tabulating Machine

In the late 1890s, The United States gained rapid growth in the economy, acceleration in urbanization, rapid expansion in population, making it hard to manage census data. After graduating from Columbia Institute of mining technology, Herman Hollerith had participated in census work and won the appreciation of Walker, the general superintendent, who recommended him to be a mechanical engineer at the Massachusetts Institute of Technology. Then Hollerith researched like mad, in an attempt to develop a machinery automation equipment for census work.

The tabulator designed by Hollerith is as follows [9]: He first makes the census data into "punched tape." There are several items in everyone's survey data, including gender, nationality, and age. He can put all review articles in order and then bore a hole into each person's corresponding element according to survey results. When all columns of punched tape are bored holes, it is a detailed record of the review results. Hollerith described the method in his patent application as follows: use appropriate holes to record everyone's different statistical projects. The holes got distributed on a paper tape that moves forward under the traction control of bootable disk.

After unremitting efforts, Hollerith finally completed the first tabulator in 1884. The machine equipped with a counter, whose circuit gets switched on and complete a cumulative statistic once places with holes go through the surface of the drum-like reel when the punched tape is undergoes traction to move. However, there are still a wealth of problems remain to be improved. Hollerith's tabulator enjoyed an extensive use eventually after continuous failure and improvement and the solving of statistical classification and drilling problems step by step.

In 1888, the tabulator first got applied to the military surgeon in Department of Health and War, New Jersey. Later, it was adopted by other states. In 1889, it got a roaring reputation when exhibited in places such as Berlin and Paris, and hence sold to Europe. In the 12th American census in 1890, it defeated other competitors and thus obtained an extensive use. The census processed a large amount of data, saving about $5 million for the Census Bureau.

For all the achievement, the scientists Hollerith were not satisfied. He made improvements to the machine tirelessly according to different countries and different industries. Therefore, the machine got to march into markets including railway, finance, and retail after being applied to the census, health department, and military. In this arduous process of scientific research, Hollerith applied for four patents and put his market profits into technological transformation. With the improvement of machine function and the constant expanding of application market, he founded his tabulating machine company, the predecessor of IBM, topping in its competitive with a variety of similar products.

Although tabulator almost has no other purposes except for statistics table, its punched card is the first to change the complex data into binary information, which still gets represented in today's computer.

With the thriving application and development of tabulator, the wheel of mechanical calculation keeps going forward. In the 1930s, *On computable numbers, with an application to the Entscheidungsproblem* [10], an academic paper published by Mathematics Journal of London Authority, prompted a sensation at the time. Because the work gets regarded as the theory and model of electronic computer, creating the new era of computer. In honor of the article and its genius author, later generations established "Turing Award," which we call the Nobel Prize in the industry of computer. The genius is none other than Turing.

1.2.2.5   Turing Machine

Alan Mathison Turing, born in outskirts of London on June 23, 1912, showed his outstanding mathematical talents when little. He did average grades in other subjects but was especially high in mathematical ability. After graduating from senior high school in 1931, Alan went to the Cambridge "King's College" to study mathematics and ranked the first in the examination for a degree in mathematics when graduating, winning the honorary title of "Wrangler." In 1936, he won the Smith Prize for his published paper which is on the same subject as his graduation thesis.

It was in 1935 that Turing developed an interest in mathematical logic, which is also known as formal logic or symbolic logic. Mathematical logic, an important branch in logic, uses mathematical methods to study human thinking process and the law of thought. Leibniz, the origin of mathematical logic, believed that mathematical logic, mathematics, and computer were all for the same purpose, that is, to realize the calculation, computerization of human thinking process or even computer. A lot of people tried to describe further what kind of machine should the computer be, what its components were and how should it calculate and work by Leibniz. With volumes of work done by those mathematicians and logicians, mathematical logic got to be developed and improved gradually and had many clearer concepts and frameworks. However, no one can explain the problem before Turing.

In 1936, in his paper—*Analysis on Computable Number and its Application in Decision Problem,* Turing mentioned the theoretical model of computer incidentally. He claimed that reasoning could get transformed to some simple mechanical operation by using the model, which was called as "Turing machine" by later generations [11].

Now everyone gains an understanding of the particular structure of Turing machine. Put in an easy way, the Turing machine is an infinitely long paper tape that got divided into small checks, each with different contents. A machine head, which moves back and forth in the paper tape, has a set of internal state and some established procedures. At each moment, the machine head needs to read a grid information from the current paper tape and then look up method table according to its internal state, so as to output information to the tape grid according to the procedure and switch its internal state to move forward. It will shut down after reading the valid information on the tape.

The computation function of Turing machine appears to be very weak, but as long as there are enough steps and space, it can to calculate any feeble visual and calculable function in theory. Alonzo Church, a well-known American mathematician, and logician, also believed that any calculation could be realized by Turing machine if there is an efficient process. The great proposition gets called as Alonzo Church scheme, which is sometimes collectively referred to as Turing-Church proposition.

The design of Turing machine aroused the attention and wonder of various scientists and laid the foundation for the emergence and development of the modern computer. Later generations have made some computers based on this idea.

With the continuing war throughout the world, all countries put their top technology and invention into war to gain an advantage and enhance their combat effectiveness. It was precisely because of the demands and needs of the war that the first electronic computer got created. Hence, the era of electronic computers kicked off.

1.2.3   The First Generation (1946–1957): Age of Vacuum Tubes Computers

The computers constructed in this period are characterized by using vacuum tubes as the building blocks, using fluorescent tubes or mercury delayed circuits as memory units and punch cards or tapes as input–output interfaces. They were huge, power hungry, slow, having little memory to offer, relatively unreliable, difficult to maintain and extremely expensive to build. In its software level, these computers usually recognized machine code or assembly language. Thus the computers in this era were often used for scientific computation.

The circuit structures of these computers used vacuum tubes and the programs they executed varied from hand-written machine code to symbolic languages. These first-generation computers represent the start of the revolution of computational tools. The binary representation and stored programs structures make up the cornerstone of modern electronic computers.

During the 1930 to 1940s, our civilization buried itself with World War II, prompting disputes globally about the claims of the creator of the first electronic computer.

We believe that the Electronic Numerical Integrator And Computer (ENIAC) developed by the University of Pennsylvania was the first general-purpose electronic digital computer.

1.2.3.1   ENIAC

On February 15, 1946, the first general-purpose electronic computer, ENIAC, was completed [12]. It was a monumental success in the history of computers, reaching new heights in the development of computational technology.

The initial design of ENIAC was introduced by a 36-year-old American engineer John William Mauchly in 1942. The primary objective of ENIAC was to analyze the trajectory of cannon shells. The US Ordnance Department funded the research and development of ENIAC and formed a research group led by Mauchly. The chief engineer was 24-year-old Eckert, one of the members Stan Siegel was a mathematician, and the other was logician Burkes. ENIAC used 18,000 vacuum tubes, 1500 relays, and other devices. It took up 90 m^3, weighed 30 tons, and used 170 m^2 of ground. It was a giant, as it needed a room 30 m long to hold it.

This computer used 140 kW of power and could do 5000 additions or 400 multiplications per second, and was 1000 times faster than relay computers. When ENIAC went on display, it used 20 s to calculate the trajectory of a bombshell compared with the original 20 min. ENIAC uses electrical components to store data, and could complete tens of millions of multiplications every day, which is roughly 40 years for a human to operate a mechanical computer. It uses decimal digits instead of binary digits for arithmetic processing, but has a few vacuum tubes for binary processing, so during its operation, it had to convert a decimal number into binary digits for calculation and convert it back to decimal numbers for output.

ENIAC got initially used for calculating the trajectory of a bombshell, but through changing the wiring could let it solve numerous problems, in doing so converting it to a general-purpose computer. One of its variants got used in the development of the hydrogen bomb.

ENIAC, despite its advantages, is also flawed. It uses externally plugged programs. Whenever it has to undertake a new program, the operators would have to rewire the programs, which would take a few or tens of minutes to hours or days depending on the program. It uses decimal digits instead of binary digits, thus increasing its logical and structural complexity and low reliability.

For a long time, most people have believed that ENIAC was the first general-purpose electronic computer. But in 1973, the US district court of Minnesota, after years of investigation, determined that the design principles of ENIAC came from the Atanasoff–Berry Computer (ABC) machine completed collaboratively by John Vincent Atanasoff and Clifford Berry, so the ABC machine should be the first general-purpose electronic computer.

1.2.3.2   ABC Machine

The reason behind the invention of the ABC machine was to reduce the time that students spent on solving linear partial differential equations.

In the 1930s, John Vincent Atanasoff, an associate professor at the Iowa State University, after seeing his students often having to face a huge amount of computation in solving linear partial differential equations, sought to use digital electronics to help lessen the load [13]. He decided to use electronic components, use capacitors to store data and conduct logical operations based on binary numbers.

It is a pity that both Atanasoff and the University did not realize the importance of this computer. In 1942 Atanasoff was recruited by the Navy and could not attend to the ABC machine. Furthermore, he did not apply for a patent, and the university dismantled the machines for the vacuum tubes.

But whether it is the ABC machine or ENIAC, the first electronic tube computers are significantly flawed and had to be improved. John von Neumann, who also participated in the construction of ENIAC, collaborated with the other participants to research for improvements, and after six months of hard work they reached a satisfactory result. Along with the other participants of ENIAC, von Neumann started an electronic computer with a new architecture, the Electronic Discrete variable Automatic Computer (EDVAC). People refer to the results of von Neumann as the first generation computers.

1.2.3.3   EDVAC

John von Neumann was a Hungarian–American pure and applied mathematician, physicist, inventor, polymath, and polyglot. He was born in Budapest, in October 1903. He was an extraordinary child prodigy in the areas of language, memorization, and mathematics. As a 6-year-old, he could divide two 8-digit numbers in his head. By the age of 8, he was familiar with differential and integral calculus. He received his Ph.D. in mathematics in Budapest at the age of 22 and simultaneously earned a diploma in chemical engineering in Switzerland. After that, he arrived in the United States, and in 1931 he became the first tenured professor at Princeton University.

In 1944, John von Neumann met a lot of computational problems in the first atomic bomb research work in the United States. Thus, he joined the ENIAC research team. In the process of research, Neumann discovered the ENIAC shortcomings of the project and tried to improve them. At the end of June 1945, he wrote the draft plan of EDVAC [14]. The later provided good conditions to improve the computing speed.

Under the guidance of this theory, the construction of EDVAC took a full swing and got successfully delivered to the Ballistic Research Laboratory in 1949. After some adjustments and improvements, EDVAC was fully operational. The computer took 45.5 m^2, weighed 7850 kg and used approximately 6000 vacuum tubes and 12,000 diodes, which is much less than ENIAC while having a similar running speed. During its operation, it could run up to 20 h a day, with an error rate of one error every 8 h on average. It remained in service until 1961 when it was replaced and gets acknowledged as a reliable and buildable computer.

This architecture is still in effect today. Our computers today still uses the principles of stored programs and program control, so nowadays computers are also called von Neumann architecture computers. Von Neumann got honored as "the father of computers" to commemorate his role in developing electronic computers.

First generation computers such as ENIAC and EDVAC use vacuum tubes as the core component and mercury delay lines for storage, then gradually they shifted to magnetic storage devices, using punched cards as input and output devices, and first system software. During this period, the cost of a computer is very high, the skills it takes to manufacture and operate are very complicated, and the size of the machine is huge, so the usage of computers are limited to military and research.

But as science and technology progress, in the next few decades, we will see computers becoming miniaturized, cost-effective, and user-friendly. Next, we will discuss how computers changed from generally military use to an ordinary commodity.

1.3   From Laboratory to Household

With the world's first general-purpose electronic computer ENIAC was born in 1946, we ushered in the era of computer. From the first-generation computers with Vacuum Tubes to the second generation of a computer with transistors, the third-generation computers with integrated circuits, then to now the fourth generation of a computer with silicon chips, computers are smaller, cheaper, and easier to use.

The computer gets along people's life step by step, and it is changing the production and way of life. Step by step, we entered the information age based on computer.

Reviewing the history of computer's development and looking forward to the bright future of the information age can provide us with a good knowledge of the development laws of technology and software.

1.3.1   The Second Generation (1958–1964): Application of Transistors

In addition to the first generation of the vacuum tube computer, the transistor is one of the great inventions in the World War II which gets widely used in the second generation of computers.

In the mid-1950s, the emergence of transistor enabled computer manufacturing technology to gain a fundamental development. With transistors replacing that of vacuum tubes as the primary device of computer, magnetic core or drum as storage, there is a vast improvement of overall performance compared with the first generation computers. At the same time, programming language emerged, such as advanced computer languages including Fortran, Cobol, and Algo160. With the transistor computer applied to scientific computing, it also began to be used in data processing and process control.

Ever since then, we started to use transistors as the components of the computer. Transistors can not only achieve tube functions but also has advantages of small size, light weight, long life, high efficiency, low heat generation, and low power consumption. After the use of the transistor, the structure of electronic circuit got a significant improvement, making it easier to make a high-speed electronic computer. We will start from transistor to talk about the results of this stage.

1.3.1.1   Transistor

As early as 1929, the Engineer Lillian Field had obtained the patent for the transistor [15]. However, due to the technical level at that time, the manufacturing materials of the device did not meet the purity required, leaving the transistor unable to be manufactured.

During the World War II, many labs were in the manufacturing and research on silicon and germanium material, laid the groundwork for transistor's invention. After the end of the World War II, to overcome the limitations of tubes, Bell's lab stepped up the study of solid-state electronics.

In the fall of 1945, Bell laboratory set up a semiconductor research team led by Shockley, the members of which included Bratton and Bardeen. As early as 1929, Bratton began to work in this laboratory. He engaged in semiconductor research for such a long time that he accumulated a wealth of experience. After a series of experiments and observations, they gradually realized the reason of the amplification effect of semiconductor current. Brattain found that there would be significant changes in the present one if we connected electrodes in the surface of germanium, inserts a fine needle and apply some current, and then let another fine needle be as close as possible and apply a weak current. A small change in a weak current will exert an enormous impact on the other current, which is the so-called the "amplification" effect.

Bratton and others also come up with effective measures to realize the amplification effect. They first entered a weak signal between emitter and base. And then it amplified into a strong signal at the output that existed between collector and base. The amplification effect of triode transistor mentioned above enjoys an extensive use in modern electronic products.

The original magnification of solid-state device made by Bardeen and Bratton was approximately 50. Later, they substituted gold contacts with two close (a distance of 0.05 mm) tentacles contacts to create "point contact transistor." In December 1947, the world's first practical semiconductor device finally made its debut. It is capable of carrying the amplification of the audio signal to 100 times in its first test. Its appearance is shorter than a matchstick, but thicker.

Considering the resistance transformation characteristics of the transistor, that is, it gets worked through low input resistance to high resistance output transfer current, Walter Brattain named it as the transformation resistance (trans-resister), later abbreviated "transistor". So far, the transistor has existed for more than 60 years, it has been smaller and more delicate. In many areas, the transistor still plays a significant role.

Besides functions of the vacuum tube, the transistor has more advantages such as small size, light weight, long service life, high efficiency, less heat loss, and low power consumption. All of these tremendously improve the effectiveness of the computer. Therefore, the Bell's laboratories used transistors in the development of computer and the transistor era of computer started.

1.3.1.2 TRADIC

TRADIC stands for Transistor Digital Computer, and as the name suggests this was the first machine to use all transistors and diodes with no vacuum tubes [16]. It was built by Bell Labs for the U.S. Air Force in 1954. The machine consisted of 700 point-contact transistors and 10,000 germanium diodes. During 2 years of continuous operation, only 17 of these devices failed, a vastly lower failure rate than vacuum tube machines of the time. Compared with the first-generation vacuum tube computer, TRADIC meant more robust, more reliable, less expensive, less floor space, and less heat loss.

After the invention of TRADIC, the transistor computer developed rapidly.

In 1955, the intercontinental missile in the United States got equipped with small computers whose main components are transistors. Ten years later, due to the integrated circuit components, the weight of the same type missile was reduced to only 1/100 of the original, volume and power consumption was reduced to 1/300 of the original.

In 1958, the American IBM company made the first computer RCA501 that used transistor entirely. Since the second generation of computers uses transistor logic elements and fast magnetic core memorizer, computer speed increases from thousands of times to hundreds of thousands of times and the main memorizer storage from several thousand to more than 100 thousand. In 1959, IBM Company produced the electronic computer IBM7090 that used transistor entirely. From 1958 to 1964,there is a broad range of development in transistor computer. From printed circuit board to circuit unit and random access memory, from theory of computation to programming language, constant innovation offered an improvement in transistor computer. In 1961, the world's largest transistor computer ATLAS finished its installation.

Compared to the rapid development of computer industry in developed countries, China lagged behind due to the lack of electronic industry and years of wars. At that time, Chinese electronic components factory could not produce the essential electronic components. Crude production equipment and weak technology are major impediments to the development of computer in old China. Reassuringly, as the central government emphasized on computer science and technology, Chinese scientific researchers began to strive for the development of the computer industry.

Finally, Chinese kept up with the pace of the world. In 1958, Chinese Academy of Sciences together with industry departments and defense agencies developed the "BaYi" universal computer (also known as the 103 machine). In 1964, the Chinese people's liberation army military engineering college successfully made the first all-transistor electronic computer 441-B, which established the preliminary foundation for China's computer industry.

1.3.1.3 Chinese 441-B

In September 1961, the deputy director of the department of electronic engineering in Harbin Military Engineering University, Yungui Ci visited the UK. He noticed that the general mainstream development direction of the computer was on the transistor. However, a whole tube computer got designed in China, and he had signed an agreement of the manufacture of it. Yungui Ci felt nervous and shame. He thought that Chinese computer business ought to catch up with the world advanced level. Then, he wrote a letter to China to suggest to stop the development of the electronic computer and to design the transistor computer. Finally, he completed the architecture and basic logic circuit design of transistor computer before returning to China. After returning to China, he wrote a report to related leaders and got support immediately. Rongzhen Nie marshal instructed that it is important to use home-made transistors to develop general computer as soon as possible.

To overcome the quality problems of the domestic transistor, Yungui Ci put forward that the first task of developing the new computer was to improve the circuit in three aspects: the primary circuit, the system reliability design and production processes. First, after repeated experiments, he invented the isolation block type push–pull trigger technology, which is more reliable and more stable and could efficiently solve circuit problems. This invention caused a big sensation in Chinese computer industry at the time. Then, Yungui Ci developed a set of scientific testing methods of the domestic transistor and carefully tested every transistor. Since then, they have developed 8 bits and 20 bits arithmetic units and core memory models. They finally finished the 40 bits machine.

At the end of 1964, they used local semiconductor components developed Chinese first general electronic transistor computer. In February 1965, this computer got international identification. It could continuously run 268 h without failure, and its stability reached the international advanced level. At the end of 1965, they successfully developed 441 B/II computer.

In January 1966, Yungui Ci led Chinese computer delegation to the UK and visited British computer companies and British national physical laboratory. They saw many transistor computers in the UK. From then on, Yungui Ci began to design the new transistor computer structure. Although he had a hard time in the "cultural revolution," he still came to work in the laboratory to carry out more research. At the beginning of 1970, 1970 B/III type computer got successfully developed. This computer was the first computer with a time-sharing system and the standard library in China and could also compile assembly language and FORTRAN computer language.

Since then, the development of computer did not stop. Nearly 10 years later, the third-generation computers showed up, which was the application of integrated circuits.

1.3.2 The Third Generation (1965–1970): An Era for Small and Medium-Scale Integrated Circuit Computers

In the middle of 1960s, with the development of semiconductor technology, integrated circuits were successfully manufactured. Small- and medium-scale integrated circuits became the main components in computers, and semiconductor storage gradually got used as the central storage devices. Compared to the previous phase, the volume, as well as the power consumption (while calculating) of a computer got significantly reduced. Due to the reduction of solder joints and connectors, computers' reliability got improved further. Regarding of the software, with standardized programming languages as well as the man–machine interaction like Basic language, computers' applications got further expanded.

In this chapter, we firstly introduce the integrated circuits.

1.3.2.1 Integrated Circuits

In 1959, the early stage of the development of the second generation computers, J. Kilby at Texas Instruments had first proposed the integrated circuits with multiple transistors, diodes and resistors combined on a silicon plane [17]. Although it did not look beautiful, the fact proved that it could perform a much higher working efficiency than those discrete components. The invention of the transistor made up for the shortage of tubes, but very soon engineers just found another new problem. To produce and use electronic circuits, engineers had to personally hand-assembled and connected a variety of discrete components, such as transistors, diodes, capacitors and the like. Obviously, this approach was very much impractical. Therefore, Kilby suggested the design of the integrated circuits.

After that, the founder of the Fairchild (Fairchild Semiconductor, The Power Franchise) Robert Noyce proposed a new model named "semiconductor device and lead structure". In 1960, the Fairchild produced the first integrated circuit ready actually to get used. Eventually, the method proposed by Noyce got extensively applied in the mass production of integrated circuits, as a practical technique. Both Kilby and Noyce are awarded the "National Medal of Science" in the States and got recognized as the co-inventors of the integrated circuit. After several years' arguing, the patent of the integrated circuit got finally granted to Kilby and Noyce, and integrated circuits indicated the future developing direction of computers.

Developments in this period also included the use of the operating system which realized the simultaneous operation of several different programs under the control of the coordination center of the computer. Therefore, computers produced from 1964 to 1972 got called IC computers.

The integrated circuit is a revolution in electronic computers' development. It has fundamentally changed the manufacturing process of the electronic computer. It can integrate tens of thousands of electronic components on the thumb size of the silicon wafer, which makes a faster memory and processor of computers and reduces the costs. Small companies could use the computer at this time.

In 1964, Dr. Moore published a three pages essay, predicted that the number of transistors in integrated circuits could be doubled every 18 months at a steady speed, and the momentum will keep for decades. It is known as "Moore's law," which becomes "the first law" of emerging electronic industry.

Although integrated circuit has distinct advantages, it did not get applied in industry for a long time. Instead, it aroused the interest of military and government departments first. In 1961, Texas Instruments developed the first computer based on integrated circuit, i.e., the so-called "molecular electronic computer" for the United States Air Force. National Aeronautics and Space Administration (NASA) also started to show a keen interest towards the technology. At that time, both "Apollo navigation computer" and "star monitor detector" adopted integrated circuit technology.

In 1962, Texas Instruments developed 22 sets of integrated circuits for "militia-I" and "militia-II" missile guidance systems. It was not the only first time that integrated circuit got applied in missile guidance systems, but also the first time that transistor technology got applied in the military field. By 1965, the U.S. Air Force has surpassed NASA, becoming the world's largest consumer for integrated circuits.

Application of the early development of the integrated circuit is the most important field of computer technology. The development of the third generation of computers got based on integrated circuit technology, the various hardware components of the microprocessor, memory to input and output devices, is the crystallization of the integrated circuit technology.

During this period, one of the most famous computer was designed by IBM in 1964 the IBM System/360.

1.3.2.2   IBM360

In 1995, Bauer science prize, the one with the largest award amount in the United States, was granted to a computer scientist—Frederick Phillips Brooks, who was a professor at North Carolina State University, for the first time. He was known as the "father of the IBM360" since the 1960s. Sources also present that there is another computer expert—Dr. Gean Amdahl who is called as "the father of IBM360". He claimed to adopt large computer systems IBM 360 made by integrated circuits, which occupies a unique position in the history of computer.

In the early 1960s, faced with fierce competition in the computer industry, Thomas, Watson Jr., the President of IBM, gave an instruction to develop computer series composed of integrated circuit, so as to eliminate outdated transistor machine. Vincent Lilson sent a car to send engineers to a motel in Connecticut to concentrate on work the moment he received the order. On December 28, 1961, a report as long as eight pages was finally completed, the bold headline of which prominently reads "electronic computer with IBM 360 system". The new computer system takes 360 as its name, representing a circle is 360 degrees. It not only represents the general application of 360 computer from the industrial and commercial field but also indicates IBM's purpose, i.e., to provide users with an all-round services. Lilson made a rough estimation of the costs: $0.5 billion for development cost, $1 billion for production equipment investment and $3.5 billion for selling and leasing underwritten, which means 360 planned a total of $5 billion investment! Mind you; it only took $2 billion for the United States to develop the first atomic bomb in the "Manhattan Project".

However, Watson Jr. embraced the bet. To develop IBM 360 series models, IBM recruited more than 60,000 new employees, created five new plants and invested billions of dollars. On April 7, 1964, IBM Company's $5 billion "big bets" won IBM 360 computer series for the company at the same time old Watson's company celebrated its 50th anniversary after four years of ups and downs. IBM 360 series, holds a total of six types of large, medium, and small computers. Forty-four new types of equipments are put in the big hall in a standard order, ranging from the weaker 360/51 minicomputers to 360/91 supercomputer 51 times that of 51 type. All of them make a homogeneous "compatible machine." At the then-computer market, software and peripheral equipment were unable to be used interchangeably, which brought great inconvenience to users. "Compatible machine" stands for all the big difference in its type compared with that of 360 computer series. They have to be capable of using the same method to process the same instruction, enjoy the same software, configure the same disk drives, tape drives and printers, and can be able to connect with each other to work. It was a great concept transformation at the time, bringing technological progress to modern computer development. So far, it still plays a huge role.

IBM 360 sold 32,300 units computers within 5 years, creating a miracle in the history of computer sales. Soon came to existence the IBM 370 machine compatible with the 360 computer, among which the most high-end is 370/168 model, whose computing speed has reached up to 2.5 million times per second.

IBM360 was a sign of the third-generation computers. Compared with the second-generation computers, in the aspect of hardware, the small-scale integrated circuit was the central part of the third-generation computers, a high level of integration of semiconductor memory got used in the main memory. Also, the third-generation computers became smaller and lower power consumption. And in the aspect of software, there are database systems, distributed operating systems, etc. Software development has become a huge industry nowadays.

At this time, computer language has already transformed from machine oriented language geared to the human oriented language and high-level language comes up. Some of the popular languages are being used by the majority of computer manufacturers and solidified in the computer's memory, such as the BASIC language. In addition to BASIC and FORTRAN language, there are more than 250 high-level languages such as COBOL, C language, DL/I language, PASCAC, ADA, etc.

In this era, the small computer got widely used. In addition to the IBM System/360, PDP-8 machine, PDP-11 machine and VAX-11 made by DEC also had played a great role in the promotion of the computer. In addition to the United States, the Soviet Union also launched EC ЭBM system, and CM ЭBM system. The ICL of UK also introduced a general computer ICL 2900. Computer development in Europe and the United States was getting better and better, while Asian countries were relatively backward.

And as Moore's law predicted, with time goes by, the chip can hold more and more electronic components. Until 1980s, VLSI can accommodate hundreds of thousands of parts. Then the giant of ULSI expands numbers to millions of level. It heralded a new era of computer—the arrival of the fourth generation of computer.

1.3.3   The Fourth Generation (1971 and On): Application of Large-Scale and Very Large-Scale Integrated Circuits

The elements of the fourth generation computers are the same with the third generation integrated circuits. However, the integrated circuit improved it greatly; it contains hundreds of thousands to millions of transistors, known as Large-Scale Integrated Circuit (LSI) and Very Large-Scale Integrated Circuit (VLSI).

With the successful production of large-scale integrated circuit and its application in the computer hardware manufacturing process, compared to that of the third-generation one, the volume of the computer gets further reduced, and its performance is further improved. As an internal storage, a bulk semiconductor memory with higher integration develops parallel technology and multi-machine system, prompting the emergence of reduced instruction set computer, engineered and general software system and program design automation. Microcomputer further expands its scope of application in the society, with computer omnipresent in every field.

The 1971 INTEL4004's release is a significant achievement on the LSI development process, also marks the first generation microprocessor coming out.

1.3.3.1   Intel 4004 Microprocessor

Intel 4004 microprocessor is the world's first commercial computer microprocessor. Just as the advertisement of 4004 schematic circuit diagram put it, it is "a landmark work." It integrates 2250 transistors, the distance of which is 10 μ. It can process 4-bit data, with 60,000 times operations per second and operating frequency of 108 kHz, the total cost of which is less than $100. Gordon Moore, chief executive of Intel, calls 4004 as "one of the most innovative products in human history".

Intel 4004 microprocessor Intel got originally designed for the Japanese company called Busicom for its calculator, shown in P1–14. However, due to technical reasons, Intel's delayed delivery made Busicom quite angry. At the same time, the competition in the calculator field was increasingly fierce, when Intel fully completed Intel 4004 chip design and sample production, Busicom required Intel to discount, and they attached a requirement: Intel can have a free sale of 4004 chips except for calculator market. So Intel Company completed the transition from a single memory manufacturer to microprocessor manufacturer.

The original Intel 4004 use microprocessors golden white ceramic package, later it uses the regular black ceramic and plastic packages (Intel microprocessor production's first convention) Golden white pottery is divided into ordinary white pottery, gray traces of white pottery, and five departments of white pottery. Among them, the gray trace white ceramic version is the most precious. Intel has also developed 4001 (dynamic memory DRAM), 4002 (read-only memory ROM), 4003 (Register) and 4004; they can architect out of a microcomputer system.

Integrated circuit developed in super-large-scale direction since 1971. With the advance of history, integrated circuit has already given way to the microprocessor. Intel's 4004 microprocessor, though not the first commercial microprocessor, is the first computer component that sold on the open market. According to Hoff, the computing power of 4004 microprocessor is no worse than electronic digital integration computer but is much smaller than that of ENIAC. Thus came the era of microcomputer based on a microprocessor.

At this time, more and more powerful microprocessors continue to emerge. In 1972–1973, the 8-bit microprocessor come out, and first appeared Intel8008. Its performance may not be perfect, but it demonstrated the infinite possibilities that drove many manufacturers to compete, the microprocessor has a dynamic development. Later appeared Intel8080, MOTOLOLA6800, and ZILOG's Z-80.

Since 1978, 16-bit microprocessor has emerged, the microcomputer reached a new peak. INTEL, MOTOROLA, and ZILOG Company have continuously introduced new products with the microprocessor innovation. Especially INTEL Corporation, after the introduction of the 8086, has successfully developed 80286, 80386, 80486 Pentium, Pentium II and Pentium III. It is because of these microprocessors paving the way to the emergence of many traditional computer in this era.

From the first large-scale use of the logic elements and memory computer as LSI, the United States' ILLIAC-IV computer successfully developed ICL2900 computer. Following was Fujitsu's M-190 machine, and the University of Manchester in 1974. In 1976 was the successful development of DAP series machines. In 1973, Germany's Siemens, France, and the Netherlands, Philips international information company jointly set up a unified data firm. Together they developed the Unidata7710 series machines. The foreign developed countries therefore started to develop the new generation of computers.

In 1977 United States APPLE's Apple II computer was one of the earliest personal computers, as the first microcomputer with color graphics, it is priced at $1300 and start to sale in June 1977, the processor is 1 MHz, Memory is 4 KB. This computer in the United States caused widespread sensation, and led the company to become the US microcomputer king. In 1981, IBM introduced the first personal computer PC, creating an IBM PC computer standard, and win the Apple computers standard in the fierce competition to become the ultimate industry standard, that is the beginning of a new millennium.

1.3.3.2 IBM PC

On August 12, 1981, IBM launched the world's first personal computer 5150, which marks the reality of personal computer into people's work and life, and more the beginning of a new era.

At that time the personal computer is priced at $2880. The first IBM PC uses Intel 4.77 M 8088 chip, is only 64 K of memory, using low-resolution monochrome or color monitor, with the optional cartridge tape drives, having the two-sided 160 KB floppy drive, and using Microsoft's MS-DOS operating system. The product is characterized by comprising a number of innovations. Each screen can display 80 characters in the column, with the case-character keyboard, you can expand the memory, the parts can be purchased from other manufacturers, other personal computer manufacturers can follow IBM's standard production models to produce IBM compatible computers, which is called "clones" and so on.

5150's design abandoned complex parts from the IBM standard workflow, which is to fight with the popular Apple II. IBM 5150 achieved great success, listed only one month, and its orders reached 240,000 units.

Although it is not IBM that first invented the desktop computers, nor HP who claims its first use of the "personal computer" term in 1968. Many analysts and observers believe IBM PC 5150 is less good than the Apple's Apple II and other systems, but IBM 5150 is widely regarded as the ancestors of modern personal computers, it was later established as the industry standard IBM PC standard and laid the foundation for the future promotion of personal computers.

With the invention of the personal computer, the computer, on the one hand, began marching toward miniaturization. From the desktop to the laptop computer, to the emerging tablet computer, miniaturization of the computer is popularizing step by step in people's daily life, as bringing a variety of convenience. Meanwhile, the computer is also developing towards the direction of giant size, trying to improve the calculation and data processing capabilities of the computer, make a greater contribution to high-tech and cutting-edge technology research field.

1.3.3.3   China's First Million Integrated Circuit Computer

In 1973, Yang Fuqing developed China's first million integrated circuit computer—150 machine operating system successfully, which was China's first multi-operating system designed by him.

Early this year, China's successful first million integrated circuit electronic computer, which was developed successfully by relevant units including Beijing University, Beijing cable plant and burning department, enjoys 48 bits word length and 13 KB storage capacity. In January, *The First Professional Meeting for Electronic Computer*, which was held by the fourth Ministry of machinery industry in Beijing, determined to make the development of computer series as the current development direction. In May of the same year, the computer DJS100 was developed successfully with self-design hardware and compatible software based on 16 bits minicomputer technology of American General Data Machine Company. As of 1973, there were altogether 250 sets of digital computers, 323 sets of Analog computers, 133 sets of machine tool control equipment, 1520 sets of desktop computers, all of which were applied in more than 30 industries.

1.3.3.4   Super Computer

The concept of "supercomputing" first appeared in the report in *New York world* concerning Columbia University's large tabulator constructed by IBM in 1929 [18]. Super computer commonly refers to as the computer that is composed of hundreds of thousands or even more processors (machines) that can calculate ordinary PC, and that the server is unable to complete large and complex subject [19].

If compare the operation speed of conventional computer to that of adult's walking speed, then super computer achieves the speed of a rocket. Based on such operation speed, people can predict and explain natural phenomena that cannot be tested previously via numerical simulation.

In 1975, American Cray Company launched the world's first supercomputer—Cray-1. This is a vector computer that can not only do vertical and horizontal processing but also can do vector operation and scalar operation. It inherited the style of Cray CDC7600 and CYBER76, with 12.5 ns clock cycle, 64 bits machine word length. It can execute approximately 50 million instructions per second on average, and 80 million floating-point operations when in efficient state. If the procedure adapts to the characteristics of adaptive vector calculation, the speed will be higher. Like a supercomputer, its speed increases five to ten times that of personal computer IBM 370 unveiled at the same period, while cost performance being three or four times that of the latter.

This machine compact is assembled well, and is the smallest one during such supercomputers, only about 6.5 m^2. The software is an operating system and Fortran compiler system. Its function is adamant, but it is not complicated. Craig said: "I designed the same computer as the design of sailboat I strive to be simple." Cray-1 has only limited command of scientific computing; instructions are simple and easy to master. Most of the central processor have only an integrated circuit chip, power supply, and cooling design are very simple.

The launch of the supercomputer gained a great success. U.S. Department of Defense officials called Cray as "the mastermind of American nation." For commemorating the leading computer practitioners in the computer industry, people in that industry honored Cray as "the father of mainframe computer".

After that, supercomputer became the most prominent tool showing the scientific and technological strength of a country. It started to act well in high-tech fields such as weather forecasting, genetic analysis of life sciences, nuclear industry, military, and aerospace. So that the National scientific and technological elites therefore engaged in research and development of exascale supercomputers.

Indicators of supercomputers have such provisions: First, the computer's processing speed should be more than 10 million times per second; second, having the storage capacity of 10 million or more. Development of supercomputer is an important development direction of the computer. It marks a degree of national development level of science and technology and industrial development, reflecting the strength of the country's economic development. Some developed countries are investing a lot of money and workforce to research and developing the mega computer which can reach computing speed up to several hundred billion times.

Eight years after the United States launched the first supercomputer, China launched its first "Galaxy" supercomputer systems. It is an important means of petroleum, geological exploration, and long-term numerical prediction, satellite image processing and large-scale computing research topics and national defense construction, and plays a crucial role to accelerate China's modernization. Currently, only a few countries can develop a giant computer. "Galaxy's" successful development makes us two years ahead of the goal of the National Science Conference in 1985 high-speed supercomputer will be put into use, making that our country stepped into the ranks of the world supercomputer countries, marking China development of computer technology have stepped into a new stage.

November 1983 China's first billion times giant computer, named "Galaxy", was born after 5 years at the National Defense University. Its successful development announced to the world: China has become a country after the United States, Japan, and other nations to design and manufacture supercomputers independently.

After less than a decade, in November 19, 1992, the "Galaxy-II" 10 billion times supercomputer developed by the National Defense University in Changsha had been through the national identification.

Thus, our country has achieved a leap from vector supercomputers to parallel processing supercomputer, becoming a national after the United States, Japan, and the third to complete building one billion times supercomputer. In 1994, the Galaxy II supercomputer was put into formal operation at the National Weather Station, for the use of the medium-term forecast for the weather.

On June 19, 1997, the "Galaxy-III" parallel supercomputers developed by the National Defense University in Beijing had been through the national identification. The machine uses a distributed shared memory architecture, for large-scale scientific and engineering computing and large-scale data processing, primary word is 64, having a peak performance of 130 billion times. The machine has some domestic leading technology; integrated technology has reached the international advanced level.

Currently, only a few countries in the world have mastered the technology to develop high-performance supercomputers. The successful development of supercomputers "Galaxy-III" making China reaching the world advanced level in this field.

In 2000 Galaxy IV supercomputer was composed by 1024 CPUs and has a peak performance to 1.0647 trillion floating-point operations per second; the indicators have reached the international advanced level, which enables the development of China's high-end computer system to arrive at a new level.

"Galaxy" series of supercomputers is now widely used in weather forecasting, aerodynamic experiments, engineering physics, petroleum exploration, seismic data processing, and has produced tremendous economic and social benefits. National Meteorological Center will use "Galaxy" supercomputer for the mid NWP systems, making China one of the few countries able to publish 5–7 days mid NWP.

Over time, various countries are gradually paying attention to the development of supercomputers, faster and more powerful supercomputers are also emerging. China's "Galaxy", "Dawn", the United States' "Sequoia," "Titanic", "Blue Gene" series, Japan's "Jing", Germany's "Juqueen" and so on, the major countries are always making development and improvement of supercomputers. Every year, the International Supercomputer Conference will assess the world's supercomputers and published the latest global Top 500 supercomputer list. United States, Japan, China, Russia, and other countries are on the list, fighting for the first position. In 2013, the International Supercomputing Conference released the 41st session of the World Top 500 supercomputer rankings, developed by the Chinese National Defense University's supercomputer, "Tianhe-2", sustained a computing speed of among the 339 million billion times per second, which is nearly twice faster than last year's first. Therefore, it wins the first place.

At the same time, the super computer has also entered into local colleges and universities for teaching and scientific research. On October 23, 2015, the super computer "Pi" system joined into online operation in Shanghai Jiaotong University. The use of GPU technology acceleration will support high-end research projects such as the so-called "artificial sun" inertial confinement fusion project. We say that "Pi" peak performance can reach up to 263 trillion times, ranking the 158th in the latest global TOP500 list. The system, designed and constructed by Langchao Company, will focus on support for the teaching and scientific research of Shanghai Jiaotong University. Once the system goes online and becomes the super core support platform for "IFSA inertial confinement fusion science and application of Collaborative Innovation this Center", becomes the fastest supercomputer in China.

At the same time, exascale computing has become the development direction of the super computer. The U.S. Department of Defense Advanced Research Project Agency (DARPA) is redoubling its efforts to develop exascale (the 16th power of 10) supercomputer, which can conduct exaflop floating-point operations per second, about 1000 times that of world's current fastest computer Jaguar. Darpa notes in a statement that the ultimate goal of the research program is to "make the computer have a radical transformation."

According to BBC reports, at present, the computing speed of supercomputer Jaguar in the United States Department of Energy Oak Ridge National Laboratory is 1.75 kM petaflop per second (1 kM petaflop is to have floating-point operations to the 15th power of 10 s). Darpa, who has authorized the Intel Corporation, Nvida Corporation, Massachusetts Institute of Technology and Sandia National Laboratories to work together to create the super computer, expects to develop prototype successfully in 2008. Darpa said that the new super computer is mainly used to analyze the mass data generated by military equipment and sensors. The new research project got called as "universal high performance computing (UHPC)" aiming to break the shackles of Moore's law.

Also, according to Intel's Web site, Intel will work with the French Research Institute to establish the European Exascale research and development (R&D) center to develop super computer with exaflop level together.

As early as 2006, Japan education ministry was engaged in developing a new generation of super computer, in the hope of developing the first exascale super-computer in 2012, with 12.3 billion yen as its predetermined R&D costs.

To reach exascale per second in super computer operation speed is not only a milestone in computer development history but also will enable many disciplines to leap to a new height. Scientists and doctors to better understand volumes of data, scientists to develop new technology to make cloud computing achieve a certain scale to allow large distributed computer to simulate reality. It can also help researchers to create three-dimensional visual images rather than video game to run the endless of putative scenario, so as to increase the accuracy of details, just as the "holodeck" described in the film *Star Trek Series* and so on. Exascale supercomputer systems will also distinguish itself in high-resolution climate model design and manufacturing, bio energy products development, smart grid research, and development as well as the melting energy design prowess.

With the growing computing power of supercomputers, how we use it to the maximum extent of their ability, and how to design them better and fully utilize the outstanding performance of supercomputers algorithm are the development directions which most countries constantly strive to.

1.4   Peripheral Devices of Computer

Along with the booming of the computer, to make more people use computers more conveniently in daily life, to facilitate computers and human interactions, to realize more functions, many external equipment adherences to computers come into being as well.

The computer people used ordinarily are equipped with basic configurations keyboard, mouse, computer monitors, mainframe and various Universal Serial Bus (USB) flash drives as external storage to store huge volumes of data for us. Multimedia devices like speakers, sound card bring us rich and colorful enjoyment of multimedia. Network devices such as network card (network interface controller) and router bring us into the world of Internet. A great many computer external equipment makes our life even better. However, these are unimaginable back to the time first computer being produced. It is inline with the trend of history, comply with the development of computer culture, dose these configurations develop together and become an inseparable part of computers, imperceptibly popularize in people's life.

The computer people used ordinarily are equipped with basic settings keyboard, mouse, computer monitors, mainframe, and various USB flash drives as external storage to store huge volumes of data for us. Multimedia devices like speakers and sound cards bring us rich and colorful enjoyment of multimedia content. Network devices such as network card (network interface controller) and router bring us into the world of Internet, a great many computer external equipment makes our life even better. However, these are unimaginable back to the time first computer being produced. It is inline with the trend of history, comply with the development of computer culture, dose these configurations develop together and become an inseparable part of computers, imperceptibly popularize in people's life.

Following we categorize them and introduce their process of development in order.

1.4.1   Input Devices

In the early stages of electronic data processing systems, punched cards were widely used. A punched card is a piece of stiff paper that contained either commands for controlling automated machinery or data for data processing applications. Both commands and data were represented by the presence or absence of holes in predefined positions. As have mentioned above, Herman Hollerith invented the recording of data on a medium that could then be read by the machine. After some initial trials with paper tape, he settled on punched cards, developing punched card data processing technology for the 1890 US census.

However, punched cards have its limitations. Punched card is time-consuming, cumbersome, and difficult to save and the data storage capacity is relatively small. Therefore, with the passage of time and the development of science and technology, keyboard, mouse, scanner, and other more convenient and fast input devices continue to produce. Due to space limitations, we only introduce the familiar keyboard and mouse.

1.4.1.1 Keyboard

The keyboard is one of our most common computer peripherals. It remains a question mark as to when was the first keyword produced, but the long history of the keyword is known to all everyone. As early as 1714, people in Europe and the United States began to invent a variety of typewriters, which can be said to be the prototype of the keyboard.

With the development of the computer, someone began to introduce the keyboard input tool into the computer to serve as a kind of external input mode of the computer. In the early AT/XT PC era, most of the keyboard was 83 keys and adopted mechanical design basically in its internal design. A mechanical keyboard is a relatively sophisticated method that is easy to implement. It is similar to metal contact switch principle, which can obtain keyboard input signal through the connection and blackout of electric shock. The advantage of this keyboard is that it is easy to design and mature in relevant technology, and easy to repair and clear in tactility. However, its shortcomings are obvious, i.e., it is easy to produce a lot of noise during the input process.

With the progress and development of computer technology, 83-key was unable to meet people's demand for fast input. Therefore, the keyboard keys began to increase, and new keyboard standard for 101-key began to emerge. The added key is convenient for people to use the keyboard to input. In the meanwhile, a variety of software enhanced their functional keys by keyboard standard, which enriched the application method of the keyboard.

The emergence of capacitance changed the design principle of the keyboard. Capacitance keyboard adopted a control method similar to capacitive switch to change capacitance through changing the distance between electrodes via keyboard, which conditions to allow oscillation pulse to go through temporarily. The keyboard eliminates the shortcoming of loud noise in mechanical keyboard and will have a little loss during long-term usage. As for those that use the capacitive keyboard of high quality, it is far better than that of mechanical one in tactility, which can meet the needs of a variety of users to a greater extent.

After that, with the launch of Windows 95 along with the increasingly powerful and sophisticated graphical interface, the number of keyboard keys began to increase again, resulting in the birth of Windows keyboard commonly used nowadays, i.e., 104-key keyboard. The keyboard adds two Windows keys and an attribute Association key by the original one, allowing for more convenient and efficient operation of Windows. Most of the keyboards we use today are of the same type.

To make keyboards easier to use, the wireless keyboard was invented.

In fact, the arrangement of keyboard keys we use is not the most scientific. Why does the keyboard become so? Let us go back to the typewriter era.

In the early age of typewriter era, the productive power is not very high. To extend the lifespan of the typewriter and prevent card slot problem caused by typing too fast, the "father of the typewriter" Christopher Latham Sholes invented the QWERTY keyboard [20]. He placed the most commonly used letters in opposite directions, which can slow down typing speed. With people widely received this keyboard, the QWERTY layout has become the mainstream.

After that, there are many people tried many more scientific keyboard layouts, such as DUORAK keyboard and MALT keyboard. Although they can reduce finger exercise and improve typing efficiency, they still failed to replace the QWERTY keyboard layout.

1.4.1.2 Mouse

Although mouse now seems to be a computer peripheral that we take for granted, it did cause a huge sensation in the IT sector when the first mouse was unveiled.

On December 9, 1968, at the world's largest professional technology institute of Institute of Electrical and Electronics Engineers (IEEE) conference, Dr. Douglas C. Engelbart showed the world's first mouse (there was no "mouse" name at that time) [21]. It is a wooden box with only one button and two mutually vertical rollers inside. Its working principle is to use rollers to drive shaft the rotation and use the rheostat to change the resistance, which can produce displacement signal, prompting the movement of the cursor indicating the position on the screen after computer processing.

IEEE Association lists the invention of the mouse as one of the most significant events during the birth of the computer for 50 years, which sufficiently indicates the high impact of mouse towards the development process of IT.

As the mouse was dragging a long tail, Dr. Engelbart and his colleagues jokingly called it as "Mouse," or the Chinese "Shubiao." After the birth of computer in the world, then it function was far from perfect compared with today's one. Those expensive luxury goods were mainly used in fields such as scientific research and military. For all this, as a visionary inventor, Dr. Engelbart had realized that, along with the invention and popularization of the computer, the computer would play an integral part in the development process of human history. No doubt that mouse might be widely used. Therefore, he applied for a patent and named it "position indicator for system X–Y display. Perhaps due to the name "mouse" is concise and vivid, so the name "mouse" has been handed down. Of course, the then mouse is not only considerably different from today's one in appearance but also needs an external power supply to provide power.

With the emergence of the third generation of computer, more and more computer companies equip their new products with the accessory—mouse. In April 1973, Xerox Corporation launched the world's first operable Alto computer with a graphical interface, which is the world's first computer to use a mouse. On April 27, 1981 after nine years, the world's first commercial mouse appeared. It was launched along with Xerox Corporation's Xerox Star 8010 computer. However, due to the unpopularity of the computer, very few people knew it. Although the market operation of the computer is not successful, its appearance has already meant that mouse will become one of the necessary computer configurations.

In 1983, Apple Corporation launched the world's first personal computer—LISA computer with graphical interface and mouse. It is the first time that Apple Corporation configured a mouse in its computer after the mouse has been invented for 17 years. It was because of Apple's behavior that so many users recognized the importance of mouse. In 1984, Apple introduced Lisa computer upgraded product —Macintosh computer, which is not only a milestone for Apple but also a sign of significance in computer development history. As Macintosh computer created huge profits for Apple, it also enables the mouse to enter into tens of thousands of households. After that, the use of OS/2 and Windows system further established the position of the mouse as computer standard peripheral. Hence, the mouse started to be well-known and became one of computer peripherals. That is how mouse and PC forge an indissoluble bond that is more than words can express.

As mouse becomes part of the computer culture, it began steadily upgrading towards a more convenient and more accurate direction.

To overcome wooden mouse disadvantages such as comfortable to wear and quiet precision, in 1983, Logitech invented the first photoelectric mechanical mouse, that is, today's mechanical mouse, the mouse structure of which became the virtual industry standard. After that, there appeared various types such as Bluetooth mouse and laser mouse gradually, which overcame the bothersome "tail" and made constant innovation in operation. In 2009, Apple launched the new Magic Mouse that even removed all mouse buttons and rollers. The whole piece of multi-touch trackpad can be able to provide functions equivalent to that of left and right buttons and 360° roller. It offers greater possibilities for mouse operation through only two fingers to achieve more gesture functions.

With the advent of the laptop, the touchpad gradually enters into people's lives. Through gestures, people can achieve many functions in touchpad exactly as the same as mouse. Perhaps mouse will slowly go out of people's life or will bring a new revolution, in any case, the aim that computer will serve people better will not change.

1.4.2 Output Device

As the terminal equipment of a computer, the output device can represent all kinds of computing results data or information in the forms such as digit, character, image, and sound. When the computer was just generated, the related output device was very limited. At that time, computer input device was often punched card reader to lead instructions and data into internal storage, while output device for results storage was tape. With the development of science and technology, there are ever-growing output devices types, without which computer will indeed become unintelligible, and the convenience and happiness brought by computer will be greatly reduced.

Conventional output devices are monitors, printers, speakers, etc. Here we will only make a detailed introduction of printer equipment due to the limited length.

As the external equipment of computer, printer plays a significant role in our daily life and work. Charles Babbage made a driven apparatus for his difference engine in nineteenth century, which is regarded as the first computer printer [22]. After that, printers with various technologies stood out, providing a lot of convenience in transforming electronic data in a computer into paper ones. The conventional printers in today's market are stylus printer, inkjet printer, laser printers, etc., each of them occupies parts of the market with their unique advantages, holding up the printer market together.

The history of inkjet printer can be traced back to 50 odd years ago. As early as 1960, some people put forward inkjet printing technology. However, it was not until 16 years later when IBM produced the first commercial inkjet printer that printer appeared officially. The most original IBM 4640 adopts continuous inkjet technology that was developed by Professor Hertz and his colleagues of the Swedish Institute of industrial technology in Europe. The so-called continuous inkjet is first to produce ink droplet continuously and then recycle or scatter ink droplet of non-lithographic image no matter it is a lithographic image or non-lithographic image. However, this technology is almost to print ink dot on a paper drop by drop, which is rather easy to imagine its weak effect, making it of none practical value in reality.

In the same year with IBM 4640, Zoltan, Kyser and Sear, three pioneers of Siemens Technology successfully developed an electric pressure ink control technology and applied it to their products–Siemens Pt-80. The printer was put into production sales in 1978, becoming world's first inkjet printer with commercial value. Hence, printer entered into the public view.

At the same time, both HP (Hewlett Packard) and Canon Corporation researchers developed new inkjet printing technologies. With Canon Corporation applied bubble jet technology in Y-80 inkjet printer for the first time in August 1980, the history of inkjet printer made its debut.

Nevertheless, people were not satisfied with this. To pursue more colors and larger format, HP launched world's first color inkjet printer–DeskJet 500C. To seek a better print quality, Epson put forward technologies including variable-sized droplet technology, natural color reproduction technology, and ultrafine droplet technology, while Canon proposed professional photo optimization technology and four-color control technique. HP presented richly layered graph technology and intelligent color enhancement technology, which further enhanced the technical content of inkjet printer. To pursue faster printing speed, Lenovo adopted inkjet head supported by micro-electro-mechanical systems, which made it unnecessary for the print head to move around when printing, boosting print advantage in speed.

As another major type of printer, the laser printer is constantly updating its own technology during the decades of its birth. After the launch of the first laser printer, Xerox Company made 9700 electronic printing system. Companies such as IBM, HP and Lenovo have been under trial and reform and have launched new products including double cassette desktop laser printer, LAN printer, Chinese laser printer and color laser printer that supports automatic two-sided printing. With the vast improvement of movement performance, the increasingly perfect control technology and the significant decrease of price, a laser printer is constantly optimizing its cost performance in its way to provide more convenience for people's life.

Apart from the several external devices, input and output devices mentioned above, numerous computer peripherals are devoting themselves to our convenience in using a computer. It can be predicted that, with the passage of time and the further development of science and technology, there will be more computer peripherals, offering more and richer help for a better and more convenient life. The computer peripherals developed along with computer development, providing more or less help for us to use computer better. Perhaps one day they will become history, or perhaps they will accompany human for a longer time. In a nut, they will leave their marks in computer development process, enriching the whole network culture tree with their own unique cultural forms.

1.5 The Influence of Computer

Computers greatly accelerate people's computing speed, provides possibilities for faster, more accurate and wider range calculation.

With the help of a computer, through decades of rapid development, there is a radical change in people's life in great powers like the United States. The emergence of high-performance computers enables people to realize more complex designs, such as the Lunar Probe Project which can only be achieved in the legend. Factories under computer's automatic control liberate workforce and it helps to make production activities much more efficient. Through the Internet, computers connect people all over the world and provide a platform for the integration of various cultures. Electronic storage is convenient for sharing information, which is changing the way people access to knowledge. The emergence of e-commerce provides a more convenient and more efficient style for people to trade. Also, due to the generation of the computer, IT industry has become one of the industries which many countries are incredibly paying attention to. It also offers many jobs and provides countless new products to create new value.

The computer has brought great influence to our society and culture, people have become accustomed to using computers to solve their problems, to use computers to share their lives with others, to use computers to work or entertain. All these indicate that the computer will continue to bring greater influence to our lives.

1.6   Summary

In the long history of human civilizations, since the demand of the commerce, measure and qualification, the pursuit of computing never stopped and become a part of culture eventually. In this chapter, we tried to go through a lot of stories to lead you into the developing process of calculation. The finger-counting, abacus, slide rule, various mechanical calculators or even the development of computers, they are the crystallization of human wisdom. Human's development promotes the development of computing, in turn, calculating lays the foundation for human's development.

The computer was born from requirements of calculation. Based on the progress of material and the continuous development of science and technology, to meet the growing computing demands, we have experienced the generations of reform and innovation. This includes the first generation of computers which are the application of vacuum tubes, the second generation of computers which are the application of transistors, the third-generation computers which are the use of integrated circuits and the fourth-generation computers which are the application of large- scale- and gigantic-scale integrated circuits. However, time will not stop at the moment. With time goes by, computers must have its new development. There will be new generations of computers which will provide better convenience to people's lives. The culture of computing and computer will be passed down from generation to generation. Computer also promote other domain of science, for example, high polymer material, bioengineering, nuclear engineering, and numerical mathematics. With no doubt that the computer is the product of culture in the one hand and it will promote culture itself in the other hand.

References

1. Marx, K (1844). The economic and philosophical manuscripts.
2. Pullan, JM (1969). The history of the abacus. Hutchinson.
3. Cajori, F (1909). A history of the logarithmic slide rule and allied instruments. Engineering News Publishing Company.
4. Napier, J. (1889). The construction of the wonderful canon of logarithms. W. Blackwood and Sons.

5. Chapman, S (1942). Blaise Pascal (1623–1662): Tercentenary of the calculating machine. Nature, 150(31): 508–509.
6. Trogemann, G et al (2001). Computing in Russia. Vieweg Wiesbaden.
7. Babbage, C (1970). Father of the Computer.
8. Babbage, C (2011). Passages from the Life of a Philosopher. Cambridge University Press.
9. Backus, J (2011). http://www.columbia.edu/cu/computinghistory/backus.html. Accessed 2 Sept. 2017.
10. Turing, AM (1937). On computable numbers, with an application to the Entscheidungsproblem. Proceedings of the London mathematical society, 2(1): 230–265.
11. Turing, AM (1948). Intelligent machinery, a heretical theory. The Turing Test: Verbal Behavior as the Hallmark of Intelligence, 105.
12. McCartney, S (1999). ENIAC: The triumphs and tragedies of the world's first computer. Walker & Company.
13. Edwards, J (2010). EE Hall of Fame John Atanasoff and Clifford Berry: Inventing The ABC, A Benchmark Digital Computer. Electronic Design, 58(16): 58.
14. Wilkes, MV (1956). Automatic Digital Computers.
15. Vardalas, J (2003). Twists and Turns in the Development of the Transistor. IEEE-USA Today's Engineer Online.
16. Irvine, MM (2001). Early digital computers at bell telephone laboratories. IEEE Annals of the History of Computing, 23(3): 22–42.
17. ROSTKY, G (1999). Micromodules: the ultimate package. Electronic Engineering Times (1093): 42–43.
18. Da Cruz, F (2013). http://www.columbia.edu/cu/computinghistory/packard.html. Accessed 2 Sept. 2017.
19. Prodan, R, Fahringer, T (2007). Grid computing: experiment management, tool integration, and scientific workflows. Springer-Verlag.
20. Foulke, AT (1961). Mr. Typewriter: A Biography of Christopher Latham Sholes. Christopher Publishing House.
21. Engelbart, D (2014). http://www.dougengelbart.org/firsts/mouse.html. Accessed 2 Sept. 2017.
22. BBC News (2000). http://news.bbc.co.uk/1/hi/sci/tech/710950.stm. Accessed 2 Sept. 2017.

Chapter 2
The Development of Software

Abstract Culture can be regarded to be that normative glue withholding a coterie together. It is associated to the standardized approach of reasoning and behavior of our kind. Being engulfed in the hegemony of computing, civilization indispensable vocation narrowed down to how to convey their conjectures to computers so that the latter would by dint of effective logic put together an output, henceforth software came into existence. Two centuries earlier, humanity desired hypersonic productivity, thus shepherding Charles Babbage's in 1860 with his mechanical computer to chime in machine language. As computing versatility up surged, software exigencies proliferated, thereupon siphoning the birth of FORTRAN language which expunged barricades between manifold hardware and the programming language. Computing versatility came in double edged, unquestionably overloading itself and urging for additions in its magnitude, this led to the birth of languages like BASIC, PASCAL, and C. Following the downright outstretch of software about every single niche of our turf, operating systems such as Microsoft made surface, managing data storages and of all users' interruptions and treated them with a corresponding adequate and appropriate response. Here and now, software pilot financial management tools and systems, networking systems, browsers, the IoT, and even e-commerce platforms. The appearance of each of these software services has been closely related to the evolution of the needs of mankind and its hunger for improvement and novelty. In the following chapter, we will decorticate this process with relevant examples to understand the flow process in their happening.

2.1 Culture and Software

On knowing the brief history of computer development, this chapter will make an introduction to software. We all know computer can do many things, it is an assistant in your work and a game machine in your rest time. But computer is the body, software is the soul. Without software, computers will be reduced to nothing. When you click into a virtual supermarket for software, it will be easily detected that they are various software. They are made for Curriculum Vitae editing, small

© Springer Nature Singapore Pte Ltd. and Zhejiang University Press 2018
Z. Qin et al., *Fundamentals of Software Culture*,
https://doi.org/10.1007/978-981-13-0701-0_2

businesses management, language learning, health monitoring, music processing, and even virtual adventure games, all presented on the shelves. Install a software and you can get a new function on computer.

Since the widespread use, software is changing our lifestyle and forming new culture. Communication, as an instance, is all via a software instead of face to face. Or payment, people now do it on smart phone with payment software like PayPal and go shopping without cash. Many sorts of software develop an ecotope environment, they serve many aspects in our life and generate new culture.

The software gives access to communication between human and machine, and data processing, which would consequently lead to the conduction of different tasks. For instance, when software on music composition orders the computer to display a staff on the screen, it tells the computer to memorize the notes you input by keyboard or synthesizer. After that, the computer will transform those inputs into electrical signals, and make them played by the speaker. We dare say to that the best experience computer users can possess mostly appear when he or she is skimming through computer markets or software contents for their ideal designs.

A programming language is not only a basic element but also the core of a product. Serving as the internal reflection of the software culture, it acquires a simultaneous development of the software itself. Therefore, this chapter will provide relevant knowledge on programming language together with the history of software development.

2.2   The Definition of Software

The software is defined as a systematic aggregation of computer data and instructions. It includes two categories: system software and application software [1]. Besides those which can be run on computers (here mean general computers), relevant files on computers will also be taken a part of it. In brief, the definition of software can be concluded as programs plus files. In certain cases, the word is also used to describe the social management system, ideology, political ideas, laws, and regulation.

Chinese National Standard provides a definition for software as—any computer program, procedure or rule relating to a computer system, as well the possible documents, files, and data [2].

The World International Property Organization declares in *The WIPO Model Laws for the Protection of Computer Software (1978)* that software is the aggregation of programs and their corresponding files on explanation and instructions [3].

2.3   The Development of Program Language

The programming language has a history over half a century, or nearly two centuries if we take the Ada Lovelace, the first people who wrote a program in history, as the starting point. She attempted to write a program for Charles Babbage's mechanical computer in 1860. Although she has not succeeded, at last, her name long remained in the history.

According to the dominant ideas, the development of programming language from the simple instructions for binary machines to the advanced symbolic sentences can be divided into five generations.

2.3.1 The First Generation: Machine Language

The original computer programming relied on those thin paper tape, on which small holes were punched [4]. The holes were the initial representatives of machine languages. Just as its name suggested, machine language had a close connection with the hardware. Based on binary codes "0" and "1", this language was directly read and conducted by computers. Designers only needed to operate their machines by writing in this form.

The virtues of machine language were most reflected by its flexibility, directness, and high speed. However, it possessed obvious shortcomings as well, not least the incompatibility of computer language between different products, which will lead to much redundancy. This kind of incompatibility required that programmers should remember all the instruction code with its exact meaning. And when it came to programming, they then have to work on the storage, input and output of each instruction and datum on their own.

At the same they had to learn all the steps or units they had finished by heart. It has been estimated that, through this process, the time spent on programming was tens or hundreds of folds of the exact operating time of that program. Therefore, due to the nondirective and error-prone characteristics, most people have stopped learning or using it. Only very few specialists in manufacturing houses were still required to understand it.

2.3.2 The Second Generation: Assembly Language

Before the invention of the electronic computer "UNIVAC (Universal Automatic Computer)", machine language had been most frequently used. However, just as what has been mentioned in the proceeding section, since the machine language was uneasy to identify, it was almost painful for programmers to check their works by the punched paper tapes. Upon that, people started to search for a readable and more convenient way for programming. In 1952, two Americans, John Mauchly and Grace Hopper, came up with a kind of para-natural computer language (based on English) called "Flow-Matic" an assembly one [5]. Working together with Presper Eckert, Mauchly founded up a company designing and producing electrical calculators, launched "ENIAC" and "UNIVAC" in 1946 and 1951 respectively.

Grace Hopper, an American Commodore, and computer scientists was known both as one of the world earliest program designers, and one of the world-famous female program designers. She joined the Naval Reserve Force during the Second World War in 1943, and then took a position in the Eckert-Mauchly company for the study on "UNIVAC." When she was in the Navy, Grace was assigned to the department in charge of the program development of "Mark" computer, and then took park in programming and maintenance of "Mark-II." Once in her work, she found a bug clipped in the relay of "Mark-II" which caused dysfunction. With that bug posted right on the page, she reported her discovery on the research record. From then on, any dysfunctional mistake found in the department was called "bug," and solutions "debug." That was the origin of the name of modern programming mistakes.

We could not deny that the adoption of some daily languages, numbers, and symbols in assembly language has made the programs more understandable, useful, even easier to be recognized and examined. However, it has to be pointed out that, assembly language could be read and run directly by computer without the help of a compiler—the translation machine between the assembly and machine languages.

2.3.3   The Third Generation: High-Level Programming Language

Although the emergence of assembly language was a considerable progress to computer programming, it is still heavily dependent on computer hardware, because different assembly languages and assemblers were required for different computers. That was extremely unfavorable to the development of computer program. Thus, a high-level programming language with higher compatibility was expected by the public. This section would focus on some typical representatives of this kind.

2.3.3.1   Fortran [6]

On November 10, 1954, a young man named Backus (John Bakus) in IBM invented a computer programming language called FORTRAN (FormulaTranslation) language on the IBM704 machine. Baku was born into a wealthy American family. When he was young, he did not show any interest in the study. Then he was enlisted during World War II, he was recommended to a medical school because of his good performance after wartime. However, since he was not interested in medicine, and voluntarily transferred to Columbia University for mathematics, finally came to IBM as a graduate in 1949.

In 1953, Backus suggested that a new computer programming language be developed in the IBM704 machine. Although the proposal did not win the support from the consultancy Von Neumann, the leaders agreed to the Backus's idea and confirmed the establishment of his own R&D group. The beginning of the structure of the language design was relatively smooth, but he soon encountered great difficulties in designing an appropriate compiler. They applied what they would learn from Grace Hopper and her "Flow-Matic" assembly language assembler to that of the FORTRAN, and succeeded. In fact, the biggest advantage of FORTRAN language was to get rid of hardware and restrictions on computer models. Owing to its more standardized grammatical structure, FORTRAN was named as the high-level programming language. The convenience for the expression of mathematical formulas also made this kind of language well applied in the field of scientific computing. The earliest user of FORTRAN language was the Westinghouse Electric Company in April 1974. Quite coincidently, the company used FORTRAN in the calculation of fluid mechanics in aircraft design, and found some errors in the compiler. Those errors took Backus team six months for remedy. And then a perfect FORTRAN compiler finally came into being.

For successfully designing the first high-level programming language, Bakus won a huge popularity among the computer software field, as wells as American National Medal of Science, and Turing Award. The public even praised him as the Father of "FORTRAN".

The advent of FORTRAN language has caused a huge effect in the computer industry by marking a leap-frog progress. It has brought the development of the program from the low-level assembly language into a superior one, changing the programmers' working model, and showing its great talents in the fields of aviation, aerospace, engineering, and scientific academia. The FORTRAN language also gave birth to the computer software industry, for COMT II, IPL, and IT advanced languages were all designed in the process of FORTRAN language debugging. It was FORTRAN that enlightened the whole era for software languages.

2.3.3.2   Algol [7]

The name ALGOL was the abbreviation for algorithmic language (ALGOrithmic language). It was the language for describing the calculation process, or in simple words, an algorithmic-oriented one. Developed in 1958 by an IBM R&D team, ALGO was the world's first structured language based on a sound theory, which possessed a rigorous language style under formal grammar rules. In the same year, on the International Business and Academic Computer Conference held in Zurich, Association for Computing Machinery (ACM) group and the Applied Mathematics and Mechanics Association (GAMM) from the Federal Republic of Germany suggested integrating their ALGO works into one. The new one was first named as IAL which refers to International Algebraic Language, but later recognized as the ALGOL58.

ALGOL was first successfully run on the IBM709 computer in 1959. Then in January 1960 in Paris, the Turing winner A. J. Perlis published *A report on Algorithmic Language ALGOL 60* on a world class seminar for software experts. Before long, a Dutch man Azchl Dykstra (Wybe Dijkstra Edsger) developed the first ALGOL60 language compiler, and Alan Pelis Revised ALGOL 60 again in 1962.

Compared with the FORTRAN language, the ALGOL language has two distinct advantages: first, it has for the first time used local variables in programming languages. Whereas FORTRAN language could only use global variables, and one variable in the whole program representing only one sense; local variables can refer to different meanings in several paragraphs. Second, FORTRAN has applied the recursive ideas to programming. Recursion could divide a problem into some small tasks, and the answer to the whole question will come out after all the small problems are solved. Backus, although as the designer of FORTRAN language, made some contributions to the ALGOL language as well, since his latest research findings of a context-free grammar system were absorbed in the ALGOL grammar design. In June 1959 in Paris, his thesis on that issue was discussed on an ALGOL conference held by the United Nations Education, Scientific, and Cultural Organization (UNESCO). However, disappointingly, the thesis was not involved in the symposium collection due to its missing of a deadline. On reading Backus' paper, a Danish mathematician Dr. Peter Naur was greatly inspired. He carefully reviewed and modified Backus' description language syntax, and finally gave birth to the famous Bakus-Naur Form (BNF) in the computer world. His works has been mentioned in "The Report of the algorithmic language ALGOL 60".

Before the publication of the ALGOL60 report, programming language was once seen as an informal definition describing instructions and code compilation. However, the grammar defined by Bakus-Naur Form has revolutionized this idea, for it had made the language so concise, clear and powerful that it can be explained perfectly within the length of the 17 pages, and distinctively promoted communication between computers and humans. In 2005, Naur was awarded the annual Turing Award for his pioneering work on ALGOL60.

The emergence of ALGOL language was of great importance to the development of the computer. For bringing the automatic computing into reality, ALGOL was described as "a definite miracle" and the birth of "computational science" by the former Turing winner Edsger Wybe Dijkstra.

2.3.3.3 Lisp [8]

In 1958, John MaCarthy, invented a computer programming language suitable for artificial intelligence—LISP language.

Mccarthy was born in a Communist family on September 4, 1927, in Boston. His father was a Catholic while mother, a Lithuania Jewish. In 1948, when McCarthy was in California Science Institute of Technology studying mathematics, he attended a seminar (Hixon Symposium on cerebral mechanism in behavior at CalTech) hosted by the school and got the chance to listen to an academic report on self-replicating automata from Von Neumann. This report has kindled his interest in the field of artificial intelligence.

During his doctoral study in mathematics at Princeton University in 1949, encouraged by Von Neumann, John made his first attempt to simulate artificial intelligence on the machine. In 1955, together with Claude Elwood Shannon (the founder of information theory), Marvin Minsky (the master of artificial intelligence, the author of *Society of Mind*), and Rochester (one of the designers of the IBM computer), McCarthy initiated the Dartmouth project funded by the Rockefeller Foundation. This project was not only an important event in the history of the development of artificial intelligence but also a milestone in the journey of computer science.

Mccarthy for the first time put forward the concept of "artificial intelligence" in 1956. To realize his idea, Mccarthy started from the study of the relationship between a programming language and artificial intelligence. On carefully analyzing the method of symbol processing, he summarized several advantages of conducting logic reasoning by using a table. For instance, the table could be expanded, contracted, and reorganized with logic. However, when he tried to apply improved FLPL table of FORTRAN language to list processing artificial intelligence, things did not work out, because the FORTRAN language failed to support the recursive model.

Thus, Mccarthy resolved to design a new programming language LISP which could process tables on its own, in which all the data, data structures, sentence structures would be represented by tables. It was through this language that Mccarthy started his journey on artificial intelligence, and be known as the "Founder of AI". Those two major functions of the LISP language—"recursion" and "evaluation"—were also heavily borrowed in the Algol 60 programming language and following high-level languages.

The features of the LISP language have equally solved the core problem of artificial intelligence and further simplified the program design of LISP by its exquisite table mechanism. Therefore, it has been widely used after invention in the calculation of calculus in mathematics, theorem proving, predicate calculus, game theory, etc.

Another famous design of that age was called PROLOG, a later logic programming language first proposed by a student called Kathe from the University of London, and then materialized by the research group led by Kaul Mailaoesuo from the University of Marseille in 1973. Those two were known as the two major languages in the field of Artificial Intelligence (AI) and left a far-reaching impact on AI development.

2.3.3.4 Cobol [9]

COBOL language was born in May 1959, commissioned by Ms. Grace Hope from the US Pentagon. She based the COBOL language on the early design of the assembly language "Flow-Matic", designing a new one especially for business use on data processing. As using a large number of English vocabulary and sentence patterns, the operation of COBOL was simpler and had a specialty in describing data structure. Also, having a grammar which was much closer to English, the operation and learning of COBOL became easier that even for nonprofessionals. In 1960, the official released the first edition of COBOL-60. Quite short after that, COBOL has swept the European and American countries, and been known as the world's first language for commercial use.

For the continuous 50 some years, COBOL has constantly been modified, perfected and standardized into several editions. Its wide application has ranged from accounting work, statistics, planning, information retrieval, personnel management, to data management and business data processing.

The following series of data would serve as the justification for its importance.

Four ninety two out of the world top 500 enterprises (including all of the top 100) were using the COBOL language, and the current investment in COBOL was estimated to be over \$3 trillion. More than 1000 million lines were written by COBOL, and this number was still increasing at an annual speed of 5 billion. 30 billion times of transactions are processed online by COBOL on every day. It also supported the process of 70% of the world's data, and 90% of the ATM service. For its solid foundation in the field of business, COBOL was mainly used in banking, finance, and accounting industry. Thus, even for the experienced IT companies, it was not practical or financially feasible to have other high-level languages take COBOL's place. It could be predicted that, so as long as the mainframe computers existed, COBOL would not disappear. Since it had already survived the massive impact of "Millennium Bug problem" in the computer industry, its longevity may sound quite certain to us now.

2.3.3.5   Basic [10]

BASIC language was officially released on May 1, 1964, by two professors from the Dartmouth College: Thomas E. Kurtz and John G. Kemeny. The full name of Basic language was "Beginner's All-Purpose Symbolic Instruction Code". Just as its name implied, this language was designed with the purpose to benefit the unprofessional users. The notion was first proposed on a Computer Symposium by those two professors in 1964.

As BASIC has continued the conversational form of FORTRAN and ALGOL, its simple and concise language style has made the communication between machine and people quite user-friendly. Only by spending a short period on training, a green hand would have access to designing his or her program. Novelty in BASIC language could also be reflected by its way of interpretation. Instead of a compiler, it relied on an interpreter for the procession to reduce the share of memory. However, this would at the same time have brought a decrease in the speed of BASIC, compared with its assembly counterparts as FORTRAN and ALGO.

Surprisingly, there was a story between BASIC language and the bellwether of software industry—Microsoft. In the 1970s, when Bill Gates was still at Harvard, he designed an interpreter called Altair BASIC for Altair 8800 computer with his friend

Paul Allen. This BASIC version in effect was the prototype for Microsoft BASIC and the foundation for MS-DOS operating system. In some degree, that BASIC product has predicted the primary success of the Microsoft company.

2.3.3.6 Pascal [11]

The design of Pascal language was started in September 1968 by Professor Niklaus Wirth from the Swiss Federal Institute and officially launched as the world first structured language in 1970. It was named in honor of the famous French mathematician and philosopher Blaise Pascal in the seventeenth century. Having its language style originated from ALGOL 60, Pascal language acquired a strict structured form, a sufficient amount of data supply, high working efficiency, and the error checking ability. As a kind of self-compiled language, PASCAL was comparatively excellent in reliability.

With its conciseness and compactness in language and structure, PASCAL was also widely used in many schools for teaching purposes. It gained a large popularity within a short period in Europe and United States and was taken as an important milestone in the history of the high-level programming languages. Beyond that, Wirth also wrote a large quantity of books on program design, algorithm, and data structure, winning the "Turing Award" in 1984 for his outstanding contributions in the field of computer.

2.3.3.7 C Language [12]

The emergence of C language could be traced back to design of combined programming language (CPL) in 1963, which was revised on the basis of the ALGOL by the University of Cambridge, UK. At that time, C language could directly control the computer hardware but was not easy to operate due to its large scale. Then in 1967, still at the University of Cambridge, Martin Richards successfully simplified its design and worked out the BCPL language. Retaining the function of hardware control, the BCPL language gained a much higher readability. Before long, this version was copied to Ken Thompson from the Bell Laboratory, and further simplified into a B language (B came from the first letter of "BCPL"), and issued in 1970. However, the B language only covered partial functions of BCPL owing to its rather highly simplified form.

Then in 1972, based on the B language, Dennis. M. Ritchie from the Baer laboratory started his redesign, subsequently launching the C language (named after the second letter of "BCPL") in 1973. Compared with the last generations, while keeping the hardware control, the C language was more powerful in function, richer in data, and more efficient by introducing a new concept called "pointer". Thus, this language was so well received by the majority of programmers and widely applied to fields as software development, scientific computing, system writing, 2D and 3D graphics, microcontroller and embedded system development.

2.3.4 The Fourth-Generation Language

The fourth-generation language [13] was made to meet the demand of business. This notion first appeared in the advertising and product introduction of software companies in the early 1980s. Therefore, products in the fourth generation of language were quite different on its performance and functions compared with its older counterparts. In 1985, the United States held the nation's fourth-generation language seminar. By taking this opportunity, many famous computer scientists started their comprehensive study on the fourth-generation language and brought it to the research field of computer science.

The fourth-generation language possessed many specialties as a good user interface, problem-oriented design, and quick learning period. At the same time, serving as a highly nonprocedural language, it significantly reduced the quantity of code and improved the productivity of software by order of magnitude. In order to improve the efficiency of execution and powerful ability of the tasks, many fourth-generation languages such as LINC, NOMAD, IDEAL, FOCUS, and NATURAL have made a smart combination between the procedural and nonprocedural statements.

It is normally held that ADA is one of the best representatives of the fourth-generation languages. ADA was born in the 1970s. During that time, the embedded computer system project was led by the US. Defense Department saw a gradual increase on programming language procession. The Department became quite anxious that many current languages were either too old or hardware-dependent to support the modular programming on security issues. Consequently, in 1975, they set up a High Order Language Working Group (HOLWG) to design a suitable language, demanding that it should integrate all the programming languages currently operated in the military system.

After nearly 20 years, the HOLWG group eventually came up with a programming language called Ada, credit to the world first programmer Ada Lovelace. Unlike other popular ones, Ada did not only reflect but also practice many principles of modern software development. Therefore, the use of ADA could promote the clarity, reliability, validity and maintainability of the software system in a significant way.

The appearance of Ada marked the successful entry of software engineering into the national and even an international scale. To some extent, by getting rid of the "Von Neumann thinking mode," it carved out a new ADA culture together with its support environment (APSE). Now it has been appointed by the US Defense Department as the only language for military system development. China has also adopted ADA for military use and launched its standard in *GJB 1383 Program Design Language ADA*.

2.3.5 The Fifth-Generation Language

The fifth-generation language [14] was usually considered as the natural language, knowledge base language, or artificial intelligence language. It was the one which assembled people's natural. Strictly speaking, the real fifth-generation language has not appeared by now. Some people may put the LISP language and PROLOG language as the fifth-generation language. In effect, those two were far from being the natural ones.

Owing to the specialties on the treatment of artificial intelligence, it was necessary to develop an exquisite language for this certain field.

Generally speaking, artificial intelligence language should acquire following characteristics:

(a) The ability to process symbols (i.e., non-numerical processing capacity);
(b) Suitable for structured program design and easy to program; (the ability to decompose the system into several small units, which were more convenient for understanding and independent procession);
(c) Recursive and backtracked functions;
(d) Human–computer interaction (HCI) ability;
(e) Fitted for reasoning process;
(f) Blending ability while dealing with process and descriptive data structure, together with a pattern matching mechanism for data identification and control confirmation.

Traditionally, all the knowledge for solving a certain problem was expressed by different models in fixed programs. However, this was not the same with the AI technology, in which we usually build a knowledge base (including facts and reasoning rules) instead. The knowledge base would empower the program to decide its actions according to the changing environment and the input information. Therefore, AI program was in effect a reasoning process run under the environmental model, which had great flexibility, dialogue ability, self-explanatory ability, and learning ability.

By this method, many unstructured problems without clear conditions or goals (i.e., the poorly formalized or described ones) could be better solved. Compared with the traditional ones, this model was more proficient at heuristic strategies.

2.4 The Development of Software

There are mainly four periods on software development: first, the production of customized software programs for key accounts; second, the launching of individual software products; third, the prosperity of enterprises solutions companies; forth, the "shrink and hidden" software for the mass market.

2.4.1 The First Stage of Software Development (1949–1959): The Embryonic Stage of Software Products

Within this period, there was no real sense of commercial software in the market. In fact, the first batch of independent software companies was the ones who provided solutions for private users. In the United States, this development process was promoted by several major software projects, first founded by the US. Government and later subscribed by some large companies. While taking a leading role in that age, those mega projects provided important opportunities for the earliest independent American software companies to gain experiences.

2.4.1.1 "The Universities for Programmers"

Sage [15]

Semi-Automatic Ground Environment (SAGE) was a super large computer projects developed from 1949 to 1962. Its research and development expense amounted to $8 billion.

In the early 1950s, the United States established a Semi-Automatic Ground Air Defense system for its own security issue on its border with Canada. That system was called SAGE system. The development of SAGE software program was at that time one of the noblest careers, and 700 out of 1200 programmers in the US were working for it.

The United States established warning radar on the US–Canada border, automatically recording the messages of azimuth, distance, and height of planes in the sky, and converting into the binary digital signals. All those messages would then be sent to the information processing center of the North American Air Defense Command via data communication equipment. In NORAD information processing center, large computers automatically received this information, and then worked out the flying direction, speed and instantaneous position of the aircraft after data procession. It also could be used to distinguish invading enemy planes. By sending that information to the Airforce and Artillery units, the military would have sufficient time for battle preparation. In short, it was all about "automatic" in the SAGE system. It was equally the first time in history that the computer and communication equipment had been well matched. Today's worldwide network is also based on the important combination of those two technologies.

In 1951, the Massachusetts Institute of Technology Lincoln Laboratory began to design a semi-automated ground air defense system called SAGE for the US Air Force. This system was divided into 17 zones. Each defense command center was equipped with two sets of IBM computer, connected with all the radar observations, airports, air defense missiles and antiaircraft gun positions by a communication line. It has formed an online computer system which allowed the computer program to assist the commander in decision-making, automatically gave guidance to intercept aircraft and missiles.

In 1959, Rand Company set up another individual branch "System Development Corp" (SDC) for the further development of SAGE, which estimated to have over 1 million lines of code. SAGE was, in fact, the pioneer in several aspects, including the use of a human–computer interaction display, developing a small computer form of the front-end processor, setting up the initial procedures for data communication, and providing a variety of paths for algorithm selection. Built in 1963, this system was considered the earliest example of the combination of computer technology and communication technology.

Sabre [16]

Till the middle 1970s, to cope with the fierce competition in the aviation industry, American Airlines, and United Airlines separately developed two sets of computer booking systems: SABRE and APOLLO. Beyond the great profits brought by those two systems, the two airlines have in fact almost monopolized of the airplane ticket sales at home.

In 1954, American Airlines required IBM to develop another aircraft booking system SABRE. This was the first industry-funded software project, employing about 200 software engineers, and consuming $30 million to complete in 1964. After that, SABRE system gradually grew into a network system with more than 30 thousand travel agencies, and 3 million online customers. Through SABRE, connections between computers have been for the first time realized by the Internet, on which people around the world can enter data, process information requests and expand their business. Meanwhile, the system has revolutionized the entire travel industry by introducing a comprehensive system into the sale of travel services. Also, SABRE could be seen as the predecessor of E-commerce which later bloomed in the 1990s.

The idea of SABRE system was proposed quite by accident at a meeting in 1953. A young salesman, R. Blair Smith, took a flight from Los Angeles to New York to attend the professional training. During the journey, he unintentionally had a conversation with another passenger about the information cards, but he had no idea that, the one he talked to was just C.R. Smith, the Chief Executive Officer (CEO) of American Airlines.

At that time, airline tickets booking service solely depended on the written information on cards stored in separate boxes. However, as the service developed, the information soon became a burden. Smith-Blair pointed out that, the old computer in American Airlines could only track the number of available seats on the plane, but nothing about the consumers' information. Blair Smith told C.R. Smith that he intended to learn and use a better computer when he came back to LA. More ideally, it should have the ability to record the passengers' names, travel flights, and telephone numbers. With great interest, Mr. Smith C.R. took out a card and wrote a special phone number on the back and responded, "Well Blair, I invite you to visit the reservation center of LaGuardia airport after the study. When you arrive, please write a letter to me about your ideas."

During the training process, Blair Smith met IBM CEO Thomas Watson Jr., and told him about his experience on the road. Watson replied to Smith that he should no doubt follow the requirements of the president of American Airlines, and send a copy to himself later as well. Smith then wrote the letter to suggest that IBM and American Airlines should jointly develop a project to create a computer reservation system. This was then definitely confirmed by C.R. Smith.

Based on their experience of constructing the large SAGE air defense computer system in the middle 1950s, IBM completed SABRE reservation system in 1960. Initially, equipped with two IBM 7090 computers, SABRE was run only in Briarcliff Manor, NY for testing. By the end of 1964, this new system had already become able to deal with 7500 transactions per hour. In the old system, the average time spent on a single booking transaction is 90 min, while SABRE whittle down the time to just a few seconds.

Till the middle 1960s, SABRE had become the largest private real-time data processing system, merely second to that own by the US. government. *Fortune* magazine reported the amazing ability of SABRE in an essay published in 1964 that, "Things may seem just the same as before when the LA customers make phone calls to the United States airline ticket counters for booking. However, they have been benefited by this 30-million dollar system within 0.4 s in their dialogue. Not only because they can have the correct flights reserved one year ahead, but also for the future close tracking of every step in the journey. No matter it is meal booking, car rental or transfer reservation, as long as the name has been recorded, everything would be safely guarded till one reached his destination."

That SABRE had made American Airlines so competitive consequently forced other airlines to choose IBM for their reservation system. In 1976, since the United States Airlines marketed SABRE to travel agencies, the agencies could then now book the tickets directly on the system, which could at the time store the fares of over one million tickets. Then in 1985, American Airlines built another "easy SABRE" system to allow consumers to get access to online service via the Internet or CompuServe. A year later, SABRE once again made a breakthrough in the industry by launching the first revenue management system, which helped the companies get the maximum income from the ticket sales. Even in today, that revenue management practices created by SABRE is still widely used. Ten years later, SABRE established its web site Travelocity in 1996. It was then in 2000 when SABRE finally left the United States Airline and became an independent share-holding company.

It could be noticed that, in every stage of the whole process, SABRE did provide people with the totally fresh experiences. To some extent, the real-time transaction processing, and the tracking functions on available tickets, prices, and customers are in effect the foundation for the prosperous E-commerce in the 1990s. At present, SABRE is still the bellwether in global travel technology products and services. It operates 24 h 7 days without a pause. More than 57000 travel agents around the world log on SABRE desktop per day, while SABRE alone deals with more than 42000 transactions per second.

SAGE and SABRE were also nicknamed as the "Universities for programmers". They enjoyed unparalleled positions in the early software industry in the United States. On learning from those two gigantic projects, many developers in past later built up their companies when they came back home. Since Europe or Asia did not have similar experiences as America, the early software industry was almost led by the US.

2.4.1.2 The Old Remington Rand Versus the Young Blue Giant IBM [17]

The operator of Remington Rand Corporation, James Rand, was born in a business family. His father ran a company which produced account books banks. After James Rand had graduated from the University, he started to work as a salesman for many companies selling office equipment. A few years later, he returned to his father's company and invented Kardex, a patented system which equivalent to the current visual documentation system for a computer database. Since he had a different idea on selling strategies with his father, James set up his company just named after Kardex and swiftly gained success within few years. Later on, he started to merge a large number of companies, including the one owned by his father.

Till the end of the 1920s, Kardex had already become a competitive company with a wide variety of products. Especially in the office equipment market, Kardex was long being the rival for IBM in typewriter and adding machine in the early 1930s.

As time marched on and technology developed, Remington Rand Corporation missed two development opportunities on of office equipment: the electric perforation technology applied on punched card tabulating machines and the rental service on selling office equipment. Thus, it lost the competition with IBM in the 1940s. However, the acquisition of Eckert-Mauchly Computer company was Kardex's action of fighting back. By entering the new computer market, Remington Rand Corporation resolved to strive against IBM on manufacturing and selling of office equipment. The fact later proved that the gambit made by James Rand was quite decisive and foresighted. By setting up a milestone on the computer industrialization, his old rival IBM was also so shocked to change their direction for products.

After the acquisition of Eckert-Mauchly Computer company, Remington Rand Corporation immediately raised a large amount of money to invest in research and manufacturing work of a computer. The improvement of the engineering measures, the development speed of the UNIVAC machine was greatly accelerated. The first UNIVAC machine was born on June 14, 1951. This UNIVAC was then delivered to the United States Bureau of population statistics, successfully dealing with the U. S. census data in 1950. The high reputation won by UNIVAC symbolized the computer's entrance into the practical stage. Instead of being an experimental equipment, the computer has now developed into an application with a variety of practical uses. Just as the Remington Rand Co. said in its advertising slogan, "UNIVAC machine will bring business into the electronic era." From another aspect, this fully reflected the expansion of UNIVAC on application field.

What surprised the world was the second UNIVAC computer, which helped the tally of votes in the election of American President in 1952. Then the vital use of the computer began to sink in, and UNIVAC became a household star. Remington Rand Company had also been brought to the center of the limelight. In that era, the Rand Company had become the namesake for electronic computers.

Since the great success of the UNIVAC machine from Remington Rand Corporation was twice proved by its wonderful performance in the population statistics and 1952 presidential election votes in the United States, IBM became quite nervous. Because although IBM had the history of cooperating with Harvard University in the past on developing MARK-I and mechanical computer of "the program selective" design, it, in fact, had not put much emphasis on this aspect.

On the one hand, that IBM's had already taken the leadership in calculation by calculating machine and punching machine blurred the vision of Watson and IBM. They failed to notice the bright future and potential market of electronic computers. On the other hand, the electronic computers were primarily used in scientific computing. The old Watson predicted that this expensive technology would not leave an impact on the commercial computing field, or made any profit.

In fact, in 1946 the large and bulky image of ENIAC left a very bad impression on young Watson. However, by a sudden chance, his prejudice against the computers was totally changed. The sudden event took place just within a few weeks after his visit on ENIAC. As young Watson one day casually wandered into the patent development room on the first floor of the headquarters, he came across a new equipment called "multiplier" by the engineer. It was a concise shape of tubes, over one-meter high, and the shell of which resembled a box.

Connected with IBM's high-speed punching machine, it could do the multiplication just by inserting statistics shown on punched cards. Its speed in doing multiplication was so fast that the time of operation was only one-nineth of that use on imputing numbers. This demonstration of calculation greatly surprised young Watson, and he decided to sell those machines on the market. With the consent of his father, young Watson put up an attractive ad on the "New York Times" after several months of preparation. The ad was published in September 1946, accounting for a full page. Watson named the equipment IBM 603 electron multiplier, claiming that IBM had successfully developed the world's first commercial electronic calculator. As the advertisement was well received by the majority of users, IBM started its business on a monthly rental of the machine at $350. Within a short time, over 100 appliances were borrowed. The IBM 603 electronic multiplier hallmarked a new starting point of IBM company, leading the company into the industry of electronic computing.

By the spring of 1954, IBM could nearly match Remington Rand Corporation on the technology on electronic computers. In April, IBM held a grand conference to launch his 701 type of computer. 150 first-class scientists and business leaders were invited to participate, including J. Robert Oppenheimer ("the father of the atomic bomb") and Von Neumann ("the father of the computer"). Oppenheimer even pointed out in his speech that, "IBM701 computer is the masterpiece out of human's extreme wisdom".

Meanwhile, as Remington Rand Corporation being advanced in the field of computer science, its strength was distributed to other products, such as an electric shaver, industrial television system, punching card machines and so on. This caused the often delay of delivery time of its computer products. By contrast, IBM's strict and dependent capacity on the industrial production line and business promotion began to sink in.

At first, IBM started a large scale of recruitment ranging from the East to West coasts. Graduates from Massachusetts Institute of Technology, and talents from California University, Stanford University, were all invited to the company. When they found that the west coasters would become reluctant to leave for the good local environment, IBM even set up a local laboratory to attract them. Based on that, only a year later the launching of 701 models, the 702 came out. That computer had already gone beyond the Remington Rand new products.

Subsequently, IBM704, 705 computers had been produced to meet the needs of customers. Whereas Remington Rand Corporation was still fixed on the large machine, IBM decided to divert into the medium-sized computers. This seemingly better deal soon won a loud applause from the market.

Although IBM did not have naturals like Mauchly or Eckert in their research team, congregation among some first-class talents was enough to work things out. Without the lofty and isolated characteristics, those people actually could be better integrated into IBM sales culture. This could be detected even from the names from their works. Without choosing those obscure names as ENINAC and UNIVAC, they preferred the clear serial numbers such as IBM701, 702, 650, which more tuned to the tastes of business customers.

The IBM computer at that age was already made in the modular idea. That was to say, the machine was composed of a series of boxes which could be randomly assembled, and the size of each box was made to fit the space of the standard elevator. Apart from the convenience of transportation, this design could better optimize the assembly for consumers' different requirements. However, what yielded by the Remington Rand Company at the same time were still clumsy and huge like ten years ago.

Under this great pressure, Remington Rand's competitive strength waned. In 1955, it was finally merged by the marine equipment manufacturer Sperry Corp, replaced by the Sperry Rand Co. Then in 1956; IBM subsequently took Sperry Rand's place on the CBS's prediction of the U.S. presidential election.

2.4.1.3 The Emergence of Small-Medium-Sized Software Development Companies

While large computer makers were conducting large software projects for their important customers, the medium-sized customers were neglected. This vacuum was soon detected and filled by some programming companies.

In 1955, and even before the time when the term "software" was coined (1959), two former IBM colleagues founded the Computer Usage Company. It was considered to be the world's first software services company independent from the vendors. With its venture capital of $40000, CUC's first project was a program designed to simulate the flow of oil. It formed the California Research Company and then completed in 1955. Then in a certain period, they went on to develop software for the insurance and retail chain corporation for a single customer. Soon after that, many other people joined the company. In 1959, CUC already had 59 employees and was listed in 1960. Until the end of 1967, the company already had 12 offices in the country, with over 700 staff members.

Before long, many other entrepreneurs walked into CUCS's steps. For example, in 1959, Fletcher Jones and Roy Nutt founded the Computer Sciences Corporation (CSC) in 1959. In 1963, CSC became the world's largest independent computer Service Corporation, with revenues of nearly $4 million. In the same year, it went public on the New York stock exchange as the first listed IT Service Corporation. Even in 1997, CSC still listed in the world's largest software Service Corporations, yielding $6.3 billion.

Other companies established at the same period were: applied data research firm founded in 1959, Electronic Data Systems, EDS in 1962, American Management Sciences Inc. (MSA, which diverted its focus to software products after the bankruptcy in the early 70s of the twentieth century) in 1963, California Analysis Center Inc. (CACI) in 1962, and the Keane Inc. in 1965.

Early 1960 saw a boom of the professional software service companies, and great progress on the computer technology, such as running speed, the size of the outlook and the number of owners. As the global desire on software increased rapidly, many manufacturers started to outsource most of their development projects.

For instance, CUC had a group of 20 people working for the software on IBM/360 system, while CSC was a major software sub-contractor for Honeywell. By 1965, there were about 45 major software contractors in the United States. Some of them employed more than 100 programmers, with the annual income of $100 million. There were also numerous small software contractors living under those big guys, which often had only a few programmers. In 1967, an estimation showed that there had been 2800 software Service Corporation in the US. Europe was left behind on this field. Although its large software contractors caught up in the 50s and 60s, they were a few years late.

France's SEMA was founded as a joint venture of Loichot Marcel Management Consultants Co and the Bank of Paris in 1958. Its early orders mainly came from oil and sugar refining industry, or defense mechanism. Most chose SEMA rather than the foreign competitors for its deep local experience. In the 1960s. SEMA already had nearly 120 employees.

In the UK, in addition to several computer services companies, there was another two large software services company coming out in the early 1960s. One of them was a Computer Analyst and Programmer company (CAP) which founded in 1962 and merged into SEMA group company in 1988. The other was Logica started in 1968 by, which participated in a big project of the European terminal on an American based housing reservation system. Those two companies are still quite active in today's world.

2.4.2 The Second Stage of Software Development (1959–1969): The Birth of Software Products

Ten years after the establishment of the first batch of independent software services corporations, the first generation of software products was born. Since the traditional idea in the 1960s held that software alone could not yield profit, they used to be customized ones or even for free. IBM's CFO (Unified General Features) program framed in computer1401, for example, was one of that kind. Although it was widely accepted as the most successful insurance software in 1964, most computer managers did not realize its market value. Only very few entrepreneurs had foreseen the potential of business in rewriting software for different customers.

2.4.2.1 The First Patent and License for Software [18]

In 1964, the hardware manufacturer RCA turned to Applied Data Research Inc. (ADR), the first software products company founded in 1959 by seven programmers, for the development a new design. It should serve as a flowchart program, in which the logic process of equipment was presented. Finally, this software became the first software product in the real sense. RCA sold numerous copies of it to the customers and built up important development and marketing segments for it.

Since RCA itself was not interested in this program, ADR at first intended to reclaim its 10000-dollar investment by selling 100 permits of the RCA501 computer to the users. However, only two of the customers bought their program at the price of $2400. This gave ADR a hint. It started to write a program for IBM1401 and then rewrote the program for IBM/360. The later trial was a huge success that ADR software was soon applied to thousands IBM computers. In 1965, with an already good fame, ADR came up with a new design AUTOFLOW (one could produce flow chart automatically) to hit the market. At this time, ADR succeeded. Its product AUTOFLOW was also seen as the ground zero of software industrialization.

In March 1962, three employees from Ramo-Wooldridge company founded "Informatics", the company famous IV Mark software product. IV Mark was their first database product.

Informatics used to be an ordinary software contract firm founded in 1962. In 1964, the company realized that most computer manufacturers were weak on the aspect of the database. Thus, at the expense of $5 million, it took 3 years to develop the IV, Mark. When the product went public in 1967, most users were stunned by its price of $30000. By the end of 1968, it had barely succeeded by selling 44 products. However, after it left IBM, Informatics' selling began to surge up. The number rose from 170 in the spring of 1969, reached 300 in 1970, and rested at 600 in 1973. IV Mark also formed up its product cycle and user groups called "League IV".

In the next 15 years till 1983, Mark IV remained the world's most successful software products with its sales over 100 million US dollars in total. One of the major challenges for Informatics was to determine what should be included in the price. Influenced by IBM's old view of packing services in the prices, Informatics initially provide free product maintenance and upgrade. However, four years later, as it saw the real value of those services, they started to price them.

On aware of the unauthorized software copies on the market, ADR and Informatics were both eager to protect their rights and interests. Goetz, as ADR's product manager, decided to apply for a patent for AUTOFLOW. This absolutely was the first application for software patent in the history. It was a turning point of the software that it had become a product and not a service any longer. Informatics simultaneously developed a license for customers to use the software, but strictly held the ownership of program code in Informatics. This has in the future become the industrial software mode, which was still valid in modern time.

In summary, those software pioneers 1960s set up the foundation for today's industry. They not only defined the basic concepts of a software product, such as pricing, maintenance, and legal protection but also further differentiated the software project from software product companies. However, the software product industry was still in its infancy. By 1970, the sales of software products were estimated to be less than $200 million.

2.4.2.2 IBM 360 [19]

IBM System/360 was a mainframe released by the IBM company in 1964. It symbolized the coming of a common language shared by the computers worldwide. The language was coded for OS/360. (OS refers to operating system), but it was not one tuned for every single piece. This language was designed to be run on the whole series of products. That was later found by the company the key to success. IBM 360 then served as the first standard platform within the field and put up a solid base for the company's future prosperity.

In April 1964, the new IBM/360 system appeared to be the first computer "family" which allowed computer software and edge devices exchange. It also became the first stable standard platform, accounting for nearly 80% of the market between 1969 and 1971, and now possessed 50 thousand computers for writing and testing programs. IBM/360 has brought $26 billion in revenue and $6 billion in profits for the company in total. In addition to this standard platform, IBM also developed freest software in the market, which was normally sold with its hardware.

In 1960, IBM already became the giant in the computer world. Since IBM started the development and sale of the computer from 1950, its sales increased to nine folds of the past. Thousands of sets of IBM computers were widely used in the financial sectors, governments, national defense and scientific research institutions. Only from the monthly rent ranging from $2000 to $50000 per machine, IBM earned 2 billion dollars a year. Besides that, the company has successfully achieved transition technology for replacing the vacuum tubes with transistors. The IBM's stock performed outstandingly as well.

However, this did not make President Watson joyous for he became aware of the lurking danger that IBM did not make further progress in this expanding market. While its turnover is increased by a speed of 20%, the profit in effect dropped rapidly to 10%. If the growth in turnover ceased at the end, IBM would be crowded out by the more advanced rivals with lower pay.

In 1960, there were only eight transistor computers and some vacuum tube computers showed in the IBM's catalog, and another six transistor computers were still asleep. All of those computers had nothing related to others for they all used different internal structures, processors, program design software, and external equipment. Moreover, their functions and performances varied as well. That was not special for IBM, but the general phenomenon of the whole computer industry in 1960.

Users subsequently started to grumble on this issue for every time their business developed; they need to change many things. What's more, it was too expensive and time-wasting to buy computers with exterior appliances and rewrite programs. Numerous complaints towards IBM were focused on the useless rewriting process of software made up by the overwhelming comply language. What drove the users crazier was that, no matter after somewhat optimization, the rewritten software did not operate 50% quicker than the old one, but only got a bare increase of 10%. IBM actually knew the reason quite clear—they needed another half year to optimize the external device to match the high-speed computer.

As different components needed to be made to suit all the models, the manufacturers were toiled over on those tediously repeated works. Although the company had spent much energy and cost merely on the management and quality control, the reality was that nothing would further irritate those talents beside rewriting the old program for a recorder. Market department sounded the alarm too, for they thought the mutually incompatible products of IBM would hurt itself by destroying the integrate image and market promotion.

It was clear that IBM now was lagged behind in the research and development. Becoming aware of the chaotic situation, Watson realized that what had been forgetting was IBM's core value—the overall optimizing ability. This kind of ability used to unite the research, production, marketing, and sales department within the company and lead them all together towards one direction. Only by reclaiming this kind of coordination could IBM be able to return to the arena.

He called up for vice president T. Vincent Learson who was responsible for the development and production and required him to find the cause of conflicts between several departments as soon as possible because IBM only had 2 years to live on their existing products. The company ought to release new products for revival. With this heavy task, Learson has authorized a complete right to all the all of the information and resources in IBM.

This decision made by Waston later proved to be the turning point for both IBM and the whole computer industry. Its far-fetching influence even shaped the modern field. At first, Learson conducted a comprehensive survey on the situation of the company. The bad news came out in May 1961 that no existing technology could tackle the compatibility challenge. However, there was a piece of good news sound quite exciting. Some technicians, especially the analysts and core members proposed a concept of "computer family". This may probably take effect, but no one had attempted to do so. Even those talents could not be certain about its feasibility. What's more, it was impossible to complete the "computer family" before 1962. It would at least cost two years longer. On knowing those conditions, Learson adopted two risky measures. First, advising the business department to adjust their planning to sell the current products for another two years. Second, demanding the core group to place "computer family" project as their priority.

As time went on to October 1961, although the positive attitude had taken the lead, the company still did not arrive at a common idea to launch the program. Learson found that it was time to make a resolution. He organized a special working group consisted of 13 researchers, technical managers and marketing directors, and left them with the task of completing the overall scheme of "computer family" before the new year. The group was even sent to a hotel in Connecticut for their private and intensive research.

On December 28, 1961, a common document titled "Processor Products—the Final Report of SPREAD Working Group" finally accomplished after two months. It was later used as the overall scheme of the renowned IBM S/360 computer system.

The implementation of the S/360 system was led by that special group as well. Some group members continued to exert a major impact on the development of computer technology. Bob Evans, the group leader later became the vice president who took charge of technology. Gene Amdahl invented the theory—"Amdahl's Law"—by applying a faster running component, the level of improvement on system performance depends on the use frequency of that new segment, or the time of its operation. Brooks Frederick on his own discovered "Brooks Law".

No matter judging from which point of view, the overall design of the S/360 computer was an amazing piece of work. Anyone who wanted to design computer hardware or software, or intended to write a product definition report would largely benefit from it. Owing to its profound influence on the development of the computer, this document has been recorded as the milestone in history. (the complete version could be found in *Annals of the History of Computing IEEE*, Vol. 5, No. 1, 1983, or china.computer.org.)

The report had the following characteristics: First, quite contrary to the lengthy and flawed report in the modern time, this text was quite refined, concise, but quite accurate and comprehensive in expressing meaning. Within the space of 20 pages, it is equally satisfied the demands of technicians, managers and marketing staff. Second, the report was a skillful combination of innovation between market and technology. It has reached four objectives of defining a brand new series of products; setting out dozens of rules for design, engineering, and implementation; program design must comply with; devising the period of launching new products, and proposing the management and monitoring mechanism to guarantee implementation of working plans.

In addition to its universality, the most prominent feature of S/360 was the application of "computer family". It means that all appliances within the system enjoyed the same "systematic structure". To analyze from the perspective of assembly language and external devices, they shared the same standard instruction system, address format, data format, and interface to external devices, which altogether enabled them to "mutual compatibility". In this way, upgrading or downgrading of a computer would not demand any exterior changes. Models on different prices could now share the identical computing environment, and technical staff from IBM finally put and ending to their long time dedication to rewriting programs.

The first generation of S/360 computer family encompassed five products for customers with various needs on cost effectiveness. Those five computers based on the same structural system showed distinctive differences in functions and performances. The operating speed between two adjacent levels of the machine was about 3 to 5 folds. If we take the comparison algorithm "Is A bigger than B?" as a benchmark test program, the computing time of the five gears could be listed as 200, 75, 25, 5 and 1 µs. That is to say; the most advanced S/360 could computer 1 million times per second.

Another feature of the overall program is to distinguish the system definition from its implementation so that technical personnel will have enough innovative space in the future to give full play to their talents in the design and implementation of the project. The Working Group divided rules into three categories deliberately: The first category is significant contents related to the overall situation, including address formats and data formats, which the working group made mandatory and clear provisions. The second category rules that are unnecessary to be detailed in the overall scheme, which the working group made relatively general but examinable provisions. The third are encourage rules that technical staff can make innovations beyond the rules. For example, working group hopes that all products use a new technology—"micro program". However, they do not need to use the micro program if technical personnel can realize the same function with other method and can prove that the cost performance of the method exceeds 33% of micro-program one.

2.4.3   The Third Stage of Software Development (1969–1981): Independent Enterprise Solutions

In this period, great enterprise solution providers appeared. IBM's decision of pricing software and hardware independently reaffirmed the independence of the software industry. In the ensuing years, a growing number of independent software companies emerged to provide new products for all sizes of businesses and the services provided by these products surpassed the hardware products. Eventually, customers started to find the source of software products instead hardware vendors.

2.4.3.1 IBM's Spin-off Decisions Promoted the Development of Independent Software Company

In the late 1960s, it was IBM that accelerated the development of independent software industry once again. On June 23, 1969, it announced that from January 1970 IBM would provide software services and hardware in separate prices. Although we never exactly understood that whether the decision was made under the pressure of the antitrust laws or it was just a new business strategy, its impacts on the growing software industry were huge. Although the software product had already appeared a long time before 1969, IBM's "spin-off" enables independent software companies to develop and market their products much more easily. Thus, customers had to pay for the software, even if it came from their hardware sellers. Insurance application software market was the first one changed by IBM's spin-off decision. Before 1969, the insurance companies must develop their solutions, or use IBM's CFO'62 which bundled together with its hardware. This situation left little development space to independent software companies. However, after IBM's spin-off decision, new software companies came up immediately. For example, Cybertek computer products company which was founded in 1969 by an IBM CFO'62 team members. Tractor Computing (TCC) was founded in 1969 and it had Life70 which was a unified functional system to compete with IBM's products.

In the early 1970s, database market was the most active. Since 1972, numerous software packages have been developed by the independent companies. As reflected by a 1972 software catalog, most of the products were offered by the insurance industry software. Most of other industries still relied on software which bundles with hardware. However, this situation was about to change. The emergence of the independent database company was one of the big powers behind it. The database system was very complex in techniques, and almost all industries needed it. However, since the system provided by the computer manufacturer was considered inadequate, independent providers invaded the market, making it one of the 1970s' most active markets.

One of the most successful companies in the first batch is Cullinane Company, which was founded by a former IBM database expert John Carlin in 1968. Cullinane, a typical of a young man in new software product market, is totally product-oriented rather than software contracting or computer service. As a typical example for other new kit software companies, Cullinane is organized by entrepreneurs who are proficient in technology and is in contact with venture capital. In 1973, Cullinane developed IDMS—a database for IBM host based on the network model. The company sold IDMS database system and became the first publicly listed software companies in 1978.

At the same time, European companies also marched into the market. In 1969, six members of the Application Information Processing Research Institute in Darmstadt, south of Frankfurt, Germany, founded Software AG. New companies developed and marketed its database system-ADABAS (Acronym for Adaptable Data Base System), which was an elastic database management system. In 1972, it entered into the U.S. Market and sold its featured products all over the world soon afterward. Then, other software companies followed suit. Companies that played an important role in the market were Cincom System Company (founded in 1968), Computer Associates (hereinafter referred to as CA, founded in 1976), Oracle (founded in 1977) and Sybase (founded in 1984), all of them advertised their products in business magazines and direct mail in early stage. In these companies, CA, which distinguished itself with its unique and successful corporate strategy, was one of the big companies in the first batch that determined to take merger and acquisition strategy as company's strategy to gain growth. All CA's actions were aimed at obtaining "products with a large volume of sales" rather than the most capable technology. By 1987, CA had acquired 15 companies, including the world's second largest software company-Accel, with a total of $629 million.

By 1992, CA had become one of the few traditional business software vendors that turned to new markets for personal computer software via acquisition. The demand for a standard enterprise application is as follows: although large software service corporations continue to provide customized application services to customers, there is a constant increase in demand for a standard enterprise solution application suite. Standardization means that software developers do not need always to start with a sketch in programming software for some common tasks, such as accounting revenue and expenditure, wages, orders, and material management. In the spring of 1972, the most successful SAP (systems, applications, and products) company was founded by five former IBM employees, who believed that they could develop software in a faster and cheaper way based on a new product that could be used by various companies. Eight years later, SAP's revenue reached $60 million and had 77 employees. Also, of Germany's 100 large-scale industrial enterprises, 50 were SAP's customers. Eight years later, SAP enjoyed a revenue of about $200 million and approximately 1000 employees when it was listed. Today, there are products of R/3, who is the leader of an evident market branch. Bann, a Dutch consultancy founded by two brothers-Jan Baan and J. G. Paul Bann in 1978, has similar success stories. In 1982, the company released its first corporate solutions and put much investment to establish a non-European standard later. In 1996, it enjoyed $388 million assets. The third winner is a database company founded by Larry Allison in 1977, which was Oracle.

In the 1980s and 1990s, many solution providers companies turned from mainframe computers to new platforms such as Unix (1973), IBM OS/2 and Microsoft NT and other proprietary operating system platforms. This change earned great profits from users of their software. One of them is PeopleSoft. Founded in 1987 by Ken Morris and David Duffield, PeopleSoft was originally headquartered in Walnut Creek, California before moving to Pleasanton, California. Duffield envisioned a client–server version of Integral Systems' popular mainframe Human Resource Management Systems (HRMS) package. PeopleSoft version 1, released in the late 1980s, was the first fully integrated, robust client–server HRMS application suite. Under the HRMS, PeopleSoft could explore some vertical market functions through the acquisition (such as health care and financial services), which made himself a strong competitor to traditional enterprise solution providers. At the same time, most electronic public relations (EPR) system company relied heavily on co-workers to assist with the restructuring of their products. These partners usually got 2–6 times incomes of the EPR seller's in the installation of large systems. Thus, both sides benefited from the huge market growth since the early 1990s. In the camp of EPR's partners, especially the big accounting firms, a very active merger-centralization happened in the 1980s and 1990s. The merger of KPMG's in 1987, and more recently, the merger of PricewaterhouseCoopers in 1998 seemed to be the signal of the worldwide industrialization of professional software services.

2.4.3.2   War in Database Market [20]

It has been a long time that people pay a lot of attention to collect and save data. From the nineteenth century to 1952, US census had been using punch cards to record each person's situation, demographics, and statistics through the card tabulation processor. As inception, the computer was an important tool for processing information, the most famous example is the UNIVAC election ballot statistics which got the correct result. People begin to have high hopes for computer; they want the computer to complete the management of data. Till the 1960s, scientists began to study to meet this requirement on how to use computers to store and retrieve data information, which was the study of database technology.

The earliest one is network database management system software which records data as storage units, each data is connected with other related data records, like a spider web, crisscrossing in the database. First developed forming network database management system IDS by Charles William Bachman Group in 1964. After this database, network database system got a rapid development after the 1970s. Many companies developed products of the database system, of which the most famous systems were DMS1100 database of Univac, IDS II database system of Honeywell, IMAGE database system of HP and IDMS database system of Cullinet, who was formerly known as Cullinan. Cullinet became the then world's largest independent software company by this system, creating a sales volume of $184 million in 1984.

In June 1970, one of IBM's researchers Edgar Frank Codd released a new model-relational model. The relational model for database management is an approach to managing data using a structure and language consistent with first-order predicate logic. Sometime after that; Codd continued to study and enrich the theory, prompting a huge impact on the computer industry. At that time, many scientists were busy establishing a standard specification for the database by taking network database as a model, on which the emergence of new theory caused a great impact. Therefore, a debate over database technology was unfolded between Codd and Bachmann, the result of which was that relational database theory gained the upper hand. A relational database can solve the difficulties in using network database and can obtain the records need to be checked without being given path. However, being only a theory at that time, it still had a long way to be realized. Many companies began the research work of relational database, in the hope of obtaining a technical lead in this area to gain profits. Honeywell, one of the companies that began this work at an early time, was the one who first developed commercial relational database system products. In June 1976, the relational database launched by them was called as Multics Relational Data Store (MRDS), which was programmed in PL/1 language and adopted Codd's relational model. It was able to run in the multi-task operating system and employed command interface in database and structure definition.

As the first company to raise relational model, IBM will not lag behind. The company organized a team of 40 people to develop this sort of relational database system. At the beginning of the development, they named the database system as R system, with R standing for the first letter of the English word "relationship". The first step was to develop a language that can realize the database system. The team members named the language as structured English query language, SEQUEL for short. Later, they changed the name into SQL after they got to know that a British aircraft company had registered the trademark. In 1974, SQL language got developed successfully. It can complete a series of functions such as definition, operation, query, and control, which facilitates the communication between computer users and computer. The success of SQL language did excite the research group, but they dared not to relax for a single moment in that they knew that there was a development team of the University of California who was also in the midst of relational database systems development. The team, led by Michael Stonebraker, was composed of a group of professors. People in the two teams knew each other very well. After studying Codd's relational database theory, these professors considered it promising. That is why they agreed to develop a similar database product, the project of which won the support of the government. The professors named their database products as Ingres system, and they also developed a query language (QUEL). Soon IBM's research team built the R database and put it into use in 1977. Nevertheless, the hierarchical data base product IMS of IBM was popular at that time and made great profits for the company. Therefore, the company was unwilling to launch system R too soon to affect IMS sales. On top of that, with the bureaucratic system of IBM, it was still too soon to put system R into the market. However, it did not stop IBM's development team to unveil its own research results. The team introduced the working principle of R system publicly in myriads of journals and read out papers to introduce system R at professional conferences.

A small company called Software Development Laboratory took note of this information. Software Development Laboratory Inc. was founded in 1977 in Santa Clara by three programmers, Larry Ellison, Bob Miner and Edward Oates. The three men were originally Alex Impey company's staff; the company produces audio and video equipment. At that time Alex Impey company was developed a trillion-bit memory system for the CIA, which was called "Oracle" and they wrote codes for this system. Ellison is the leader of this team. In 1944, he was born on August 17, in a rural southeastern Manhattan. Ellison grew up in Chicago with his aunt. In 1962 18-year-old Ellison was admitted to the Illinois State University, two years later he was ordered to leave the school. After that, he is entered the University of Chicago, during which he learned computer programming. Because he was not interested in school study, he left school in 1966 and came to Berkeley,

California to become a computer systems programmer. Although he worked for many companies, his works are basically around IBM's computer, which allowing him to gather experience of using and programming in IBM's mainframe. When he worked for Alex Impey, Ellison found that the one trillion Alex Impey storage system had no future and he switched to another company and became vice president of system development. When the company was going to develop a new type of data storage and retrieval device, his workload was gigantic. Under this situation, outsourcing must be considered. Then, Ellison decided to start his company. He found two colleagues in Alex Impey, Bob Miner, and Ed Oates to establish the Software Development Lab and take over the outsourcing tasks together.

They earned a lot on this project, and the company got money. On December 1, 1978, they moved the company office to the heart of Silicon Valley - Solomon Industrial Sand Hill Road No. 3000, rented a nearly 300 square meter office which is convenient in transportation, has beautiful scenery and is surrounded by the rich. At that time there were only five members. After moving, they gave their company a new name, Relations Software Co., Ltd. (RSI). They found the description and specification of the SQL language, carefully studied it and finally they decided to take advantage of this excellent language to develop database on the DPD-11 aircraft. After a few months, the first version of the relational database software came out; they named it as Oracle, which was the same as the name of the one trillion memory system project in Alex Impey.

2.4.4 The Fourth Stage of Software Development (1981–1994): Popsoft Era

The emergence of the personal computer created a new kind of software called Popsoft, which required a different marketing and sales strategies. At this time, some new companies aimed at this market. Among these, Xerox PARC, which was founded by Xerox Corporation, used ground-breaking innovation, including black and white screen, a bit-mapped displays, button, laser printers, word processors and network to lay the foundation for personal computer revolution. Some scientists working at PARC later worked for Apple Corp and Microsoft or established their companies.

In 1975, Altair 8800, one of the first "personal" computers created by MITS. Later, in 1977, published it and sold by mail order. Apple II computer came into the market, which provided much more functions.

In 1979 Bricklin and Franks developed the first spreadsheet program called VisiCalc for the Apple II computer, together with the "trump card application." However, both of them did not last for a long time.

In contrast, IBM's personal computer (IBM PC) released in1981became the leading platform. With the IBM PC, a new software era began. It was also the birth of independent software industry. There is no doubt that Microsoft is the most successful and most influential software company in the era.

2.4.4.1   Operating System [21]

Microsoft was by founded Bill Gate and Paul Alan in 1975. The company became a limited company in 1975 and went public in 1986. In 1981, IBM decided to authorize its personal computer operating system to Microsoft, which paved the way for the great success of the company located in Redmond. Ironically, Microsoft did not even develop the product's core, which was bought from Seattle Computer product company, a century deal with only $50,000. Microsoft's MS-DOS, as well as the later Windows, became the leading market standard, providing and strengthening the company's status and income in the personal computer market.

In fact, Microsoft did not have products in the operating system, but Bill Gates quickly bought 86-DOS operating system from a highly innovative small company along with its technology and talents and made improvement for 86-DOS based on the advantages of CP/M. Then, Bill Gates offered a very tempting cooperation condition for IBM, ie.,Microsoft would fully observe hardware standards and specifications of IBM and Intel, and design PC-DOS operating system especially, with each computer charging less than $50 for authorization. IBM was so overjoyed that the two clinched a deal immediately.

Surprisingly, Microsoft was not tied to IBM or became some nobody who paved the way for IBM due to the success of this big deal. IBM had thought that they could take control of the 20 odd Bill Gates. However, it turned out that the pretentious IBM become the unlucky one who paved the way for other people. Bill Gates, who grew up in a lawyer family, was very familiar with the complex commercial contract law. It was due to his insistence that Microsoft could be lucky enough to both retain the exclusive rights of PC-DOS and authorize other hardware vendors to use MS-DOS that was slightly modified based on PC-DOS. Bill Gates had wonderful insight in the transaction, enabling Microsoft to gain an advantageous position of a free ride, flexible autonomy and smooth, which buried the seeds of success for Microsoft's future growth.

In 1981, IBM officially launched its personal computer (IBM PC). By the well-known prestige of computer giant and its marketing network, IBM personal computer gained popularity all over the world. Global computer makers vied to develop application software for IBM computer, making Microsoft DOS that was closely related to application software became software industry standard with just a small effort. Apple's Macintosh operating system could only lose the golden opportunity helplessly since it was not compatible with DOS standard. The CP/M operating system of Digital Research Inc., though being slightly better than Microsoft's DOS version 1.0 at first, had to be paid with an extra high price, which explained why the vast majority of users preferred to use the pre-installed DOS. Hence, Bill Gates' business principle of "throw a sprat to catch a whale" had DOS version 1.0 sold together with IBM computer with a low price was totally "in virtue of the wind, rush into the sky", enabling Microsoft to step into the world's fastest road to success.

After the domination of IBM personal computer in the market, it offered a loophole for a group of small companies producing IBM compatible computers due to insufficient supply and high price. Manufacturers such as Compaq and Dell (DELL) introduced the use of Intel microprocessors and pre-installed Microsoft MS-DOS by small companies' momentum and flexibility first. The 386 computer, who claimed to be fully compatible with IBM, posed a serious threat to the dominance of IBM Dynasty, leaving the personal computer market in a hegemony situation resembling that of the Spring and Autumn period. Due to the huge structure, slow pace, and constant loss of IBM, the personal computer was pushed into a corner where nobody cared. Since Apple authorized other hardware vendors to use Macintosh operating system to produce Apple compatible computer in 1994, it did not only miss the golden opportunity in dominating the market share of operating system but was also pushed gradually to the brink of bankruptcy due to lack of support. Nevertheless, the repeated defeat of IBM posed no negative impact to Microsoft, who got rich by depending on IBM. In the meanwhile, the astonishing increase of IBM compatible computer sales provided an unprecedented stable position of the industry standard in Microsoft's DOS family. Market share rate would soar automatically easily without advertising and marketing. With the constant upgrading and yearly increase the price of DOS function and version, the authorization fee for DOS pre-installment from global PC makers flooded like sea tide, leaving Microsoft in a fantasy state winner-take-all where it could collect money easily and "difficult in being poor".

Later, Microsoft launched the advanced terminal operating system NT to enter the enterprise solution industry. The new IBM platform attracted a large number of new software reference program entrepreneurs, among them most personal computer software branch quickly dominated by new comers. On the other hand, the existing vendors rarely made a successful transition to the public-oriented software market. Among those successful new comers, some are Adobe, Autodesk, Corel, Intuit, and Novell.

2.4.4.2   Wars in the Field of Electronic Forms Processing Software

In 1982, Mitch Kaper founded the Lotus Development Corporation and designed Lotus 1-2-3, which made IBM PC became a commercial user's choice. Founded in 1983, Novell, created the computer network era. In 1989, it released the multi-channel local area network system, which runs on major operating systems, including IBM's OS/ 2, Unix and Apple Macintosh. Novell Inc. is an old network company which grew very rapidly in the 1980s and 1990s and almost monopolized the entire network market. However, after Microsoft's Windows operating system adding network function, Novell's business was affected. Once results low. Later, to improve its sales performance, Novell focused on the development of Internet products, and this strategy worked.

2.4.4.3 Word Processing System [22]

Speaking of word processing, we will think of Wang Laboratories, which was founded by Dr. An Wang. Dr. An Wang. Wang An company marched into mini-computer market by developing 2000 minicomputer successfully in 1971. Since then the company had been considering the development and marketing of innovative products to improve the ability of competition. In 1976, Wang An took a fancy to the word processor market, which was basically controlled by IBM. In addition to its electric typewriter, it is a word processor system that connected by some terminals with mainframe or minicomputer. This word processing system is installed with word processing software to process text messages from one terminal time, with other terminals can only be in a wait state. Its work efficiency is so low that it can only edit files line by line. Wang An saw the problem in the existing word processing system, so he decided to develop a dedicated word processing system. After the company technical staff's efforts, the Wang An company's word processor came out in June 1976. They named it the word processing system (WPS). The word processor is installed with a microprocessor chip and a cathode ray tube, i.e., the television screen display. Users can fully modify, adjust and move the text appears on the screen by using word processing software to complete text processing function. The software also enjoys functions such as error reminding and limited printing. Word processing system aroused people's interest the moment it appeared in computer trade fair. There were long queues in the front row of Wang An company's exhibition stand. People there scrambled to visit and observed the new word processing system, whose good performance and convenient use made word processing system of Wang An Company gained popularity among word processing people such as writers and secretaries, who ordered in succession to replace their original typewriters, prompting the company to win huge profits. By the word processing system and knock-out products such as the VS microcomputer and screen display system introduced in 1978, Wang An company marched into the top 100 companies list by Fortune magazine. In 1980, the company's turnover was up to $3 billion, ranking the eleventh in the national computer business. Wang An also earned $1.6 billion and became the fifth richest person in the United States.

2.4.4.4 Novell—The "Microsoft" in the Field of LAN [23]

Novell is the first company to get involved in network operating system. Under the leadership of its president Noorda Raymond, Novell created a glorious history in network operating system. He also led the competition between Microsoft.

Speaking of the development history of Novell, we cannot fail to mention the popular NetWare. In 1983, Novell launched Netware operating system, which had dominated in network operating system market, accounted for 70% of its share. There are numerous NetWare operating system versions, the most representative of which are Netware 3.11 SFT III, Netware 3.12, Netware 4.1, Netware 4.11, IntranetWare, Netware 5 and Netware 6. Its advantages are low requirements for network hardware, compatible DOS commands, similar application environment with DOS, rich application software support, perfect and reliable technology, the establishment in diskless workstation and so on.

To talk about Novell, inevitably we should introduce 3COM first. A few years before microcomputer (PC for short) appeared, most users were different ones who were independent with others' computers. Personal computers are nothing more than to meet the needs of personal entertainment (such as games), learning, word processing, daily management, and simple industrial control. The networked computer system used by commercial enterprises (such as a bank) is almost without exception composed of main frame and peripheral terminals (all calculations are completed by central main frame, while peripheral terminals are just input and display devices). The central main frame adopts the time-sharing operating system and serves for multiple end-users. Before the 1980s, no one intended to substitute large computer system with a microcomputer.

However, in 1979, something occurred, though it did not draw people's attention at that time, and it had a far-reaching impact on future computer development. That year, several scientists of the world-famous Xerox's Palo Alto laboratory who had invented Ethernet founded the 3Com Corporation and developed Ethernet adaptor, which was commonly known as a network card. Although 3COM originally designed network adapters for large or small central main frame such as IBM and DEC, it soon extended its business to main frame field with the popularity of computers.

In the mid 1980s, IBM PC/AT and its compatible personal computer were able to replace the original DEC PDP and VAX minicomputers in myriads of tasks. Also, the cost performance of microcomputer was one order of magnitude higher than minicomputers. With networking, data and hardware resources sharing, microcomputer was able to replace the minicomputer-based system. Unfortunately, the initial design of microcomputer did not think of resource sharing, with zero network function. The Ethernet servers and adapters of 3COM Company made up for the deficiency and solved the insufficiency. Nevertheless, the cost was very high. It was highly unlikely for a small enterprise with dozens of people to afford VAX minicomputer and terminal computer system. In the mid-1980s, VAX system with 20 to 40 users costed nearly 2 million yuan. In addition to hardware investment, minicomputer system also needs special rooms and administrative staffs, who must undergo training of Hardware Company. Although minicomputer speed is quick, its calculation speed is slow when allotted to each user. Minicomputer is the heart of the whole system, and the entire system will not breakdown once it malfunctions. The microcomputer can replace minicomputers in many times after networking.

In the so-called microcomputer local area work (PC LAN) system, there is a network server, which is usually a high-performance microcomputer and can also certainly serve as a minicomputer or workstation. It is mainly used to manage network and storage shared data to serve as the bridge of data exchange between microcomputers. The calculation is largely completed on a microcomputer, and some documents unwilling to be shared can also be saved in the local microcomputer. Because each computer has its independence, the microcomputer can work offline even if network server even goes wrong. Although each micro-computer is slower than a minicomputer, the total computing capacity of dozens of microcomputers can surpass that of minicomputers'. Also, microcomputer local area network is much cheaper in completing systems with the identical functions. In the mid-1980s, the investment for hardware with 40 microcomputers was only 60,000, 70,000 yuan. What's more, microcomputer system does not need special administrators and has low operating costs. Generally speaking, compared with a minicomputer, the computer system based on microcomputer network has more advantages than disadvantages in most applications. Hence, since the mid-1980s, it became an irreversible trend for microcomputer local area network to replace minicomputer system, which is why DEC failed later. 3Com Company, though developed microcomputer local area network, the goal of which was not clear and its business ranged from the network adapter, network server to network operating system. The possible reason might be that at the beginning of its foundation in the early 1980s, the then most profitable thing in the computer industry was hardware, while 3Com Corporation was actually based on hardware, with software as its supplement. Although it failed in the network, it was still accustomed to being hardware-oriented and bought the parent company US Robotics of the company whose production was Palm personal assistant system—Palm Pilot. Since the standard of Ethernet is open, its adapter is so easy that everyone can make it. Moreover, Ethernet network server is actually a high-end PC that any PC manu-facturers can make. Therefore, various compatible network cards and network servers appeared after the emergence of 3Com Corporation, leaving microcomputer LAN market as chaos like that of microcomputer one and had fierce competition. In fact, the most critical technology in microcomputer LAN is network operating system, which requires a company similar to Microsoft to unify. That is why Novell conformed to the historical trend and accepted the mission. Novell Company, born in 1979, became a network company and changed its name to Novell in 1983, a time when 3Com had been the boss of LAN. The goal of Novell after its entering into network field had always been very clear, i.e., to specialize in the operating system. If the status of 3Com in microcomputer LAN field is considered to be something like that of Apple's, then Novell can well be the counterpart of Microsoft.

Novell developed an operating system named as NOS which refers to Network Operating System in corresponding to Microsoft's DOS. It adopts DR-DOS iden-tical to Microsoft MS-DOS, so its network operating system can actually run completely independent of Microsoft's software and be compatible with Microsoft's DOS. Although a network card company bought by Novell later also made hardware, its attention had always been placed on network operating system. With the ever-growing popularity of Novell's network operating system in microcomputer local area network, Novell is in an advantageous position similar to that of Microsoft, that is, users can use Novell's operating system regardless of PC and network hardware brands used by them. Novell network operating system is not only easy to install, but its project in establishing local area network is also so easy that non-professional staff can do by just taking a look at the specification. Soon, Novell operating system in local area network was as popular as DOS in the microcomputer. From the 1980s to the early 1990s, Novell went so smooth that it would not only surpass 3Com Corporation soon but also had monopolized the whole microcomputer local area network operating system market by 1990, with a turnover equivalent to that of Microsoft's ($900 million Vs. Microsoft's $1.1 billion). Because microcomputer networking had become a trend and compared with the network in UNIX servers, workstations, and TCP/ IP protocol, microcomputer local area network was more promising in small and medium-sized enterprises. Novell was highly likely to become another Microsoft, i.e., it might monopolize enterprise operating system. Over the next five years, the annual growth rate of Novell was 20%. In 1995, the turnover of Novell exceeded $2 billion, equivalent to 40% that of Microsoft's.

Novell was very successful in the whole 1980s by selling expensive Ethernet card at the cost price aggressively to increase its primary market, and by forming monopoly position in nearly any companies needing a network in 1990s. Novell began to obtain and build services in its top NetWare operating platform as the market leader. Those services extended the capabilities of NetWare on certain products such as the use of NetWare, Novell multi-protocol router, GroupWise and BorderManager by SAA. In the late 1990s, due to the mistakes of company strategy, Netware's market share became increasingly narrow. Today, Novell is still an important software company that bought numerous small companies. Especially after its acquisition of SUSE in 2003, it began to transfer Linux's new strategy, with the main products including SUSE Linux Enterprise Server, SUSE Linux Enterprise Desktop, SUSE Linux Enterprise real time, SUSE Linux Enterprise thin client, etc.

2.4.4.5 Personal Finance Management Tool: Quicken [24]

Intuit, founded by Scott Cook and Tom Proulx in 1983, is another market newcomer in this era. In 1984, it released its personal finance software Quicken and is still leading the market with its products. In short, the software industry in the 1980s was developing with an exciting annual growth rate of 20%. The annual income of American companies increased to $10 billion in 1982, $25 billion in 1985, 10 times higher than that of 1979.

In the 1980s, Microsoft did not have sufficient knowledge in addition to the browse, and it did not realize the of potential business opportunities of personal finance management tools, which gave a chance for Intuit. Thus, Intuit had enough time to develop software, broaden the market and gain experience. In 1989, when Microsoft recognized this opportunity, it wanted to get this field easily with the acquisition approach which is its usual way. However, Microsoft's merger proposal was rejected by Intuit. Under this circumstance, in 1991 Microsoft decided to produce a competitor to Quicken called Microsoft Money.

The situation was tough for Intuit, with only 50 employees and an annual sale of $19 million. Moreover, the Windows version Quicken developed by it was worse than Microsoft competitive product-Money. It is unknown how many people at that time were for Intuit. As a result, Intuit remained 60% of the market share by 1993, while Microsoft was at a loss. The competitive Microsoft Money software was prolonged in its design cycle due to its design personnel's shortage of experience. Thus, Intuit combated Microsoft by taking advantage of experience in shortening the launch cycle of upgraded products. Also, Microsoft did not go all out to seize the Intuit market. On the surface, Microsoft embraced a "luxury lineup" of the programming team. However, judging from personal finance software field, over 1000 employees of Intuit specialized in personal financial software and other related software research, while only 60 people specialized in the same field in Microsoft. Microsoft extended too wide, which is another problem with Microsoft, that is, too scattered strength. Readership who want to know further the competition of this round can read *How to Fight against the Longer Odds: to See Competitive Strategy for Small and Medium Sized Enterprises from Intuit's Victory.*

In 1995, Microsoft proposed to acquire Intuit Software Company once again. This time, Intuit's shareholders approved the move, in the hope that they could obtain Microsoft's investment through the acquisition and share benefits by taking advantage of Microsoft's huge international distribution network, whereas Microsoft hoped obtain Intuit to develop Quicken software that had accounted for nearly 70% of personal property software market share. However, the U.S. government worried that Microsoft would dominate the nation's personal property software market after the acquisition, which, in the long run, would damage to the benefit of society as a whole. Therefore, the U.S. Government insisted in bringing a suit, which eventually led to the abortion of the transaction.

Now Microsoft and Intuit become a partner all of a sudden. They will develop software that can transfer MS Money data to Quicken platform smoothly.

2.4.4.6   The Fifth Stage of Software Development (1994 and on): Internet Value-Added Software Takes the Lead

The Internet which provides unlimited interconnection has created a new era. Most software companies will face the challenge caused by the coexistence of some different standards and platforms. At the same time, software industry may be faced with the challenge caused by new business opportunities of World Wide Web. The company which shaped the Internet era most is the Netscape.

2.4.4.7   Netscape Communications Come Out [25]

James H. Clark and Marc Andreessen founded Netscape in 1994. Two years ago, Andresen had created NCSA Mosaic, which is an Internet browser whose graphical user interface simplified the navigation of the Internet. The company was growing almost as fast as new technology. It went public in the 16 months after its establishment. Moreover, over the past 2 years, it had hired more than 2000 employees worldwide. The company's history largely represents the new pace of the Internet industry.

In 1993, National Center for Supercomputing Applications (from now on referred to as NCSA) of University of Illinois in Illinois, U.S. released a browser that named "Mosaic" and gain huge popularity at that time. The appearance of Mosaic was one of the kindling sparks that ignited the Internet boom later. On April 4th, 1994, Marc Andreessen, the key figure in developing, and Jim Clark, the founder of Silicon Graphics Incorporated (SGI for short, Chinese translation is "Shi Suan Ke Ji" or "Gui Tu") established MOSAIC Communication Corp in California, U.S.

The development team needed to completely rewrite browser code after the establishment of Mosaic. The reason was that NCSA of the University of Illinois owned trademark and copyright of Mosaic, and the University had transferred the technology to Spyglass Entertainment. On October 13, 1994, the browser Mosaic Netscape version 0.9 developed by the company was released. Although it is still the old version of the beta, the browser gained a huge success and became the most popular browser at that time. To avoid trademark ownership issue with NCSA, it renamed Netscape Communications Corporation (from now on referred to as Netscape) subsequently. On December 15 of the same year, Netscape browser version 1.0, which was renamed as Netscape Navigator, was officially released. Netscape Navigator was sold in the way of shareware because functions were added quickly. Therefore, it had an incredibly high market share. Netscape became the top one in browser market share after constant user accumulation of subsequent versions.

Soon afterward, the company's initial public offering gained a huge success. The original stock value was $14 per share, but due to a temporary decision, the stock price doubled to $28 per share, which rose to $75 after the first day close, becoming almost a record "good start" at that time. In 1995, the company's revenue enjoyed a quarterly double.

2.4.4.8 The Browser Wars [26]

Later on, Netscape tried for many times to create a web application system that could allow users to operate through the browser, which drew the attention of Microsoft, who feared that Netscape might pose a threat to its operating system and application market. Therefore, Microsoft bought the authorization of Mosaic from Spyglass Entertainment in 1995, and developed Internet Explorer based on it to march into the browser market, which unfolded the competition between the two companies. The competition between Netscape's Navigator Netscape and Microsoft's Explorer Internet was later called as "browser wars." Before 1995, Netscape was the absolute standard of Internet browser. Although its official version was not free, the evaluation version was free to be downloaded and was free. Although Microsoft released IE version 1.0 from August 1995, its recognized one by the market was IE browser version 4.0 published in October 1997, which observed the Internet standards proposed by the World Wide Web Consortium (W3C) better than Netscape and was able to provide functions such as MP 3 player and the like. Since then, IE gained a vigorous momentum. With Microsoft's huge financial and human resources, Netscape was finally sold to AOL at $4.8 billion in 1998. Later, Netscape was changed into a facade of AOL's ISP business, at which point Netscape's core team had all left, announcing the big victory of Microsoft in the first round of "browser wars." However, it was far from the end there. In 1998, Netscape disclosed its browser source code and renamed it as Mozilla, with all program having been rewritten. In 2002, it released its first version. In 2004, the debut of Firefox based on Mozilla source code kicked off the second browser wars. Microsoft's browser share dropped from the highest point of 96% to 85%, mainly because of the strong market offensive of Firefox. Therefore, Microsoft fought again by quickly releasing its Internet Explorer version 7.0 which was scheduled to be coordinated with Longhorn Windows version ahead of time, so as to compete with Firefox.

2.4.4.9 Competition in the Web Search Engine Market [27]

Search engine refers to the system to gather information on the Internet, which can provide search services and show the retrieved relevant information to users after information organization and processing, based on certain strategies and specific computer programs. Search engines include full-text index, catalog index, meta search engine, vertical search engine, set search engine, portal search engine, free link list, etc.

In the early period of Internet development, the website classification directory query represented by YAHOO was very popular. Web Site Directory, which is arranged and maintained by human, is classified into different catalog after selecting the best web sites on the Internet and making brief descriptions. Users can search the websites they want by layers of clicks when searching. Some people also call the search service website based on the catalog as a search engine. However, technically, it is not a search engine.

In 1990, teachers and students in School of Computer, University of McGill developed Archie. At that time, Wide Web World had not yet appeared. Moreover, people shared exchange resources through File Transfer Protocol (FTP). Archie can collect and analyze the file name information in FTP server on a regular basis, and provide search for documents scattered in each FTP host. Users must enter the exact name of the file to search. Archie told users which FTP server can download the file. Although information resources collected by Archie was not a web page (HTML file), they are the same as the basic operation mode of search engine: automatic information resources collecting, index establishing and retrieval services providing. Therefore, Archie is recognized as the originator of modern search engines.

The history of Excite can be traced back to February 1993 when six college students of Stanford University thought of analyzing words relationships to make more effective retrieval for volumes of information on the Internet. By mid 1993, it was a complete investment project. They also released a search software version, which was later called as Web Servers Excite, for webmasters to search on their websites.

In April 1994, Chinese American Jerry Yang and David Filo, two doctoral students of Stanford University, co-founded Yahoo!. With the increase of page view and included links, Yahoo directory began to support simple database search. Since Yahoo data was by-hand input, it could not be virtually categorized as a search engine, but a searchable directory in fact. The websites included by Yahoo! Improved search efficiency significantly due to the attached profile information. Yahoo! Almost served as a synonym for the Internet in the 1990s.

In 1995, a new search engine form-meta search engine appeared. Users only need to submit one search request, which will be submitted to multiple pre-selected independent search engines after conversion process by meta search engine and gather all query results returned by independent search engines to return to users after processing.

The first meta search engine—Metacrawler was developed by Eric Selberg and Oren Etzioni, two postgraduates in Washington University. The idea of meta search engine is very pleasant to hear, but the actual search results are always not ideal, which explains why no meta search engine has ever owned a strong position.

On September 26, 1995, teaching assistant Eric Brewer and doctoral student Paul Gauthier of University of California Berkeley co-founded Inktomi. On May 20th, 1996, Inktomi Company was established. Thus the powerful HotBot made its debut, claiming to be able to draw over 10 million pages per day, so it enjoyed new contents that far outperformed other search engines. HotBot also enjoyed extensive use of the personal search preferences of cookie storage users.

In December 1995, DEC officially released AltaVista, which is the first search engine that supports natural language and realizes advanced search syntax (such as the application of relations including AND, OR and NOT in search terms). Users can not only use AltaVista to search newsgroups' contents and obtain articles from the Internet but also can search the texts in the picture, Titles, Java applets and ActiveX objects. AltaVista claimed to be the first search engine to support users to submit or delete Uniform Resource Locator (URL) to web page index library on their own and to be able to be online within 24 h. One of the most interesting new functions of AltaVista is to search websites whose all links are pointed to a URL. As for the user-oriented interface, AltaVista also made many innovations. It put "tips" that constantly upgrading below the search box to help users to express better their search formulates. After searching for several times, users would find numerous interesting functions they might never have known. This series of functions were gradually widely used by other search engines. In 1997, AltaVista released a graphics demo system-LiveTopics, which helps users to find the information they want from thousands of search results.

In August 1997, Northernlight search engine officially made its debut. It was one of search engines that possessed the largest database. It does not own Stop Words but has excellent Current News, Special Collections composed of over 7100 publications and good senior search syntax. It is the first search engine that supports the simple automatic classification of search results.

Before October 1998, Google was just a small project-BackRub in Stanford University. Doctoral students Larry Page began to learn search engine design in 1995 and registered the domain name on September 15, 1997. At the end of 1997, BachRub began to provide Demo with the joint participation of Sergey Brin, Scott Hassan, and Alan Steremberg. In February 1999, Google completed the transformation from Alpha version to Beta version. Google took September 27, 1998, as its birthday. Google evaluated the importance of web pages based on PageRank, which greatly enhanced the relevance of search results. The geek culture atmosphere-"Don't be evil" ideas of Google won high reputation and brand reputation for it. In April 2006, Google announced its Chinese name as "Gu Ge," which is the first Google had a name in non-English-speaking countries.

Fast (Alltheweb) company, founded in 1997, is a by-product of the academic research of Norwegian University Science & Technology (NTNU). In May 1999, Fast released its search engine–AllTheWeb. The Fast's goal that to be the world's largest and fastest search engine remained nearly unchanged for several years. The web search of Fast (AlltheWeb) can adopt ODP automatic classification, support Flash, and PDF search and multi-language search, provide news search, image search, video, MP3, and FTP search, having extremely powerful advanced search functions. (On February 25, 2003, Fast's Internet search division was acquired by Overture.)

In August 1996, Sohu was set up. Sohu (Chinese: 搜狐; pinyin: Sōuhú; literally: "Search-fox") is a Chinese Internet company headquartered in the Sohu Internet Plaza in Haidian District, Beijing. This company and its subsidiaries offer advertising, a search engine, online multiplayer gaming and other services. In August 2004, Sohu created an independent domain search sites "Sogou".

Openfind was founded in January 1998. Its technology originated from GAIS laboratory led by Professor Wu Sheng of Taiwan University. Openfind initially only did Chinese search engine and provided Chinese language search engine for the three famous portals-Sina, Kimo and Yahoo simultaneously in its heyday. However, after 2000, the market was carved up by Baidu and Google gradually. In June 2002, Openfind relaunched Beta version of Openfind search engine based on GAIS30 Project and introduced PolyRankTM, claiming that it drew an accumulative 3.5 billion web pages. Hence, it began to enter into English search field.

In January 2000, two Peking University Alumni-Li Yanhong, the hyperlink analysis patent inventor and former senior engineer in Infoseek, and his friend Xu Yong, postdoctoral in University of California, Berkeley co-founded Baidu Corporation in Zhongguan Village, Beijing. In August 2001, they released Baidu search engine Beta version (previously Baidu only provided a search engine for other portals such as Sohu, Sina, and Tom). On October 22, 2001, they officially released Baidu search engine focused on Chinese search.

Other features of Baidu search engine included Baidu snapshots, page preview/ full page preview, and relevant search words, spelling correction, MP3 search and flash search. Its technology upgrading was accelerated significantly after the beginning of Blitzen Project in March 2002. Later, it launched a series of products, including post bar, know, map, Sinology, Wikipedia, documents, video, blog and network disk, which enjoyed tremendous popularity among netizens. On August 5, 2005, Baidu went public at Nasdaq, with its issue price being at $27.00 and code name BIDU. Its opening price was at $66.00 and the close price at $122.54, an increase of 353.85%, which made the highest increase record of the new share in U. S. stock market in 5 years.

On December 23, 2003, the YUANCONGHUI search engine claimed independent operation officially and established China Search. In February 2004, China Search released desktop search engine NetPIG 1.0. In mid-March 2006 NetPIG was renamed IG (Internet Gateway).

In June 2005, Sina formally launched self-developed search engine "Love Asking" Since 2007, Sina "Love Asking" began to use the Google search engine.

On July 1, 2007, Youdao search integrated the comprehensive search and Web search, which used self-developed technologies of NetEase. You do web search, image search and blog search provided service for Netease search. Among them, the Web search technology used the natural language processing, distributed storage and computing technologies which were self-developed by NetEase. Image search can search images with the brands and models of camera brand or advanced search conditions such as the seasons. Compared with similar products, the blog search has advantages of Comprehensiveness and promptness; it can also provide new functions such as "previewing" and "blog archives."

2.4.4.10   Amazon—The Rise of E-commerce [28]

It is a household story for the garage entrepreneurial myth that HP and Apple gained huge success in their garage startup business, which keeps inspiring waves of young people in venturing onto the entrepreneurship road. At the end of the twentieth century, another garage entrepreneurial myth was born and people took delight in talking about it, i.e., Amazon founded by young man Jeff Bezos in garage. Jeff Bezos was born in a Cuba immigrant family on January 12, 1964. Jeff Bezos, whose father immigrated to the United States in the early 1960s to work in Exxon, was fond of science since little and liked to fiddle with things, which nurtured his strong practical ability. In 1986, after graduating from American's prestigious Princeton University, Bezos entered into a new high-tech company in New York. Two years later, Bezos hopped to a New York Bankers Trust to manage computer system worth of $250 billion and became the youngest vice president of this company when he was 25. From 1990 to 1995, Bezos, together with other people, co-founded the world's most advanced, most successful hedge fund trading Management Company and became the company's youngest senior vice president in 1992.

In 1994, once when he was surfing the Internet, Bezos stumbled into a website and saw a number-2300%, meaning that the number of Internet users is growing at this rate. At that time, Seattle's Microsoft had grown up gradually. Bezos's eyes were shining when saw the figure, hoping that he could be like Microsoft to gain success in the IT industry and be a wave rider in the Internet tide.

Bezos made a list of 20 odd commodities and eliminated them item by item by simplifying them into books and music products. Finally, he chose to sell books first. Books are particularly suitable for display on the web. Also, as large publishing country, the U.S. owns books as many as over 1.3 million, while music products are only 20,000 to 30,000. What's more, book industry market space is relatively large, with an annual sale of $260 billion. However, America's largest chain book shop and also the world's first big bookstore which owns over 1000 subbranches has annual sales of only 12%.

A few weeks later, he refused the generous salary and embarked on a road of entrepreneurship. Bezos noticed moving company that he would inform them once he had chosen places in Colorado, Oregon and Washington State. He then rushed westward. He let his wife drive while he drafted a business plan in his laptop hastily. Moreover, then he could not wait to contact startup capital raise with his mobile phone.

In 1995, Bezos moved from Seattle to New York. The reason why he chose Seattle was that there were ready-made technical personnel and was also close to Oregon warehouse of Library Department in Ingram, the large channel distributor. Bezos spent $30,000 startup capital to put up America's first network retail companies—AMAZONCOM in the garage rented in the suburbs of Seattle. Bezos used the world's largest river to name his company, hoping that it could become the genuine "Amazon" in Books Inc.

In the initial stage of AMAZONCOM, Bezos spent a year's time to establish website and database to make Amazon gain a firm foothold in various competitive pressures in traditional bookstores. In the meanwhile, he carried out humanized transformation of the network interface to give customers a comfortable visual effect, which facilitated selection services. Of course, there were 1.1 million books available for chosen. Moreover, he was more cautious in the establishment of a database, which cost three months in software testing. Time proved that Bezos's practice was right. In July 1995, Amazon officially opened its "virtual business door" by these advantages.

From the very beginning, Amazon was faced with many challenges, the largest of which was the competition of traditional giant-Barnes & Noble, which Amazon had no intention of fighting for the market with, but had to face the tit-for-tat situation. The reason is that Barnes & Noble strongly resisted the fact that an opponent without foundation and had "unreal existence" seized their market. On the other hand, this is a confrontation between traditional and modern culture and the concept.

In this confrontation, the advantage of Amazon gradually highlighted. First of all, Amazon is one of the cheapest bookstores for its daily discount, being almost the world's largest book discount seller with over 30,0000 books available to be purchased and get discounts. Indeed, it did not like traditional bookstore business without intermediaries taking dividends, prompting Amazon to sell books or other goods at a relatively modest price. Of course, there were also a few other bookstores whose price was lower, but their difference is minuscule. Because being the cheapest was not the most important, what's important is that there were books that are cheap and convenient, which made customers unwilling to look elsewhere for a little difference. Thus they only chose Amazon. Moreover, it provides a far more convenient service model than that of the traditional ones', and comprehensive and detailed bibliographies. Due to strong technical support, one can certainly get a response within 3 s when buying books on Amazon, which greatly save customers' time. Compared with Barnes & Noble, who could provide a maximum of 250,000 different bibliographies, Amazon had 2.5 million volumes of books through the network. As Bezos put it, if there were an opportunity to print out Amazon directory in a written way, it would probably be equivalent to seven telephone directories of New York.

Its response speed also reflects in warehouse goods updating. There is almost no inventory in Amazon, except for its 200 copies of the best-selling books. Even with this inventory, the upgrading frequency of Amazon was surprising. There was data showing that Amazon changes its inventory as many as 150 times per year, whereas Barnes & Noble were only 3 ~ 4 times. The data showed not only the speed of Amazon but also its sales volume.

Bezos is a genuine innovator of the Internet. Amazon owns 30,000 thousand "agencies," who provided second recommendations for books released by Amazon on their websites. When visitors on the Internet chose recommended books on their websites through a click, these agencies could claim 15% of commission from Amazon.

At the same time, Bezos also helped to define an Internet community centered for a shopping site. The editorial contents of the community update everyday and also provide services such as "reader review" and "continue writing novels," which Bezos is the first to implement the application mode in the network. The two small innovations have increased at least nearly 40, 000 customers for Amazon.

However, Bezos did not stop his pace of expansion and innovation, to put it simply, we can define his goal as "big, and bigger." His business was not limited to books any more, and he wanted to build one of the largest online shopping centers.

Through a series of efforts, Amazon completed a transformation and was getting stronger. Bezos also had a far-sighted vision. In March 1998, Amazon opened children's bookstore, though being the largest and most famous bookstore online at that time, Bezos continued to guide Amazon to a further development of his theory. In June, Amazon music store opened and cooperated with Intuit Personal Finance Site and Selected Desktop Software in July. In October, Amazon marched into continental European markets and sold an additional videotape and other gifts in November. In February 1999, Amazon bought pharmacy site stake and invested in it. In March, it invested in pet website and established network auction station at the same period. In May, it invested in household articles website.

In January 2000, Amazon and network express company reached a cooperation agreement worth of $60 million, making it possible for goods ordered by users to be able to be delivered within an hour. The direct result of these series of initiatives was that Amazon's customers exceeded 15 million. During this process, Amazon has transformed from a purely online bookstore to an online retailer. Behind this set of data, people saw constant expansion and further expansion. However, it was during this stage that Amazon's stock price rose by more than 50 times, while its market value peaked at $20 billion.

Then in July 2002, there was no expected economic recovery or IT resurrection. WorldCom announced its bankruptcy protection due to financial scandals, leaving the global telecommunications industry riddled with groaning. Nevertheless, with other people in such a pain, the Internet Cooperation was the only green pasture. A large number of listed companies began to officially get rid of their "deficit" careers and march towards a healthy road full of profits. Major Internet companies such as YAHOO, eBay, Amazon all announced performance is exceeding their expectations. The business model held a strong foothold after experiencing severe doubts.

The dull Internet finally heard the long-lost laughter of Bezos. He admitted that what he had expected in 1994 was completely wrong since he had underestimated the power of electronic commerce. "Our initial business plan was expected to achieve $70 million in sales revenue and $4 million operating profit in 2001." Nevertheless, in 2001, Amazon's revenue is expected to reach up to $3 billion, 42 times that of its expectation. Today, Amazon is one of the Fortune 500, becoming the U.S. largest Internet e-commerce companies.

When nobody knows what "e-commerce" is, Bezos has confirmed e-commerce by his own actions. "Amazon" is the first e-commerce brands. In July 1995, Amazon was just a small site, and in January 2000 Amazon's total market capitalization had reached $21 billion, eight times than its old competitor. In less than five years, the Amazon's amazing growth rate has created a network myth.

Internet technology and graphical Web browser provide a new easy-to-use applications and service opportunities. The new company is emerging almost everyday. Providing software solutions for e-commerce companies is a good example. Many entrepreneurs seized this opportunity and set up new companies such as BroadVision, iCat, Intershop Communications, Inc., Open Market and Commerce Wave. Also, young professional service companies also take advantages of this opportunity.

The Internet is not just the miracle of the software industry. Communications, media and electronics industry also be involved in this evolution, which has brought a new dimension of the industry. Today, several platforms, programming languages, and robust key criteria co-exist, and often had to be parallel processing. This powerful standard including MVS and OS/390 which are used in the mainframe-based system, Unix, NT and Windows which are used in a medium-sized machine system, and Microsoft CE which is used in embedded software. Till now, none of other eras has experienced a similarly high degree of complexity brought by the coexistence of IT and communication structure.

2.5   Summary

Demand determines everything. Software culture is produced in the development of demand. From single computing capabilities, the software is diversifying with the functions like word processing, and entertainment. Also, with the development of demand, programming languages are in steady progress. From machine language to assembly language, and high-level programming language, the progress of the programming language makes software development simpler and quicker and promotes the optimization and evolution of software.

When people are eager to communicate with the world, the Internet was born. The value-added software has profound effects on people's lifestyle and becomes the indispensable carrier of information in the information age. Various novel network service patterns are constantly emerging, and at the same time, our life is closely connected to the network. Meanwhile, the emergence and development of software companies also contribute to the software culture. Software companies continuously promote the development of software, which brings new opportunities and challenges to the software industry. The constant mixing and innovation of these elements satisfy people's demand for software, providing new work and lifestyle and enriching the software culture. In next chapter, the book will introduce the classification of software.

References

1. Osterweil, LJ (2008) What is software. Automated software engineering 15(3):261–273.
2. Fuqing Y, Hong M, Keqin L (1999) Software Reuse and Software Component Technology [J]. Acta Electronica Sinica, 2rd edn.
3. Menell PS (1987) Tailoring legal protection for computer software. Stanford Law Review, 1329–1372.
4. Lampson BW (1965, November) Interactive machine-language programming. In: Joint computer conference, part II: computers: their impact on society, 30 November-1 December 1965, pp 141–149.
5. Priestley M (2011) The Invention of Programming Languages. In: A Science of Operations I. Springer, London, pp 185–224.
6. Backus J (1978, June) The history of Fortran I, II, and III. In: History of programming languages. ACM, pp 25–74.
7. Lindsey CH (1996, January) A history of Algol 68. In: History of programming languages-II. ACM, pp 27–96.
8. McCarthy J (1978, June) History of LISP. In: History of programming languages I. ACM, pp. 173–185.
9. Sammet JE (1978, June) The early history of COBOL. In: History of programming languages I. ACM, pp 199–243.
10. Wexelblat, Richard L (ed) (2014) History of programming languages. Academic Press.
11. Jensen K, Wirth N (2012) PASCAL user manual and report: ISO PASCAL standard. Springer Science & Business Media.
12. Ritchie DM (1993) The development of the c language. ACM SIGPLAN Notices 28(3): 201–208.

13. Englehart M, Jackson M (1994, March) ControlH: A fourth generation language for real-time GN&C applications. In: Computer-Aided Control System Design, 1994. IEEE/IFAC Joint Symposium, pp 261–270.

14. Goldstein I, Papert S (1977) Artificial Intelligence, Language, and the Study of Knowledge. Cognitive Science 1(1): 84–123.

15. Redmond KC, Smith TM (2000) From whirlwind to MITRE: The R&D story of the SAGE air defense computer. Cambridge, MA: MIT Press.

16. Copeland DG, McKenney JL (1988) Airline reservations systems: lessons from history. MIS quarterly, pp 353–370.

17. Sobel R (2000) Thomas Watson, Sr: IBM and the Computer Revolution. Beard Books.

18. Cohen JE, Lemley MA (2001) Patent scope and innovation in the software industry. California Law Review, pp 1–57.

19. Ahmed FR, Hall SR, Pippy ME, Huber CP (1966) NRC crystallographic programs for the IBM/360 system. World List of Crystallographic Computer Programs 2: 52.

20. Cespedes FV, Smith HJ (1993) Database marketing: New rules for policy and practice. Sloan Management Review 34(4): 7.

21. Deitel HM (1984) An introduction to operating systems, vol 3. Reading, Massachusetts: Addison-Wesley.

22. Bolter JD (1991) Writing space: The computer, hypertext, and the history of writing. Hillsdale, NJ: Lawrence Erlbaum Associates 363.

23. Sandhu RS, Coynek EJ, Feinsteink HL, Youmank CE (1996) Role-based access control models yz. IEEE computer 29(2): 38–47.

24. Brown ST, Lindsey JL (2011) US Patent 8,020,756. Washington, DC: US Patent and Trademark Office.

25. Kraut R, Patterson M, Lundmark V, Kiesler S, Mukophadhyay T, Scherlis W (1998) Internet paradox: A social technology that reduces social involvement and psychological well-being?. American psychologist 53(9): 1017.

26. Levy RA (1998) Microsoft and the Browser Wars. Conn. L. Rev. 31: 1321.

27. Gandal N (2001) The dynamics of competition in the internet search engine market. International Journal of Industrial Organization 19(7): 1103–1117.

28. Chaffey D (2007) E-business and E-commerce Management: Strategy, Implementation and Practice. Pearson Education.

Chapter 3
Classification and Software Culture

Abstract Peculiar to a multitude of principles, computer software could be grouped into different classes. The classification is partly based on the culture of developers and target users, and the process itself is also a reflection of the culture. Sticking to the different ages of development of mankind to analyze the different classes of software, at first were database systems. As data amount skyrocketed, those systems expressed transplanting, data redundancy, space waste and update difficulty encumbrances, which hindered their ontogenesis. As a consequence was hierarchical, grid database, relational, and non-relational database systems. Following the problem-solution patterns, DOS system ran and operated disks. Driven by users solicitation, it went through a series of redesigns, and finally its legendary predecessor, the windows OS. Together with its principal rivals, the Linux OS and apple Mac OS, they imparted variegated features in manifold ways, thence storifying the different classes of operating systems. Portable and Mobile operating systems were introduced for the sake of mobile computing. The latter interacted with users meanwhile underlying drivers systems managed device hardware. In response to the multifariousness of software systems emerged different classes of programming languages to dispatch heterogenous prospects such as object-oriented programming, script language, and many more. Compilers conjointly forked into distinctive classes transforming incommensurable codes. Game software shifted from console to networking with the proliferation of the internet. Threatens to security bred assorted target-purposed security software. In the chapter below, we will look into these classifications and how they chaperoned mankind all along.

The software was designed after the birth of the first computer in the world during the 1950s and has developed to the fifth generation thanks to the booming software industry over the world. It has deeply rooted in military, education, aeronautics, astronautics, medicine, service and many other areas. There are so many different kinds of software that we categorize for convenient management [1].

Classifying normally is proceeded according to the characteristics of things. In the preface of *Book Shun's Literature*: On the land belonging to the king, rooms are

© Springer Nature Singapore Pte Ltd. and Zhejiang University Press 2018   83
Z. Qin et al., *Fundamentals of Software Culture*,
https://doi.org/10.1007/978-981-13-0701-0_3

set, classifications are created, make Guzzo. *Biography of Kong records birth, into a family, distinguished by the family, classification coordinates them.* Poet Bai Juyi wrote in his poem: *During Tanguy, born with the family Jiang, awarded with Qi, by classification called Cui.* In Ma Nandan's book Night Talk In Mount Yan, he wrote H*ow should poem and article be distinguished? How should their forms and structures be distinguished? These are a controversial question from the past.* Therefore, Classification is social, diverse, systematic and periodic [2].

The classification of software is one branch of culture. *There are a thousand Hamlets in a thousand people's eyes (Shakespeare)* points out that there are different classifications if you see from different angles. Figure 3.1 shows ridges or peaks in the classification of software.

Readers can see from the picture above that different classifications are created by viewing software from different angles. When it comes to the problem of which classification to apply, people always have diverse opinions. In this book, the classification method combines the popular classification standard from China and other countries. International standard *ISO/IEC TR 12182* and Chinese *Computer Software Classification Code Form* are the prototypes [3].

Chapters 1 and 2 introduce the history of computer and software to the readers, followed by the this chapter illustrating the classification of software, including system software and application software. Representative system software and application cases are the keypoints. Due to the limit of the length of the book and the diversity and polytropism of software, it is impossible to cover more parts in this chapter. We are sure that readers will be curious about this chapter [4].

Fig. 3.1 Ridges or peaks in the classification of software

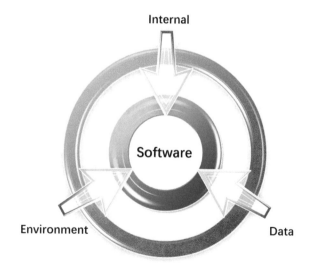

3.1 Culture of Classification

The classification of software contains a profound truth. Though we can not learn it superficially; we can try to understand it from all aspects of the characteristics it expressed. The very truth of it can be sensed well while not articulated, otherwise it would be far-fetched. Though it is hard to articulate the culture of software classification, we still try our best to illustrate the knowledge of this section.

"I get a range out of you crosswise but a summit, sidewise. Different visages, from near or far, from low or high." is a part of a famous poem in China which describes the different landscapes from different views. It means that we can draw different conclusions based on different aspects and it tells us that we can not describe a thing comprehensively with all sides. Shakespeare once said that there are a thousand Hamlets in a thousand people's eyes. Recently, a word "IP" become well known by people. In fact, IP is short for Intellectual Property which means a protection of creations. Patent, Copyrights are all belong to it. Copyrights can protect the uniqueness of some works like software, movie, book and so on. We can see software have a lot in common with the movie or other works, so they may share common culture. Given a software, we also cannot classify it into a class. Take the compiler as an example, it is used to compile the source code to generate executable application. It is combined with both application and operating system. Some people think it belongs to System Software because the ordinary users can not directly use it in their daily life and it needs a lot of components in the operating system, others stand on the another side because it is not totally a system.

The above example is about the differences between individuals in the thinking style and logical method. Only in the crowd, can people reflect their value and importance. We always believe that the culture is the inner spirits and their products shared in a group of people, which means culture is an attribute of a group rather than an individual. However, some people's points can stand for a group. The group makes the definition of an executable program and classifies it into a class. It is a simple process, but the classification process is the reflection of the culture of people in this group. We can at least find two kinds of groups in the process of software developing: the developers and the target users.

3.1.1 Culture of Developers

Most of people must know a computer game called *Counter-Strike* which is known as world most popular First Person Shooting game. It enjoyed great population when it comes up. The creator is Valve which is one of the top gaming companies. From the list of the games it developed, we can find that *Half-Life, Team Fortress, Life 4 Dead, and Counter-Strike* are all First Person Shooting games. From this we can see that this company is focused on the FPS games because of their developers. A story told that Jess Cliffe and Minh Lee who developed *Counter-Strike* as a MOD for *Half-Life* mean to let the workers in their company have fun. The developers may love the FPS so they focus on this kind of software. Another company Epic Games proposed a series called *Gears of War*, which belongs to Third-Person Shooting game. Different companies try to develop games can show their own characteristics.

From the aforementioned games we can see that a software is a product with core function, user interface, added value and the culture atmosphere it express. "Be What's Next" is the slogan of Microsoft. The products of this company can express their belief. The Office Software it constantly launched used well not only because the characteristics of product itself, but also the unique idea it tries to show us. Why this product outperforms other likewise products like OpenOffice? We believe that the complete ecosystem and the potential culture expression of the company is likely involved in the reason. The culture of one company can not only bring their ideas to the users, but also affect the style of users. The ecology circle a company creates can affect the way people solving problem and making their life better.

In the current era, nearly everyone can use mobile phone, computer, and the Internet. Countless apps appear in people's life every day and everywhere. The services and technologies behind those apps can affect us greatly. People use third-party payment tools like Apple Pay, PayPal, Ali Pay, Wechat Pay recently and feel it is more convenient than going to the bank. Going everywhere with only a mobile phone sounds cool. In fact, the high-performance servers and high-speed network connection in those companies and banks support this. The wide spread of "Cloud Service" can show us that people begin to talk with each other with "cloud" or they may feel they are out of dates. A lot of companies try to offer the service to users like iCloud that Apple offered. Without the service of computing, it is hard to offer cloud services to individuals. Without the cloud services, it is hard to develop apps which can meet the needs.

However, the effect is mutual. User preferences are the most import factor that the developers show take into account. In 2000s, the children are very happy to find a Compact Disk (CD) copy of some games. At that time, games are spread by CDs or Digital Video Disks (DVD). It is fine at the beginning but not convenient. As games are becoming more and more popular, their distribution needs to be updated urgently. Then Valve develop a platform called Steam, people can download the digital version of a game after paying for it. People have been accustomed to these methods and hardly go to the store buying a CD or DVD. All in all, the culture of developers is expressed to the users through the developing process especially the definition and classification of the products.

3.1.2 Culture of Users

People cannot directly contact the back service like servers and network connections, they usually judge an app with its user interface, fluency, effect and so on. Recently, an app called Mito Xiu Xiu become popular and rank 11 in the free application list of App Store. People share the effect of their photos after being modified by Mito Xiu Xiu on the Facebook and Instagram. People feel excited and funny because though they come from different countries, they share some common preferences on the interesting effect of photos. The app is so popular and even Mito company itself is not ready for this trend. However, some users complain that after the modification, their bodies in the photo become yellow skin though they are white skin or black skin. That is an interesting problem. Mito Xiu Xiu was first designed for Asian with yellow skin, and the built-in filters and parameters are most suitable for Asian and not perfectly fit for people living in other areas. If Mito Xiu Xiu did not succeed across the world suddenly, it is hard to realize the differences in using style between people have different cultures.

The software developers always focus on the languages of different users rather than the cultures. The aforementioned case is not hard to understand and it is not hard to go further than just language-oriented designing. A language is always a reflection of some specific culture.

People in different area have different criteria on beauty. It is generally recognized that white skin is beautiful in China, even in Asia. A white complexion is powerful enough to hide seven faults. Though an English proverb also tells the importance of white complexion, it is not regard in Western countries as important as in Eastern countries. The version oriented in the international market of Mito Xiu Xiu called Beautyplus has functions to satisfy the requirements of different users in Brazil, Japan, and so on. In which class should this app be classified? It is a tool to modify photos or an entertainment app to make fun? People can retouch the photos by adding some interesting components and share it on the SNS. If they do not care about the skin smoothing, they will think it is an entertainment app, even a social app. People can use the skin whitening and smoothing functions and classify it into tool apps. It is hard to tell but why not proposing another class? In fact, we always say Mito Xiu Xiu is a photo editing app. However, it is hard to say the problem is solved considering Snapseed, VSCO, MIX are all photo-editing apps and differ markedly with Mito Xiu Xiu. These apps focus on the light, color and composition of different kind of pictures including portrait and landscape. The classification should consider the culture, and the process is also a reflection of user cultures.

3.2 System Software

System software is the computer software designed to provide services to other software. Examples of system software include operating systems, computational science software, game engines, industrial automation, and software as service applications. There's no specific definition of system software because it includes different software in varying circumstances [5]. In Chinese *Computer Software Classification Code Form 2011*, it is defined as basic software, with validity range similar to European and American classification standards. In this book after generalizing different classification standards, we will classify system software into five categories: operating systems, database systems, drivers, programming tools, and compiling tools. We will illustrate the utility of this software.

3.2.1 Operating System

3.2.1.1 Basic Knowledge of Operating Systems

Is it possible that my computer runs ten programs simultaneously? Does my computer have access to the Internet? Can my computer keep being stable after running complex games? All these questions depend on the operating system. Because the operating system is the main controller of all events in the computer system, and one of the most important factors determining the compatibility of computer and platform. Figure 3.2 shows the position of operating system in the architecture of the computer [6].

The operating system is the interface between user and computer as well as the interface between computer hardware and other software. The functions of operating system include managing computer hardware and software, controlling the processing of programs, facilitating interaction between man and machine, and supporting other software. This makes it possible to allow all the resources in the system play a maximum role, in offering diverse user interface, bringing users a pleasant working environment and providing other softwares with essential services and interfaces. Actually, users do not touch operating system, which allocates hardware resources of the computer to the request of programs, for example, the CPU processing time, the memory division, calling the printer, etc. [7].

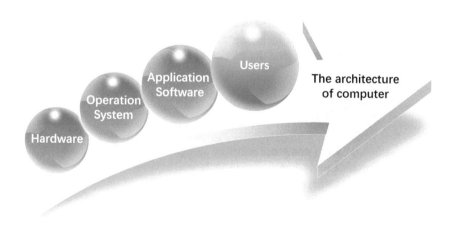

Fig. 3.2 The position of operating system in the architecture of the computer

There are many kinds of operating systems. The operating system installed in varying devices can be simple or complicated. Classified be application area there are three main classes: table operating system, server operating system, and mobile equipment operating system.

In the following part, we choose DOS system, Windows system from Microsoft, Mac OS operating system, Unix/Linux operating system, and the iOS system and Android system from mobile device system to explain in details.

3.2.1.2   Dos

DOS, standing for Disk Operating System, is the first operating system in the world for personal computers. It played a significant role on IBM personal computer in the compatible machine market during the 15 years from 1981 to 1995. If we consider it as the fundamental part of the later developed Microsoft Windows, such as Windows 95 and Windows 98, we find its commercial life lasted until at least 2000.

The DOS family includes MS-DOS, PC-DOS, DR-DOS, FreeDOS, ROM-DOS, JMOS, etc., among which MS-DOS is the most famous one. Although all these systems are named as DOS for short, none of them is named simply as DOS (An operating system on irrelevant IBM big host computer in the 1960s was named DOS). What's more, several disk operating systems that neither have a connection with DOS nor work on x86 micro computer system included the word DOS in them. On the occasion when we specifically talk about machines, there are also abbreviations DOS (For example AmigaDOS, ASMDOS, ANDOS, Apple DOS, Atari DOS, Commodore DOS, CSI-DOS, Pro DOS, TRS-DOS, etc.). However, these systems are not compatible with the executable files in DOS or MS-DOS API (Application Programming Interface).

DOS is an operating system controlled by commands. It presents users with character user interface (the communication between man and computer is mainly through text or words) and set many keyboard commands. Users familiar with the commands can input commands directly from the keyboard. When a user sends out a command, the system follows it right away and responds to the user on the screen. For instance, the user can simply input dir command from the keyboard if he wants to see what files are saved on the hard drive, and the computer will show the list of files on the screen of the monitor. Figure 3.3 shows part of the result when dir command is run on DOS operating system.

In DOS, every command is transformed into a sequence of orders that computers can direct and the process of executing a command is simply finishing the prearranged one or a few tasks with the prepared program. The paper takes MS-DOS as the research center to give a brief introduction of DOS.

DOS is an operating system for PC IBM and its compatible machines. Before DOS, some computers employed internal BASIC programming languages for their operating systems, while others embraced the CP/M operating system developed by Digital Research (which provided DR-DOS). Microsoft Corporation developed the MS-DOS after 1970, a time when the company developed similar

```
E:\>dir

Volume in drive E is
Directory of E:\

AUTOEXEC BAT              0  07-06-05  11:20 AUTOEXEC.BAT
CONFIG   SYS             0  07-06-05  11:20 CONFIG.SYS
DOCUME~1        <DIR>        07-06-05  13:06 Documents and Settings
HA-PAR~1        <DIR>        12-28-05  12:01 HA-PartitionMagic80-LDR
PROGRA~1        <DIR>        12-28-05  12:02 Program Files
WINDOWS         <DIR>        01-16-06  12:43 WINDOWS
         2 file(s)              0 bytes
         4 dir(s)    1,966,604,288 bytes free

E:\>c:

C:\>dir

Volume in drive C has no label
Volume Serial Number is 30DE-28B1
Directory of C:\

AIRENDOS EXE    6,079,239  12-12-05   5:14
         1 file(s)      6,079,239 bytes
         0 dir(s)   3,745,472,512 bytes free

C:\>_
```

Fig. 3.3 Part of the result when dir command is run on DOS operating system

basic programming languages for different computers. In 1980, IBM was in the middle of designing the earliest IBM PC and asked Microsoft to develop multiple programming languages for its new machine and CP/M became the operating system for IBM new models. While Microsoft was programming language for IBM PC, though Microsoft company improved language and application design of IBM PC, they are more aware that developing a PC operating system is their direction of efforts, which, however, did not leave enough time to start from scratch. To solve this problem, Microsoft bought an operating system 86-DOS for the 8086 processor, which is much the same as the first 8086 processors in PC IBM.

DOS 1

Based on the 86-DOS operating system, Microsoft developed the MS-DOS version 1.0, which was unveiled together with the earliest PC IBM in 1981. DOS 1.0 does not support hierarchical directory, all of the file accesses must go through file control block, and a technology followed by CP/M. DOS 1.0 supports two types of execution files: COM and EXE. All formats of COM file are similar to CP/M executable files and are limited to the 64 KB memory space used by the code, data and stack space. Also, the version 1.0 introduced batch processing file. Since the first IBM PC only has a small memory of 64 KB, command processor (command. Com) has to be employed to reduce all memory capacity. Version 1.0 divides command processor into resident and transient portion, and the latter can be covered by other DOS programs during the process of the executive program. The resident portion detects transient one when the program run is completed, and the resident portion will be reloaded into memory from disk when necessary. When Microsoft provided IBM with DOS, the user name of IBM was PC-DOS, which illustrates the close relationship between IBM and PCD.

DOS 2

In 1982, Microsoft released the second version of DOS, a version that supports double-sided floppy disk drive and was called by Microsoft as MS-DOS 1.25 and PC-DOS version 1.1 by IBM. The early single floppy disk drive can only have access to information stored on a single floppy disk. To reduce the amount of disk used, some users buy a disk that can be turned over and store information on both sides. In addition to supporting double-sided disk, DOS 1.1 also corrected some errors found in the version 1.0 and provided a programmer tool known as EXE2BIN.exe.

The earliest IBM PC is based on floppy disk system and uses area A and B in floppy disk drive. The earliest PC does not support the very expensive hard drive at that time. Microsoft developed a new file system for DOS when IBM published the IBM PC XT program that included 10 MB hard drive. MS-DOS version 1.0 and version 1.1 do not support hierarchical directory, which is a necessary directory for the hard disk.

Therefore, Microsoft chose to develop the hierarchical directory structure similar to the operating system of minicomputer—UNIX, which had come into vogue then. Because file control block did not support the space used for directory path name, Microsoft kept file control block and made version 2.0 manage file based on a file handle.

The second advantage for DOS to use a file handle is that it can realize redirection function (also an ordinary function of UNIX). IBM became very successful by using the DOS version 2.0. Also, DOS and CP/M operating systems became optional operating systems. Due to the popularity of PC machine, a wealth of hardware manufacturers developed products based on PC. In an attempt to help these manufacturers to collect products, MS-DOS 2.0 provided an installable device driver, providing a CONFIG.SYS pre-configuration file for the first time. The DOS version 2.0 contains many UNIX features. However, UNIX is an operating system that allows numerous users to run multiple programs at the same time. To provide a simplified format for multitasking, they provided memory-resident programs such as GRAPHICS and PRINT. After DOS version 2.0, Microsoft also released MS-DOS 2.01, which supports international character set. It was during this period that IBM launched its short-lived IBM PC Junior (IBM PCjr for short) computer. To support PCjr, Microsoft developed PC-DOS 2.1 for IBM. Later, Microsoft combined the last two DOS versions and produced MS-DOS 2.11. In 1983, Microsoft unveiled the MS-DOS 2.25 version, which includes the fault location and supports the expansion of ASCII character set.

DOS 3

In 1984, IBM released 80286 IBM PC ATS that used the big floppy disk drive of 1.2 MB and maintained computer settings in CMOS chip. To support DOS version 3.0, a period around 1984 became the ferment of a computer network. Although the wide application of LAN was something in the future, many DOS version 3.0 had been regarded as the supporting network. DOS version 3.1 succeed in supporting local network, though DOS version 2.0 replaced file handle with file control block, some existing procedures still used file control block (FCB). To reduce the excessive use of file control block in network process, DOS3.1 allows opening four file control blocks at a time. If the program opens the fifth files, the network server or SHARE will close the file control block opened first. DOS 3.1 adds CONFIG. SYS FCBS and also introduces JOIN and SUBST virtual command. In 1986, Microsoft released a 3.5-inch floppy drive version 3.2. Also, the DOS version 3.2 also added REPLACE and XCOPY commands. In 1987, IBM released the PS/2 series of computers. Microsoft unveiled DOS version 3.3 to support PS/2. In addition, to supporting PS/2, DOS introduces five commands: CALL, APPEND, KEYBCHCP, NLSFUNC, and FASTOPEN. So far, DOS3.3 has become the most widely used and most popular DOS version. In fact, today a myriad of users are still running DOS 3.3 in that it works well. The main shortcoming of DOS 3.3 is that it only supports disk partition not more than 32 MB.

DOS 4

In 1988, Microsoft released the DOS version 4.0 which breaks through the limit of 32 MB disk partition. In version 4.0, disk capacity can be up to 512 MB. Also, the DOS version 4.0 provides a menu-driven shell program that allows users to select file menu or use mouse to select the file. The DOS version 4.0 also introduces MEM command which not only allows users to display conventional computer memory capacity, but also shows the expanded and extended memory capacity. At the same time, the version 4.0 also modifies multiple commands to make it rather effective in using memory. To make up for the defects of the initial DOS version 4.0, Microsoft released a version 4.01. In fact, most users and manufacturers decided not to upgrade to the DOS version 4.

DOS 5

In 1987, the personal computer revolution evolved into a local area network revolution, that is, offices throughout the United States began to connect personal computers together to share information. This revolution did not last long because user program was so large that it was difficult to run in a conventional 640 KB memory limit. In some cases, the user wants to extend and expand memory. However, many programs including DOS cannot run in an address over 640 KB. In 1990, Microsoft was extremely successful in launching a friendly user interface windows, in which new users can learn how to use a computer faster, and experienced ones can improve efficiency by running multiple programs simultaneously. In 1990, other software tools opened markets with millions of dollars a year in the name of "DOS forgotten applications." In 1991, Microsoft released DOS version 5.0, which was the 10 years' improved result of the earliest 86-DOS. DOS version 5.0 addressing space not only supports the conventional, expanded and extended memory but also has a high memory block to run DOS, load device drivers, and memory retention program memory capacity. DOS version 5.0 also uses more menu-driven shell that is more powerful to replace the corresponding command in the DOS version 4.0. Besides, it also allows the user to recall the command used before quickly and define memory-resident macros like that small fast batch file processing. To provide disk applications to all users, DOS version 5.0 presents a command to recover mistakenly deleted files and allows the disk to be rebuilt after running disk formatting accidentally. Finally, to keep up with the progress of the added hard disk capacity, the DOS version 5.0 supports disk partition as high as 2 GB.

DOS 6

In early 1993, Microsoft released DOS version 6.0, which further expands software functions that the previous user must purchase from other software companies by DOS version 5.0. First of all, DOS version 6.0 provides INTERLNK and INTERSVR applications that can make it easy for portable computers to exchange files with desktop PC computers. In the future, many new computers will be equipped with power management chip supporting Advanced Power Management (APM) so as to control the use of power supply. DOS version 6.0 provides the POWER command, which allows DOS to control the chip. DOS version 6.0 also provides programs to check and clear virus and utility routine to arrange disk. DOS version 6.0 introduces the option to create a basic configuration menu CONFIG. SYS to help users configure their systems. Before publishing DOS version 6.0, Microsoft unveiled a web-based Windows version used in Workgroups and Windows which was able to allow users to share data, send and receive email and print remote files. To help users to get these functions without running Windows, DOS version 6.0 provides NET command. Furthermore, DOS version 6.0 provides a powerful menu-driven backup file utility program and disk compression software as well to allow users to multiply hard disk storage capabilities easily.

After several years, MS-DOS upgraded relevant functions along with the development and demand of computer technology and network technology. In September 2000, Microsoft released MS-DOS version 8.0, the very last version of MS-DOS. In short, DOS operating system has serviced several generations of personal computer users and has had some users in the past 20 years, creating a myth of the computer operating system [8].

3.2.1.3   Windows

The earliest edition of Windows, Windows 1.0 was built in 1985 when mouses are still not widely accepted. It has only one graphic program called the Micrographic, which was not popular at that time. After almost 30 years' extension, Windows comes to the version of Windows 6.3, normally known as the Win 8.1. History proved Microsoft to be right, and Bill Gates, the founder of Microsoft, became a billionaire at 31 and retained the richest in the world for the past years, attributing to this very personal computer operating system. It lures people to find out the magic power of Windows operating system.

Bill Gates set up the vision of Microsoft that every family owns a personal computer, in each of which, runs the Windows operating system produced by Microsoft. It seems that Bill Gates's dream has come true nowadays if you glance around and find that Microsoft has transformed from a small company founded at 1975 to the leader corporation in global software business facing antimonopoly lawsuits [9].

Knowing Windows

Over 80% of personal computers in the world run Windows operating system at present. Its name derives from the square working windows presented on the screen. Each window shows different files and programs, with multi windows, icons, menus, distant assistance and other services deployed. Users can operate in the visualized environment with input instruments like mouses and keyboards. This is Graphical User Interface (GUI), also known as the Windows system.

Microsoft Windows is a window operating system designed by Microsoft which came out in 1985. For the early versions of Windows, they were merely table environments that run on MS-DOS system. Windows systems became independent operating systems after Windows 98, and after almost thirty years' development, it conquered the major market of personal computer operating system. At 2004, vice chairman of directors Avneesh Saxena announced that Windows dominates approximately 90% of terminal operating system market. The Windows system nowadays runs in different environments, involving a personal computer, mobile device, embedded controllers etc. We will come up with these in the latter chapters of the book.

The newest personal computer version of Windows is Windows 8.1, and the newest server version of Windows is Windows Server 2012 R2 [10].

Differences between DOS and Windows

Windows system developed through a history of the 16-bit version, 16–32-bit mixed version, 32-bit version and 64-bit version. The 32-bit version Window (Window NT-structural operating system) is not based on DOS. These systems contain an NT Virtual DOS Machine, which runs a revised DOS on it. The command line interface applied by systems based on DOS is traditional COMMAND.COM, whereas Windows NT and its derivatives apply cmd.exe as their command line interface. With no doubt, lots of DOS commands are transplanted to cmd.exe [11].

User interface of 16-bit Windows

The early version of Windows system is 16-bit version, mainly including Windows 1.0 (1985), Windows 2.0 (1987) and their close relative Windows/286. Windows 1.0 is only a software application based on DOS system, and by real means, not an operating system. However, it owns a unique executable file type and supplies driver programs for its equipment (timers, graphics, printers, mouses, keyboards, sound cards) and therefore can be seen as an embryonic form of operating system.

Microsoft demonstrated to users the powerfulness of mouse with Windows 1.0. By using a mouse, users can accomplish most of the operations. Another breakthrough of Windows 1.0 is that, under the idea of parallel, users can run multi-functions simultaneously, switching from one to another. Windows produced Windows 2.0 in 1987, in which control panel was first introduced, and then went on the track of fast development.

The development of hardware empowered private computers with much greater capability than a few years ago, for example, superior processors are capable of sustaining user interface with greater visual effect. Microsoft published Windows 3.0 as the first successful Windows operating system of sense.

Window 16–32-bit mixed operating system

Dependent on the 16-bit DOS basic program to process, this series is merely an updated version of 16-bit Windows. Despite that it absorbed part of the 32-bit system features and to some extent has the 32-bit processing ability, it is single cored as same as 16-bit DOS because its structure deployed DOS code. This series, including the first version of Windows 95 in 1995, revised Windows 95 in 1996, 1997, the first version of Windows 98 in 1998 and proceeded by revised Windows 98 in 1999 and 2000. The three versions of Windows 98 all converted into Windows ME consequently. It is notable that menu, task bar, and minimize button, maximize button, and close button all first appeared in Windows 95. Besides, the symbol of the coming of the Internet Era appears when Windows 95 started supporting Transmission Control Protocol/Internet Protocol (TCP/IP) and offering access to the Internet. Leading users from 16-bit operating system to 32-bit system, Windows 98 is the last version of Windows which bases on MS-DOS [12].

Windows 32-bit operating system

Based on Windows NT structure, this series of Windows can be seen as a real 32-bit operating system. Different from 16–32-bit mixed Windows 9x which bases on DOS, Windows NT-structural operating system is an independent operating system. The design of the 32-bit operating system is purposed to fulfill the need of better performance in the commercial market. This series consists of Windows NT 3.1 (1992), NT 3.5, NT 3.51, NT 4.0, Windows 2000 (NT 5.0), Windows XP, 32-bit Windows Vista, 32-bit Window 7, Window 8 and Windows 8.1. Windows Server 2003 also expanded into an x86 version, including Windows Server 2003 R2 Datacenter Edition (32-bit x86), Windows Server 2003 R2 Enterprise Edition (32-bit x86), Windows Server 2003 R2 Standard Edition (32-bit x86) etc. Windows 2000 is an operating system with support for graphics and suspensions, prepared for computers with a single core or symmetric multi-cores 32-bit Intel x86 processor in the commercial market. Windows XP has predominant stability and has served for 13 years from 2001.10 to its retirement on 2014.4.8. Seeing the popularity of Windows XP, Microsoft released other variant versions including embedded version to the market, and these versions can still be seen now at the Windows 8 Time. Even did Microsoft publish 64-bit Windows XP system along with the update of processor structure, and as well, Windows Vista, Windows 7, Windows 8, Windows 8.1 has both x86 and x64 version.

Windows 64-bit operating system

The 64-bit operating system was first realized on small and medium computers, mostly Unix series operating systems. Since the IA-64 64-bit processor came into being, 64-bit Linux and Microsoft Windows operating system was established on this platform. Latter, AMD produced 64-bit X86-64 CPU, which was supported by Linux platform quickly and also by 64-bit Windows XP Professional x64.

The original intention of the 64-bit operating system is to meet the need of instrumental design and analysis, 3D motions, video edition and creation, as well as scientific calculating and high-performance calculating program which need big memory and float performance. Due to the differences in command bit-width, 32-bit operating system utmost support 3.25 GB of internal memory, while the 64-bit operating system can make use of at most 128 GB of internal memory. Windows 8 drew the attention of the entire market once it came out and according to reports, Windows 8 Preview Edition was downloaded over a million times in one day. It is only a matter of time when there will be 4.5 billion users of Windows 8 [13].

3.2.1.4 Unix/Linux

Linux and Unix are two interconnected operating systems, with the biggest difference: the former being a new open-source-code free commercial software, the latter being traditional commercial software implementing intellectual property protection on the source code. This biggest distinction between them is demonstrated through the fact that users have high autonomy on the previous one and have to get used to the second one. This distinction also reveals that the exploitation of the first one is in an open environment while the exploitation of the other is completely in a dark box, indicating only the related developers have access to the prototype of the product [14].

The birth and growth of Unix

A research project was launch by Bell lab and two other institutions in 1965 to design a set of operating system named MULTICS for big host computers. The plan did not work out subsequently. Nevertheless Ken Thompson and Dennis Richie from Bell who participated in the plan developed the UNIX operating system. Their article *Unix time-sharing system* on *ACM Communication* in 1974 marked the first public exposure of Unix.

Unix is still universally applied although created before DOS. Initialized on a small computer, Unix is currently used in every place from big host to microcomputers. The high portability of Unix significantly facilitated its distribution. With 90% of its core code programmed in C language, it is the first attempt of applying advanced language to build an operating system.

AT&T enhanced Unix along the road of commercial computing. Thompson returned to his mother school UC Berkeley and transplanted Unix Six to PDP-11/70 in the 1970s. A special department was established to explore Unix, and they published Unix Berkeley Software Version, with another BSD in 1978. After this, there're been two product lines of Unix, the AT&T version, and the BSD version.

When Unix Seven was designed by AT&T in 1979, computers equipped with Unix operating system appeared on the market. Microsoft produced the microcomputer version of Unix, ENIX, and pushed Unix to microcomputers. Other BSD features were attached to Unix system V developed by AT&T, encouraging the industry to take that version as a standard. Due to other companies developing their variant system based on BSD, there were about 24 different Unix versions in 1993 [15].

The development of Unix brought about positive influences to the software industry. For instance, the application of C language and latter C ++ and script languages, and socket programming under TCP/IP which has become the main stream in internet programming. What's more, Linux, an operating system combined by free and commerce was inspired [16].

The birth and growth of Linux

Linus Torvalds is programed by a Finland student who improved the operating system by adding new features after using a system Minix which is similar to Unix. In August 1991, he released the first edition of Linux. People started distributing this shared software once they found it on an internet forum and every time a bug comes out, someone would immediately fix it. Linux soon became an operating system. It was programmed following the public POSIX standard, deploying plenty of GNU software supplied by MIT and Cambridge free software fund.

There were two major groups in the market before Linux was set up. One group consist of AIX from IBM, Solaris from SunSoft and other traditional Unix operating systems, which dominates the high-end and partially middle and low-end servers along with workstations and a majority part of the personal computer market. Linux widened users' eyes, and as free software, it opened up space for its development.

It is a remarkable fact that Bob Young founded RedHat in January 1995. Designing over 400 open-source code models, focusing on GNU/Linux, he produced Linux system with a brand Red Hat Linux, which was put on to the market. Linux 2.0 core was released in Jun 1996. It had around 400,000 lines of code and supported multi-processors. At this time Linux had evolved into the practical period with 350 million people using it worldwide. In the following twenty years, Linux developed continuously and had become one of the most important products in the market of operating software [17].

Red Flag Linux in China

Red Flag Linux was designed under the background of 1992 Gulf War and 1999 North Atlantic Alliance invasion to Kosovo area in Yugoslavia Alliance. At that time, computer operating systems used by Iraq and Yugoslavia Alliance government belong to Microsoft and other foreign companies in a percentage of 100%, so the multinational army successfully paralyzed their opponents' whole communication system. This alarms the Chinese government that China should have our independent operating system and application software system. Therefore, Institute of Software Chinese Academy of sciences started developing an independent operating system based on Linux and released Linux 1.0 version which was initially used in departments related to national security.

Red Flag boomed in the beginning. On October 20, 1999, the server version was published. In March 2000, Red Flag Linux signed contract uniting in the task of publishing Red Flag Linux ISV and encouraging more software companies to transplant their solutions on to the Red Flag Linux platform. In April, Linux technique assistance center was established with Intel and software industry association. In June, ISCAS started up Beijing Zhongke Red Flag Software Technology Corporation with Shanghai Lianchuang Investment Management Corporation. In April 2001, IBM, HP, and other companies started installing Red Flag Server product. In June Red Flag safe server got the safety certification by Computer Information System Product Supervision Test Center of Ministry of Public Security and reached the third level of national standard. In July, Red Flag had over a million set of contract sales with PC hardware companies. In December, Zhongke Red Flag won the contract of Beijing government table operating system product purchase, in which Microsoft failed, and by the same time, Red Flag Enterprise Server series three was launched into the enterprising market. On May 7, 2003, Oracle China announced strategic partner relationship with Beijing Zhongke Red Flag Software Technology Corporation, publishing co-designed Red Flag Data Center Server 4.0 version. In June, Red Flag Linux was certified by Intel and became one of the manufacturers supported by Intel Itanium 2 processor and super thread technology.

Red Flag had many cooperating partners, including BEA, CA, DELL, EMC, HP, IBM, Intel, NEC, Oracle, SAP, Sybase, Symantec, Square, Tide, Lenovo, TCL, etc. Red Flag Software cooperated with these partners, devoted to building a stable, reliable, safe, open, new corporate computing platform. Red Flag produces more and better quality products, including the desktop version, workstation version, data center server version, HA Cluster Edition, embedded Red Flag Linux etc. For a time, Red Flag Linux became one of the big and mature Linux publishers in China. There were users in government, postal service, education, telecommunication, finance, insurance, traffic, transportation, power, logistics, media, manufacture, and other industries.

When we were relieved to see our Linux operating system, however, on 2014.2.10, Zhongke Red Flag Software Technology Corporation announced the decision of the board to disincorporate the firm due to difficulties in operation. The 14 years history of this domestic operating system manufacture end with this announcement and pitied every one of us [18].

3.2.1.5 Mac OS

Brief introduction of Mac OS
Mac OS X, Mac OS 9, Mac OS 8 and System vX.X is a set of operating systems on Apple Macintosh series computer. Mac OS has the first successful graphic user interface in commercial use. The newest Mac OS X is Mac OS X 10.9 published at

the WWDC in San Francisco on June 10, 2013, which might be the last edition of Max OS X for Apple.

The inspiration of Apple Macintosh computer came from the Alto plan in PARC Xerox. Steve Jobs (one of the founders of Apple) was astounding when seeing the complete graphic interface and the convenience of using the mouse as input and output when he was arranged into the PARC research center by an engineer who once worked there. After this, Jobs became a fan of GUI and determined to build a computer like this [19].

Mac OS can be classified into two series of operating systems.

One 'Classic' Mac OS (build on the first Mac sold in 1984 and its later versions, with the ultimate edition Mac OS 9) which is too old to be supported. Its core is Mach which was named 'System v X.X' before Mac OS 7.6.1.

The new OS X combines BSD Unix, OpenStep, and elements from Mac OS 9. It is based on Unix with code-named Darwin and applied part of with open-source code.

Development of the Max OS family product

(a) **Copland**: Copland, the successor of Classic operating system (the latest version Mac OS 9), was once thought to be the next generation of the operating system of Apple. Mac OS 7.5 was coded as Mozart. Therefore composer Alan Copland was used to name the next generation of operating system. Classic Max OS suffers from instability during operation, the collapse of the system, and lack of protection mode for internal storage which directly impedes the functions of the machine. The design of Copland solved all these problems, for example, adopting internal memory protection mode and multi-assignment system. This project which was started in 1994, was abandoned and replaced by Max OS X after Apple acquired NEXTSTEP operating system from NeXT in 1996.8.

(b) **Taligent**: Taligent derives from the combination of "Talent" and "Intelligent." It is a modern goal-orientated operating system. Apple began developing Taligent since the 90s last century purposed to take the place of Classic Mac OS operating system. Taligent later developed into a joint venture with IBM to compete against Cairo from Microsoft and NEXTSTEP from NeXT. It was disincorporated in the late 90s of 20 century.

(c) **NEXTSTEP/BeOS**: Based on Mach and BSD, NEXTSTEP operating system was developed by NeXT, and equipped with relatively advanced GUI. BeOS (Be Operating System) was at first designed by Be for computers in American Telephone & Telegraph (AT&T). Afterward, it was made available on PowerPC processor in Be and even latter adapted to Mac to attract Apple to purchase BeOS as the operating system on the new generation of Mac computer.

At the time, the CEO of Apple Gill Amir wanted to buy Be, but the CEO of Be requested 400 million dollars for acquisition and ruined the deal. The highest price Apple could pay was 125 million then. The board of Apple finally decided NEXTSTEP shall be the appropriate choice and offer to acquire NeXT at 400 million in 1996.

The acquisition of NeXT helped cofounder of Apple; Steve Jobs went back to Apple. After a public battle for power against contemporary CEO John Charlie, Steve Jobs regained control of the firm. Eventually, NEXTSTEP which was based on Unix became the foundation of Mac OS X.

(d) **Mac OS X**: Apple accelerated its researching process of the new operating system after Apple acquired NeXT in 1996. When Jobs demonstrated Mac OS X to the public at the world exhibition in San Francisco on 2000.1.6, its most shining attribute was the Aqua UI. Undoubtedly Aqua was favored by users. Its arc curve, anti-reshaped edge, shadow, and transparency all brought a new experience of the operating system. This widened Mac users' eyes and won Jobs thundering applauses and cheers at the publishing.

Mac OS X as an entirely new operating system is loaded with completely different structure from the past. Because its core was BSD and Unix source code, the command line was first time used to access systematic functions. Apple freely published the core of this operating system and the open-source software, Darwin.

Many designs of Mac OS X was aimed to stabilize it to prevent break-downs. Memory protection mode and preemptive multi processing support many applications simultaneously, each of which uses its own memory. If one application crashes, the other programs will not be affected and will not paralyze the whole system. Apple installed for researchers a set of new program tools, of which the most important one was an IDE named Xcode, which supports several modern programming language compilers.

Features of the newest Mac OS X

Here's a brief of some of the features of newest Mac OS X.

(a) **Full-screen mode**: Full-screen mode is the direct reflect of the advanced internet and graphic technology of Mac OS X. It symbolizes Mac OS X entering grid computing completely and almost all the applications can run under full-screen mode which brings about the better interactive experience to users by simplifying the sophistication of multi-window operation and therefore greater efficiency.

(b) **Dock**: Dock is a good-looking task bar with the default location at the bottom of the screen. It contains colorful 3D icons including not only shortcuts but movies, web pages, text files etc. The humanized design and beautiful modeling was quickly accepted by users. Surprisingly, more than merely put icons; users can even drag ongoing Quick Time movies to Dock and continue playing it.

(c) **Time Machine**: The Chinese name of Time Machine is Shuguang Ji by which one can fell its power easily. It is the backup function in Mac OS X which needs to be used together with Mac and an external CD-ROM or AirPort Time Capsule. In the default circumstance of Time Machine, Time Machine automatically recognizes the backup disk of the user and copies all the files on to the disk until it is full.

(d) **Mac App Store**: Mac App Store works in a convenient way. There is no need for users to manage it deliberately. When a user buys an application, Mac automatically installs it to the rapid start panel. This intelligent nation, for advanced users, may seem unnecessary, however, for common users, installing applications can still be a difficult task even by applying the drag system of Mac [19].

3.2.1.6   Portable Device Operating System

Portable device operating system include embedded operating system in the factory control area like embedded Linux, Windows CE, Windows WP Embedded, Windows Vista Embedded, VxWorks, uCOSII, QNX, FreeRTOS, ENEA OSE and operating systems for consuming electronic products like iOS, Android OS, Windows Mobile OS, Symbian, WebOS, etc. On 2014.1.17, director of ISCAS introduced the China Operation System (COS) which they developed with Shanghai Liantong. Since this system has not been adopted at scale by the market, we do not compare it with other systems here [20].

Relations between portable device, operating system, and desktop operating system

There are some similarities between the functions of portable device operating system and desktop device operating system, for example, allocating processor resource, managing internal memory, loading program, commanding input and output, and creating the user interface. Since portable devices usually are used to process easier tasks, therefore operating systems on it are more succinct.

Because operating systems on the portable device are small, they can be stored in ROMs. Thus there is no need to load the operating system from hard disk to RAM, and the operating system is available almost instantly after starting it. Operating system on portable devices offers functions including embedded touch screen, handwrite input, wifi access, and cellular communication.

Android system

Android system is an open-source software platform and operating system based on Linux core, mostly used on portable devices like mobile phones and tablet computers. There is still no official Chinese name of this system. The system was first established by Andy Rubin, for supporting mobile phones. In 2005.8, Google acquires it and publicly released on 2007.11.5. Afterward, along with 84 hardware manufacturers, software developers, and telecommunication service providers, Google organized Open Handset Alliance, jointly developing revised Android system. Google subsequently released Android source code by authorizing Apache open-source license. The first Android intelligent phone T-Mobile G1 was released on 2008.10.22. Android gradually expanded its market and in the first quarter of 2011, the global market share of Android phone for the first time exceeds Symbian's, rising to the largest worldwide. According to data in 2012.11, Android takes 76% of the global intelligent phone market while its market share in China was 90%. On 2013.9.24, the fifth anniversary of Android system, over a billion devices around the world was using this system.

Android equipped with the drag notification system at its first version, while Apple iOS took another three years to design another effective system to realize information distributary. The drag notification system and abundant desktop widget support remain to the latest version. The latter updated Android 1.6 Donut not only made minor adjustments to the interface of the system, supported CDMA, revealing a business opportunity for Asian service providers, but more importantly supported many screen resolutions with great revolution independence. Android 2.1 Eclair hit the market on 2009.10.26, with the universally known Google Navigator released under this version. We will introduce Google navigator in Chap. 4. Google officially released Android 2.2, coded froyo at 2010.5.20. After this, Google strived to release Android 2.3 known as the Android Gingerbread at the end of the same year. On 2011.2.3, Google released Android 3.0 Honeycomb which was specially designed to tablet computers. On 10.19 of the same year, Google released Android 4.0 with Samsung in Hong Kong China, coded Cream Sandwich. During the period between 2012.6 to the end of 2013, Google has released four editions from Android 4.1 to Android 4.5 and is expecting to release Android 4.5 in July 2014 [21].

IOS system
Developed by Apple, iOS runs on iPad, iPhone, iPod Touch and other portable operating systems. Same as Mac OS X operating system, iOS is a Unix-like commercial operating system based on Darwin. Apple released this system at the Macworld conference on 2007.1.9. This initially for iPhone designed system named iPhone OS, gradually was applied to iPad, Apple TV, and other devices. Many familiar functions were excluded in the 1.0 version and added when iPhone OS 2.0 comes out. Apple officially renamed iPhone OS to iOS at the 2010 WWDC conference. iOS 5.0 was released in 2011, with new features including backup of iCloud and supporting Twitter. The iOS 7 released in 2013 was flattened, and the release date of iOS 8 is still uncertain.

3.2.2 Database System

In comparison with operating systems, the database system came into being much latter. It grew mature during the 60–70s of twentieths century, with solid theoretical basis. IBM's creation Information Management System (IMS) based on the hierarchical structure in 1969 was significant in a database system. Latter in the book will introduce the classification of the database system [22].

3.2.2.1   Basic Knowledge of Database System

The emergence of database

The database system is a system specifically used to manage data resource. It can be described as some interrelated data and a set of programs enabling users to access and alter these data.

The early method of data processing is the well-known file system, which is programing the procedure of data processing into a program file during data processing and generating a data file with the data according to the demand of the program and finally call them. This method seems easy to be understood. However, the disadvantage of it was revealed as the computer technology developed and data amount exploded. It suffers from inconvenience in transplanting, data redundancy, space waste and update difficulty, which hindered the development of database system.

The difference between a database system and a file system is that database orients from the management of data instead of some certain application software. All the data is saved in the database of a database system. It organizes data in a scientific way and by deploying database management system and all sorts of applications and interfaces in the application system, enables users to call data in the database conveniently. A certain department in the bank needs to save all the information of clients and their deposit accounts, for example. Assuming that file storage was adopted to manage files on the computer, the system has to operate data files and applications, such as opening account, deposit, the inquiry of balance, if a user operates the information. These applications are programmed by system programmers under the instruction of the bank. However, supposing that if the bank decides to support check accounts, then the system programmers will have to program new eternal files to save all the check account information associated with the bank. Thus, upcoming problems like overdraw have to be resolved. With the developing society and increasing demand in all the time, a growing number of data and applications are added into the system.

It is conceivable that the safety of accounts cannot be secured if data is managed as mentioned above. The emergence of database system enabled all applications to invoke requisite data through the database system and realized the sharing of the data resource. A database system supplies users with an abstract view of data, concealing details about the storage and maintenance of it. A DB system usually comprises of three parts: database, database management system and application software. The database management system is responsible for maintenance and management of the data. It makes the data management more convenient [23].

Features of database

The database system mentioned last chapter consists of three parts. Database (DB) is a set of related data put together under some standards. Database Management System (DBMS) is a complex software to manipulate and manage the database and the interface between applications of users and the whole database. DBMS accepts and analyzes user's request once received and operated (inquire, store, update) corresponding data in the database. User Application Software is a set of practical programs designed under user's need with orders supplied by DBMS. For example, the operating interface is used by a bank counter worker. In the latter part of the book, emphasize will be made on the introduction of DBMS.

Strictly speaking, the database system is an operable software system designed to store, maintain, and apply data provided by the system. Normally constituted by software, database, and data administrator, it is a combination of the storage medium, object to be processed and management system. The software mainly includes an operating system, various host languages, applications, and database management system. The database is a data set in the secondary storage organized by some data models. These data sustain independent while serving multiple application software.

Database is managed by the DBMS with all the insertion, revision, and retrieval operations via DBMS. DBMS is a system software, mainly functioning to maintain database and access effectively any part of the database. The maintenance includes integrity, consistency, and security of the data. Data administrator is in charge of creating, supervising and sustaining the whole database, and to make sure the data be within the access of everyone authorized [24].

History of database system
Let us review the history of database system here. The first commercial database system came out in the late 1970s, derived from the file system. DBMS at that time was mostly adopted to data with gadgets which needs lots of inquiries and updates, such as plane ticket booking system, the banking system, corporation records etc. One significant deficiency of these early data models was failing to support advanced language inquiry.

In 1970, Edgar Frank Codd published papers about relational database system, in which he proposed in the relational database [25], that system uses a chart named relation to organizing data. At the bottom layer of the database, the data structure can be sophisticated to ensure a quick inquiry. However, the support for advanced language for inquiry eliminated users' concern of the bottom layer data structure and increased obviously the efficiency of data management.

The large scale and high concurrency of Social Networking Services (SNS) dynamic website left the development of relational database far behind. In 2010, NoSQL became popular on websites of different size pursuing high efficiency.

Application of database system
The database was universally adopted, in areas including banking, aviation, finance, telecommunication, retailing, manufacture, education, etc.

We can learn the application in banks from the example given above. The database system can store basic information of deposit customers involving credit level, account, deposit, loan, and trade records.

In the financial industry, the database system is used to store real-time market data, the possession of shares, bonds, funds and other financial products, and trade records. Clients can trade online while corporations manage to operate smoothly.

The database system has similar applications in the retail industry, recording daily sales Ps, real-time order supervisions, product recommendation charts, client information and trade information recording, etc. The membership cards offered by shopping malls which eased people's shopping process are also supported by huge database systems.

Aviation as the earliest industry using the database from geographical distribution should give credit of its booming to the use of the database, considering managing merely the booking information and flight information can be a tremendous project.

The database is also adopted in telecommunication and manufacture, in the former of which manages clients' phone records, bills, and net information, while supply chain management is supported in the latter.

Taking into consideration the teacher–student information storage and staff information storage, the database has become an essential part of all corporations nowadays [25].

3.2.2.2 Hierarchical Database System

The emergence of hierarchical database system was aimed to simulate articles arranged in a hierarchy. It also saves and loads data in the form of records. The basest relation in a hierarchical database system is a basic hierarchical relation. It represents the one-to-many corresponding relations between two record forms, also the parent–child relation (PCR). There is one and only one record form with no parent, and that is the root node. The projection from a node to its parents is unique in the hierarchical models, therefore only by pointing out the parents of each record form (except for the root node), can represent the total structure of the hierarchical model. The hierarchical model is a tree shape and the earliest used data model used in commodity DBMS.

Hierarchical database system offers many storage structures, each of which has its saving and loading method. This enables the hierarchical database system to achieve high efficiency in data storage. The common structure can be classified as hierarchical sequential (HS) and hierarchical direct (HD). Further classifications can be done according to whether index technique is used.

One famous HDBS, IMS (Information Management System) was explored and released by IBM at the end of the 1960s as the earliest product of big database system program. It was applied to banking, military, and other areas. Even data from the Apollo Plan was managed by this system. Domestic developed HDBS also stepped forward with the first HDBS designed by ourselves, SKGX, released in 1980 by the group lead by Zhou Longxiang Academician. SKGX was made into the product on DJS100 series and approved by the industry.

The HDBS is capable of describing naturally and directly the one-to-many hierarchical relationship and guarantees high access speed. Although Non-HDBS model does not support Structured Query Language (SQL) from relational database model to proceed inquiry, HDBS has similar structure to XML (eXtensible Markup Language) structure, and cane easily adapted to e-commerce. IMS v9 added support for Java tools and Web Sphere tools, and IMS v10 added OTMA. The cost of IMS system is ever decreasing and easier to operate on microcomputers. As the core product of IBM, it was adopted successfully in many industries with over 95% of top 1000 companies in the world using IMS dealing with trade amount of over 50 billion and managing commercial data with a size of about 1500 trillion.

Despite the strength and promising future of HDBS, it has obvious disadvantages especially the difficulty to depict non-hierarchical relations in the real world. Therefore, net shaped operating system seems important.

3.2.2.3 Grid Database System

Grid database system adopts grid data model as the basic structure. This grid model is a structure more universal than a hierarchical structure. It eliminates the limits of the hierarchical model, enabling multiple nodes with no parent nodes and one node with couples of parent nodes. Besides, it allows multiple connections between nodes (we call it the complex connection). Grid database system adopts set to describe grid mode, and the set is a logic presentation of one-to-many connections between realities. It is the supposed loading route when using the database, and the pointer is used to record the values in sets in the storage disk. Therefore, grid model can be used to describe the real world more directly, realizing various complicated relationships in the real world and welcomed by users.

In 1964, Charles William Bachman and his group developed the first Integrated Data Store (IDS) which was the basis of grid database and universally applied. In 1969, grid model was purposed by Data Base Task Group (DBTG) belonging to Conference on Data System Language (CODASYL). The project group put forward a milestone report on grid database system, commonly known as DBTG report. Grid database system received huge attention at the time, and Bachman was thought to be "the father of grid database" for leading the design and development of IDS system and facilitating the creation of grid database standard. In the 1970 and 1980s, massive grid database system products hit the market, for instance, IDMS produced by Cullinet Software, DMS1100 from Univac, IDS/2 from Honeywell, IMAGE from HP, DMSII from Burroughs, etc. They were extremely popular in the 1970 and 1980s dominating the market of database products and influenced the proceeding database technology.

Here's a brief on DMS1100 which was a big database management system produced by UNIVAC on its 1100 series computers. It was officially put into use in 1974 and was one of the acknowledgeable excellent DBMS in the world. DMS1100 DBMS had physical structure independent from the physical device and developed the utmost capability of operating system. What's more, it achieved query language, which is a big leap forward in the study of grid data structure.

The deficiency of gird database is also apparent. Its already existing complex structure can get only more complicated in the process of receiving more complex requirements. The operating language of this system is odd, and the independency is not satisfying. These set of disadvantages pushed relational database into being.

3.2.2.4 Relational Database

The relational model is currently an important data model which organizes data with the relation.

In 1970, researcher Edgar Frank Curd from San Jose Lab of IBM published the paper *A Relational Model of Data for Large Shared Data Banks* on Communications of ACM [26]. That was the first time the relational model was mentioned and since then was the study of relational data theory and relational database method started. Edgar Frank Curd received the 1981 ACM Tuning Award for his excellent work.

The 1970s was the age for the development of relational database theory and its prototype. Among them, System R developed by San Jose Lab of IBM and Ingres by Berkeley were typical representations. There were series of theories and appliance achievements after massive high-level exploration and research including the listed components.

(a) Clarifying the standard illustration of relational model universally accepted by people. Studying relational database theories, mainly including function dependence, multiple value dependence, connection dependence and normal forms, which established the theoretical basis of the relational model.
(b) Explored relational data languages including relational algebra, relational calculating, SQL (structured query language) language and QBE (query by example), etc. It is a comprehensible loved descriptive language being different from database languages in grid database and a hierarchical database and drew the basic print for the 1980s' database language standardization.
(c) Developing various prototypes of RDBMS, conquering the barriers of query optimization, concurrency control, failure recovery and other key techniques. It not only enriched the DMBS realization technology and database theory but more importantly encouraged the development and application of RDBMS products.

A relational database is based on a relational model which is not only simple, clear but take relational algebra as a language model and bases on the theories of data relations. Therefore, relational database system enjoys the advantage of good formalization foundation, high data independence, database language dep roc during charter, that all improve the productivity of programmers.

Since the 1980s, almost every database system produced by computer manufactures support relational model, and the even non-relational database has added relational interfaces. In the following part, some popular relational database systems will be listed in the sequence of sustainer, first initialization date, latest stable version, software authorized protocols.

After the emergence of the relational model, researchers went into depth the study of theory and development of prototype system. Accompanied by solutions of key technology, improvement of performance, standardization of SQL language, and enrichment of application developing tools, relational database system gradually took the place of grid database system and hierarchical database system, becoming the basis of mainframe database system and social informatization. The products went through four periods.

First period: In the 1970s, represented by System R produced by IBM and Ingres by Berkeley. Studies in this passage built the basic structure of the relational model and gave a formal description of a relational model. These studies solved query optimization, concurrency control, failure recovery and other key techniques, enabling the relational database to compete against grid and hierarchical database system in efficiency, and explored relational data languages including relational algebra, relational computing, SQL, QBE, etc.

Second period: In the 1980s, kinds of commercial relational database management system emerged, like IBM DB2, Oracle, Sybase, DEC RDB, etc. The release of ANSI SQL and SQL89 symbols the international standard of relational database language and different database products converged towards the standard.

Third period: In the 1990s, development in other types of database technology and widening of the area of database application, on one hand, stimulated major enhancement in the aspect of unifying of relational database management system, data integrity, and security management. On the other hand, relational database management system absorbed research result in relative areas which enriched and developed the concept, function, technology of relational database management system, such as multimedia data management, object data management, decision support and other new features. Also, many relational database products support distributed database and concurrent database features.

Fourth period: Since the start of this century, relational database management system was applied in a wide range as the rapid develop of Internet. There was an abundance of resources to be managed by the relational database, especially semi-structural Web data. Database products combined like XQuery and other XML query language standards. Driven by the demand in real life, a relational database was developed in massive data management, data assembly, mobile data management, natural language query, search engine support and data mining.

3.2.2.5 New Generation of Database System

We can conclude from the prior part that hierarchical DBS, grid DBS, and relational DBS are mostly applied to support business and data management in the processing area. However, people have higher requests for the database after their practical demand raised while the database was applied in a bigger area and multimedia technology strengthened. The combination between database technology and telecommunication technology and the combination between database technology and artificial intelligence pushed database system to step forward.

Lots of new born database system appeared after the late 20 century, including object-oriented DBS, distributed DBS, multimedia DBS, vague data DBS, concurrent DBS. We classify them as a new generation of a database system in this book because these database systems are closely interlinked, and some of them are the combination of the relational database system and new technology. In this chapter, there will be an introduction to object-oriented database and distributed database.

The object-oriented database system of the new generation of the database system is the fruit of combination between object-oriented programming and database technology. Although there are some OODB products in the markets now, like Versant, Gemstone, Objectstore, Motors, still no specific definition of OODB has been put forward now.

Versant Corporation produced Versant Object Database. There are lots of part designs in CAD and CAM which could be complicated if presented with a relational database. Versant's product aimed to acquire control of the complicated inner design of models like traffic transportation network, telecommunication infrastructures etc. They maintain high efficiency under the condition of big-scale data.

The main deficiency of OODB is a lack of unified standard. Therefore, a mature technique people use is to expand object-orient design for a relational database to realize object-relational database (ORDB). This sort of database supports abstracts data type (ADT), user-defined type (UDT), method, inheritance, and citation. Nowadays there's a variety of ORDB like ORACLE8i, CA-Ingres, and DB2-5.

Distributed database system is the combination between distributing technology and database technology. Two categories of distributed database system are common; one is physically distributed but logically centered, and the other is distributed both physically and logically. This system can support database with multiple usages and major differences, therefore suitable for data assembly. The concept of distributed database system is very complex, so we use C/S structural frame to introduce it briefly. In a broad sense, C/S is a certain kind of distributed structural for its processing assignments are done at least on two different parts. One representative of the many distributed database systems supporting C/S structure is Sybase Replication Server.

Multimedia database system is also one of the most focused database systems in the world. Nevertheless, it overlaps with OODB in many aspects and is not mature enough. Therefore we do not illustrate it here.

3.2.2.6   Non-relational Database (NoSQL)

Non-relational distributed data storage developed due to the maturity of Web 2.0 which made it hard for a relational database to adapt to the high read-write rate, high extension, and large data size requirements. NoSQL mostly explained as "non-relational" or "Not Only SQL", was proposed in 2009.

In the Web applications, real-time character and process integrity are not highly required, making relational database process management a burden under the heavy load of the database. Besides, SNS website of web 2.0 has a hard requirement for complicated SQL query, especially the amount of need for queries involving multiple charts is very small. The huge database forced queries to be the main key query or conditional queries in a single chart, thus weakened the use of SQL language and encouraged the boom of Key-Value Store DB.

Some of these databases are programmed in C/C++ while some others in Java or Erlang. The databases can be categorized by the programming language, but people prefer to classify them by performance. NoSQL databases can be divided into three kinds considering performance

(a) Key-Value Database satisfying high read-write performance need: Redis, Tokyo Cabinet, Flare.
(b) Database satisfying massive storage demand of files: MongoDB, CouchDB.
(c) Distributed Database satisfying high extendability and practicality: Cassandra, Voldemort.

Although classified into three categories above, almost all NoSQL database have the attribute of easily expanded, high performance under massive data read-write circumstance, flexible data model and highly practical.

Actually, the concept "NoSQL" was first used by staff in Rackspace Cloud, a company that played important role in the early time of NoSQL development. Its product Cassandra remained popular among people.

One American local online trade market Thumbtack used updated version of YCSB (Yahoo! Cloud Serving Benchmark) to test the performance of NoSQL database. We took the five results with the biggest amount [26].

3.2.3 Driver Program

3.2.3.1 Basic Knowledge of Driver Program

There is no unique precise definition of "driver program" yet. Basically, driver program is a software component enabling operating systems and equipment communicate with each other. A device driver, Abbe as the driver is a program allowing high-level computer software to interact with hardware. This program creates an interface connecting hardware to hardware or hardware with software and builds a system linking through the bus and another subsystem on the main-board to hardware. This system to some extent availed data exchange between devices. Whenever an application needs to read some data from a certain device, the application automatically runs function belong to the system and the system will run functions supported by driver program. According to the description above, the driver program knows how to communicate with hardware. It sends data back to the operating system which returns the value to the application.

Based on distinctive computer structure and different platforms, driver programs can be 8-bit, 16-bit, 32-bit and even 64-bit. This is to correlate operating system and driver program. In the 16-bit Windows 3.11 era, most drivers are 16-bits, and when it comes to 32-bit Windows XP, most driver programs became 32-bits (Microsoft only provide Windows Driver Model driver). As for 64-bit Linux and Window

Vista, a 64-bit driver program is essential (both WDM and WDF support 64-bit driver program). Driver programs in Linux system normally mean device driver program, including three categories of driver programs: char device, block device and internet device. All these are essential devices for a system to run, similar to the hardware supported under BIOS.

Microsoft extended one step further for the concept of driver program. The company believes that not necessarily should all driver programs be coded by corporation designing the device. Devices can be designed and manufactured following the published standard, and not all driver programs have to communicate directly with the device. In contrast, they only send requests and transfer them to driver programs at the bottom to the stacks. Some sizer driver program obeys and records relative I/O information without participation in the request. Microsoft even only call the components running under core mode the "software driver program."

Because Microsoft's expansion of the definition of "driver program" involved knowledge related to driver program development and the core of the operating system, we ignore them at this part, taking only device driver program into consideration.

3.2.3.2 Host Device Driver Program

In the Windows system, a whole set of driver programs is needed to support mainboard, disk driver, graphics card, and sound card. Why is there no driver program for CPU or memory? Because CPU and memory are essential for a private computer and can be used without driver programs. Early designers listed this hardware as can be directly supported by BIOS for they play indispensable roles. In other words, this hardware is supported by BIOS and your operating system once you install them to the machine. BIOS, in this point of view, is certain kind of driver program. However, for other hardware, like Internet card, sound card, graphics card, driver programs have to be installed to ensure they work well.

3.2.3.3 External Device Driver Program

If you need to connect other external hardware devices, an additional driver program is needed, such as for joypad, steering wheel, analogous stick, and dancing carpet. External printing machine needs printing machine driver program, access to the Internet needs driver programs for the network adapter, Modem and even ISDN and ADSL. Most keyboards, mouses, floppy drivers, monitors, and standard devices on the main board can adopt standard driver program provided by Windows. If you need to use disk driver under the DOS mode of Windows system, driver program under DOS mode is also needed. Most graphics card, sound card, network adapters and printers, scanners, external modems need specific driver programs match with certain versions. Otherwise their complete functions cannot be operated.

In this chapter, the introduction to driver program mentions some basic knowledge of software programing. Meanwhile, we comprehend software category standard from the world and attribute developing tools some sort of system software [27].

3.2.4 Developing Tools

3.2.4.1 Description Language Developing Tools

Description language developing tools mainly focus on what computers do. They are often divided into functions, data stream, logistic (based on constraints), based on models.

Developing tools for functional language

Typical functional languages include LISP/Scheme, ML, Haskell, Six, among which, LISP was most popular. Its developing tools include DrRacket and some others.

DrRacket is a commonly used developing tool with the origin name PLT Scheme. It is suitable for software from script to assignment processing tools designed by applications including graphic user interface, Web servers, etc. It is capable of supporting virtual machine of compilers, creating individual operable tools and Racket Web server, and has abundant functions in function base so that it can be easy for both professionals and starters. The graphic interface is provided with grammar highlights, compiling, single move, and other functions.

Logistic (constraint based) language developing tool

Typical logistic (constraint based) language include Prolong, VisiCale, Excel, Lotus 1-2-3, etc. Born in 1972, Prolog (programming in logic) is a logic programming language based on logistic foundation. It is universally used in North America and Europe. Japanese government once developed ICOT fifth generation of a computer system with Prolog to build an intellectual computer. In the beginning, Prolog was used in the study of natural language and evolved to study artificial intelligence nowadays. Amzi! Prolog produced by AMZI! is the best Windows version Prolong till now. There are other versions like Visual Prolog, SWI Prolog, Turbo Prolog, B-Prolog, Strawberry Prolog, Sicstus Prolog etc.

Readers practiced Excel may be surprised to learn that Excel is a programming language of Visual Basic for Applications (VBA). Sometimes, Excel macro hints bumps out, and that is the base of VBA. An Excel macro can be used to automatically runs an assignment if it needs to be operated over and over again. Limited to the length of this book, we will not introduce more about it.

Model-based language developing tools

Typical languages based on models are XSLT, where XSL means Extensible Stylesheet Language. The World Wide Web started with XSL because of its need for XML language form. XSLT is the abbreviation for Extensible Stylesheet Language Transformations, a language transforming XML document. T in XSLT means transformation and is a part of the XML standard. The popular developing environment includes Visual Studio and XML Spy. We are going to introduce the main functions of XML Spy and Visual Studio instead of the developing and adaption of XSLT.

XMLSpy is an assembly developing environment provided by Altova Corporation for XML project development. It is an XML editor that cooperates with other software to edit and operate XML and other text files. It also loads in and out XML files, convert certain types of text files between them with XML files, associate different types of XML files in a project, adopt inner XSLT 1.0/2.0 processor and XQuery 1.0 processor for processing document files. Last but not least, it can even create code according to XML file.

3.2.4.2 Command Language Developing Tools

Command language focusing on how computers should operate can be divided into three types: Von Neumann type, script type, and object type.

Von Neumann type language developing tool

Typical Von Neumann type language includes C, Ada, Fortran, etc., C language is a popular, procedural programming language. The developer of Unix we mentioned above, Thompson, used advanced languages to program operating systems. He first acquired B language based on BCPL, after which his partner redesigned B and created C language. C language compilers exist in operating systems like Unix, MS-DOS, Microsoft Windows and Linux. The design of C language influenced many following developed programming languages like C++, Objective-C, Java, C# etc.

In the early time, C environment for C language is Borland Turbo C, a set of developing environment and editor software designed by Borland Corporation. Its last edition Turbo C 2.0 was published in 1989.

Common editors in Unix and Linux, are Emacs and Vim using GNU Compiler Collection (GCC) to compile the source code. We will come to knowledge about compilers in the latter part of the book. GNU (Gnu's Not Unix's abbreviation, it is an operating system similar to Unix) official website describe Emacs in this way: Emacs is an extendable designable text editor, and more than that, Emacs is an operating platform with strong extensibility and design style.

Emacs supports many operating systems including Windows. However, the massive third-party tool applied dissatisfied users with difficulties in their installation and poor user experience. Therefore to experience the strength of Emacs, it is usually on other operating systems, like w3m on Unix system.

Script language developing tools

Typical script language includes Perl, PHP, Python, JavaScript, Ruby, Tcl, Awk, cash, bash, etc.

Popular developing tools for Perl are ActivePerl, ActiveStatePerlDevKitPro, DzSoftPerlEditor, EngInSiteerl, JPerl, OptiPerl, PerlExpress, etc.

Poplar developing tools for Python are IDLE, Codimension, Spyder, python, Eric, etc.

Popular developing tools for Javascript are Akshell, Saket, IxEdit, WebStorm, Aptana Studio3, etc.

Now we will brief about several assemblies developing environment. First, Apt anaStudio, an open-source Web integrated developing environment based on Eclipse, which supports HTML5, CSS3, JavaScript, Rails in Ruby, PHP, and Python. It is most famous for the powerful JavaScript compiler and debugs machine. AptanaStudio supports multiple AJAX and JavaScript toolboxes including JavaScript editing and debugging. Aptana also published well-functioned, iPhone-integrated developing function which meanwhile, supports RIA product AIR produced by Adobe.

Learned about integrated Javascript developing environment, let us talk about developing an environment of Python. What we are going to introduce here is the IDLE appended to Python. IDLE is an integrated developing environment created by Python initiator Guido van Rossum with Python and Tkinter. Therefore, it is essential to have Python and Tkinter installed before using IDLE. Besides, there is an editor and browser for Python, which supports auto indent, colorful coding, command history, and word completion.

Perl Express is an integrated developing environment of Perl under Windows. It is independent but strong for it contains many tools that can be used to code and debug Perl programs. Perl Express not only targets experienced advanced Perl developers but also newly hands. Since its 2.5 version, Perl Express unzipped all limits and became completely free software.

Object-oriented language developing tools

Typical object-oriented language includes C++, Smalltalk, Object-C, Eiffel, Java, etc. Microsoft Visual Studio always bumps out of a coder's brain whenever C++ is mentioned. As a developing toolbox product published by Microsoft Corporation, Microsoft Visual Studio can be used to create either Windows apps and web apps, or web service, intelligent device apps, and Office plug-in components. The target code suits Microsoft Windows, Windows Mobile, Windows CE, NET Framework, NET Compact Framework, Microsoft Silverlight and all platforms including Windows Phone supported by Microsoft. Visual Studio went through periods of changes as an ever improving developing environment.

Microsoft published Visual Studio 97 in 1997. It includes Visual Basic 5.0, Visual C++ 5.0, Objective Java named Visual J++, objective database version Visual FoxPro, and Visual InterDev for Dynamic HTML. Among these above, Visual Basic and Visual FoxPro have an independent developing environment, while others run under a unified environment.

In 1998, Microsoft published Visual Studio 6.0 and raised every developing language and environment to 6.0 version.

In 2002, Visual Studio .NET (inner version code 7.0) was published accompanied by the slogan of .NET and the Windows XP product. Meanwhile, Microsoft absorbed C# based on .NET frame (version 1.0) and evolved to objective Microsoft Basic .NET when previous Visual J++ became Visual J# in the objective .Net Framework.

In 2003, Microsoft revised partially Visual Studio 2002 and published Visual Studio 2003 (inner version code 7.1). Visio was drawn in as a UML structured app alongside portable device support and corporation models. .NET frame also updated to 1.1 version.

In 2005, Microsoft published Visual Studio 2005 which still faces .NET frame.

In 2007.11 Microsoft published Visual Studio 2008.

On 2010.4.12 Microsoft published Visual Studio 2010 and .NET Framework 4.0.

On 2012.9.12 Microsoft published Visual Studio 2012 in Seattle.

On 2013.11.13 Visual Studio, 2013 was officially published.

Java is the mark of an object-oriented language. There are many Java development environments, such as Sun's NetBeans and the famous free cross-platform development environment Eclipse.

Eclipse mentioned above is mainly used for Java development, but as supported by many plug-ins Java can also be used for other computer languages such as C++ and Python. Eclipse was originally an IDE development environment in the next generation, which belongs to alternative commercial software Visual Age for Java developed by IBM. In November 2001, it was contributed to open-source community. Now it is managed by Eclipse Foundation, a non-profit software supplier alliance.

Many software developers are familiar with a high-level programming language, but the programming language to be recognized by the computer and accepted by the machine needs to go through several intermediate processes. In the Sect. 3.2.5, we will introduce the compile tools [28].

3.2.5 Program Compilation Tools

3.2.5.1 Assembler

Assembler creates object code by transferring assembly instruction symbols into opcode and interpreting symbol names in the form of the storage location. The object code is the machine code that needs Linker to generate executable code to be able to be executed, in which symbolic resolution is the key part in assembler. Compared with high-level language compiler, assembler is much easier, with the earliest one appeared in the 1950s and many modern assemblers can support instruction scheduling optimization. The most frequent assembler in Linux is GNU Assembler, because it is the default back-end of GCC and a part of Binutils.

The earliest using language mentioned above is machine language, that is, the operation of a computer is completed by different combinations of digital string (machine instructions) of "0" and "1". This language is difficult to remember, with difficult programming, frequent errors, hard debugging, and low universality. With the passage of time, the development of computer technology, and more complex problems need to be solved by computers; new ideas were prompted. That is taking abbreviations for easy memory taking the place of the complicated machine code. These abbreviations similar to English words have clear meanings to represent the opcode, operands, and addresses and register names of chine instructions. That is how symbolic language came into being. The following is a program programmed by symbolic language.

MOV AL, DATA1:   Take the first data
MOV AH, DATA2:   Take the second data
ADD AL, AH: Summation
MOV RLT, AL: Save
HLT: Halt.

The information on a certain meaning represented by symbols is often referred to as assembly execution instructions and assembly pseudo instructions. The machine cannot identify routines programmed by assembly language directly. The role of the assembler is to translate assembly language program into machine language which can be executed by a computer. The process of assembly language program being translated into machine language one is called assembly process.

Due to different assemble programs employed by different computer models, their assemblers are accordingly different, but the principle, methods and techniques of assembly are consistent [29].

3.2.5.2   Compiler

Advanced computer language is conducive to writing, reading, communication, and maintenance. Machine language can be directly read and run by a computer. The compiler regards compiled or advanced computer language source program as the equivalent program to be input and translated into target language machine code. The source code is often high-level language including Pascal, C, C++, C# and Java or assembly language, while the goal is the object code of machine language, which sometimes referred to as machine code.

The compiler, which can be used to generate object code that runs in the same environment with the computer and operating system (platform) where the compiler itself is located, is also known as "local" compiler. Also, the compiler that can be used to generate object code running on other platforms is also called as a cross compiler. A cross compiler is very useful in generating new hardware platform. "From a source to source compiler" refers to a compiler that uses high-level language as input and has high-level language output. For example automatic parallel compilers often employs a high-level language as input to convert its code and adopts parallel code comments to annotate it (such as OpenMP) or uses structural language to annotate (such as FORTRAN DOALL command).

The compiler was created by Grace Hope in the early 1950s, a time when the compiler was called automatic programming and people doubted that it would succeed. Today, the automatic translation of programming language has been recognized as a successful fact that has formed a set of mature and systematic theory and method and developed numerous languages, environments, and tools that can be compiled.

The world's first compiler with modern sense—FORTRAN compiler mentioned above was created in the mid-1950s. It provides a source language that is problem-oriented and is unrelated to problems and machine to users. FORTRAN performed some relatively more challenging optimization functions to generate high-efficient machine code, so as to compete with assembler language programming. Languages unrelated to machine such as FORTRAN prove the vitality of advanced programming language needs to be compiled. The success of FORTRAN lays the foundation for a large number of high-level languages and the corresponding compilers. In general, the compiler will translate programming languages such as Java and C into executable machine language instructions. However, compiler technology has more extensive application. For example, text formatting languages such as TeX and LaTeX was actually compilers that will translate formatting commands into detailed typesetting commands, and PostScript language is generated by a variety of procedures. Nevertheless, in fact, it is also a kind of programming language which translates and executes printer and document preview tool to produce a readable document format. Also, Mathematica, an interactive system that combines program design and mathematical application, embraces symbols and digital forms to solve abstruse problems, relies heavily on compiler technology to deal with the specification, internal representation, and solution of problems.

Further, circuit design languages with very large-scale integration such as Verilog and VHDL use the standard-cell design of silicon compiler to specify a certain VLSI circuit layout and composition. Just as the rules of a certain machine understood and observed by normal compilers, silicon compiler also needs to understand and comply with the design rules of a given circuit when designing circuit. Also, a wealth of text-oriented programs including operating system commands, scripting languages and SQL language used in database systems will, more or less, utilize compiler technology.

3.2.5.3 Interpreter

Interpreter, also translated as a translator, is a computer program that can make a direct translation of high-level programming language line by line. The interpreter is another language processor that is different from the compiler. The first interpreter is a LISP interpreter written by Steve Russell in the 1950s based on the IBM 704 machine code. The interpreter will not translate the whole program, but rather, resembles that of "intermediary", will translate it into another language before running, which explains why interpreter program runs much slower than that compiled one.

Python, PHP, JavaScript, Perl, and Scheme use an interpreter to execute. If a platform possesses the interpreter of these languages, put the program in this platform to run directly will do. The Basic language of Microsoft Corp is also an explanation that does not need steps such as compile and link after programming to be executed. Some languages including C, C++ and Java have both interpreter and compiler. The last chapter of this book portrays various programming tools, here the book will introduce a C++ interpreter—Cint, which is an interpretive execution of C++ code judging by its name. The current analysis scope covers most script environments of standard C++ and can load and analyze code with more than 60 thousand lines quickly. It can use a mix of compiled code, which is a characteristic that each developer is extraordinarily concerned about.

As we told before, Scheme is a programming language which can be dynamically introduced into the static application via various interpreters, including DrScheme, Guile, etc. Guile, an official extension language of GNU Project, was published in 1995 with an outstanding extension that can explain scheme script. Not only can it provide dynamic configuration for Scheme script programming by binding Scheme script with compiled C program dynamically, but it can also integrate and translate C program in Scheme script. DrScheme is also a very good interpreter; we do not explore it in this book.

The differences between interpreter and compiler lies in the lexical analysis after reading the source code and the process of syntax analysis and semantic analysis. After semantic analysis, the compiler chooses to store the semantic into an intermediate language and then selects the corresponding back-end to translate into a machine language and executable program, while interpreter executes code directly. Of course, this will cause a program suffer the possibility of being compiled for many times while running in the interpreter, which explains why the interpreter is relatively low in efficiency. Java and C# are two pre-compiled languages that need to compile source code into the middle one manually before the run, and then execute in the interpreter. By comparison, it is much faster to utilize interpreter alone.

The interpreter also has its own advantages. It does not need to generate machine code like that of a compiler. Therefore, it has a great degree of machine independence. It can be used by recompiling interpreter so long as the interpreter's development language is supported on this machine. Since Lisp and Scheme mentioned above support dynamic object type, languages such as Ruby can even allow the system to modify types dynamically, making it harder for the compiler to be translated into machine code when symbolic meaning changes. Therefore, the interpreter has many advantages in this case.

Another advantage of using interpreter is of particular significance in program development process. Indeed, it is slower to run the program via interpreter than that compiled machine code. However, the direct translation is comparatively much faster than compile. This characteristic of the interpreter is very precious when programmer development is in its initial stage, or the program is in the middle of writing experimental code. The reason is that programmer will find errors during his code editing and then direct translation. Unlike compile, which can only correct errors after programming, the errors in interpreter can be corrected in a short time when executing, saving a whole lot of time [30].

3.3 Application Software

In 1996, Weisgall, Vardi and Golder Fenger, the three Israel young people who had just finished their military service gathered together and invented software that can directly transfer information more quickly than electronic mail, i.e., ICQ. It was popular around the world the moment it was launched. Nevertheless, due to its single language and simple technology, other local similar software gradually occupied a lot of market share. Take China's domestic software market as an example, in February 1999, Tencent Company developed independently instant messaging tool OICQ, which was renamed as Tencent QQ, based on the Internet. Hence, Tencent marched towards "the most respected Internet companies" gradually with its ever-growing user group.

Therefore, almost everyone will choose to install Tencent QQ, regardless of what their operating systems are. In fact, Tencent QQ is just a member of the thousands of application software. Also, the browsers people use to browse various news, the office software people use to process document or table, as well as the games played by teens in leisure time are all an integral part of our daily life.

Let us take a look at the life in the day of office workers: reading mobile phone news on the way to work, sending and receiving emails in the office, making a presentation with PowerPoint in the meeting room, having dinner after work with waiters conducting intelligent order, etc. All these jobs are done with powerful software applications.

This section is going to introduce application software in contact with our lives, showing a beautiful and large software world. The classification method in this book is according to "Computer Software Category Code Table (2011 edition)", dividing the software into general software, specialized software, and embedded software. In our daily life, we live with different software. As the ancient Chinese joint "Blossoming in the apartments, life is beautiful" described, software is either to facilitate our lives or to give our lives a new color.

3.3.1 General Software

3.3.1.1 Office Productivity Software

If you readers thought the office productivity software is just processing documents to create a table, then you may not keep up with the trend. In fact, office productivity software is a type of application software dedicated to producing information, such as documents, presentations, worksheets, databases, charts, graphs, digital paintings, electronic music, and digital video. Its names arose from the fact that it increases productivity, especially of individual office workers, from typists to knowledge workers, although its scope is now wider than that. Office suites, which brought word processing, spreadsheet, and relational database programs to the desktop in the 1980s, are the core example of productivity software. They revolutionized the office with the magnitude of the productivity increase they brought as compared with the pre-1980s office environments of typewriters, paper filing, and handwritten lists and ledgers. In the 2010s, productivity software has become even more consumerized than it already was, as computing becomes ever more integrated into personal daily life.

With population growth and technological progress, many statistics, work record and summary report occupy many work times, and many people joked that they were buried in the "mountain of the files." As there is a demand power, a lot of office productivity software have shown up in every corner of the office, caused the digital revolution in office.

Nowadays the famous office productivity software is Microsoft Office series, Kingsoft WPS series, Evermore Office series, Red 2000 Red Office, Association of CTOP collaborative OA series and Dedicated collaborative OA series. This office productivity software is used widely. From large social statistics to a small meeting, the digital office is inseparable from the assistance of office productivity software.

Currently, office productivity software is developing towards simpler and more practical and the office productivity software market can be roughly divided into two categories: office series which pays attention to all aspects of office and small software which focuses on only one aspect. Also, e-government software for the government, the tax software for tax system i also office productivity software, which is not limited to traditional typing tabulation software.

In cloud computing era, the office productivity software that based on the organizational level of cooperative has become the mainstream office productivity software, mainly used in office networks, e-government, collaborative commerce, and other fields. Founded in Fudan University Association of Software, the Chinese market first competitiveness office product-collaborative office productivity software's products have covered up to 70% market share. Its products have been an agent by the UF and Kingdee official OEM.

As we talk about the office productivity software, every Chinese will never forget Kingsoft WPS series software. As early as March 10, 1998, Chinese Guangming Daily published news which introduced the presentation of Jinshan WPS97 software—"generation of Chinese word processing system." A total of 200 Electronics Division leaders attended the demonstration. Participants thought highly of the WPS's contribution to the national software industry.

From WPS1.0 released in 1989, Kingsoft WPS now harvest the glory and also gain a storm. In 2008, the Yangcheng Evening News entitled "Bojun—never give up the competition with Microsoft office," in this assessment: "In Bojun's mind, he has not only to do a software that allows companies to make a living but to make the backbone of China's software practitioners. As a senior evaluated it: in any case, be able to fight with Microsoft for 20 years and has not fallen, which is a miracle itself."

In addition to Kingsoft WPS series, there is some OA software has been widely used in various domestic and foreign enterprises.

The following Table 3.1 compares general and technical information for some office suites.

There are multiple classification methods for office productivity software, such as classified according to the platform or classified from a brand perspective. Different classification methods can result in various types of software. From simple word processing tool to the complicated office productivity software, with the change of classification criteria, the content of office productivity software has constantly been enriched, and its covering areas are increasingly widespread. Visible software culture is having a tremendous impact on human culture, while also brings new meaning to the software itself. The word Bring Your Device (BYOD), was put forward in 2005, after several years of development in 2012 it was recognized by the US Equal Employment Opportunity Commission. During this period, the emergence of smartphones, tablet computers, and the electronic paper book make different breakthrough in software application platforms of office productivity. Before 2007, you can use office productivity software on only desktop

Table 3.1 Comparison of three office suites

Main functions	MS Office 2010	WPS	Yong Zhong
File format	*.docx	*.wps	*.eio
PDF output	Support	Support	Support
Comment	General	General	Genera and manual
Font	Windows font	Windows font	Windows font and Yong He font
File conversion (8M File)	Directly	3–4 s	3 s
File Open speed (8M file)	Directly	3 s	3 s
Interface	Different with office 2003	Similar to Office 2010	Similar with Office 2003
Resources occupied	66M	53M	34M
System support	Windows	Windows	Linux, Windows
Macro	Support	Not support	Support
Function integration	Process word, Excel and PowerPoint respectively	Process word, Excel and PowerPoint respectively	A unified interface for word excels and PowerPoint
Document displays	Opened by specific application	Tabbed MDI	Tree structure
Installation file	580M	38M	173M

computers, with operating system only Windows, Mac OS X and Linux. While in 2007, along with the development of mobile Internet technology, iPhone redefines the phone, the phone began to have features of the computer, and office productivity software first appeared at Nokia's Symbian system and Apple's iPhone system. In 2009, the Android platform, Blackberry 10 platform appeared and Microsoft developed the Windows Phone 8 platform. Of course, there is office productivity software that can also be used on many operating systems, it will be described in later sections.

3.3.1.2 Game Software

Talking about the game, I believe many people will think of a child playing with the gyro, hopscotch, and video games, and you will recall the world's popular NES in the 1980s. Until September 2003, the NES life cycle is as long as twenty years, not include all kinds of tricks reproductions, it sold a total of more than sixty million. Nintendo technology developers Masayuki Uemura said, "I am very grateful to the NES, but in some ways, it is the worst enemy of my life, because nobody can think out the reason why this particular hardware assembled will become such a popular machine." It seems that we can find the answer in this book, the reason is that NES has brought a new symbol to game culture. Regarding game, NES brings a large number of new games or created a new game category.

Nowadays, there are many games passed from generation to generation, Japan's "Final Fantasy" series, Britain's "Tomb Raider" series, America's "Diablo" series and so on, they had become a symbol of classic games culture. Usually, people combine a variety of these programs and animation software products together to refer to "game software."

In fact, many large 3D online games and web games are created by the combination of animation software like 3DMAX, MAYA, FLASH and programming languages such as JAVA, C++, Visual Basic. Therefore, they are called game software. Under the long-standing influence of game culture, it is natural to classify Internet gaming software as a console game, online game, and browser game.

Single-Player Game

Single-Player Game refers to an electronic game that can be run independently with only one computer or other game platforms. Unlike online games, it does not need a specialized server to be able to operate normally, and some can have multiplayer mode via local area network. Single-Player Game is the game that is played by players on their computers without connecting to the Internet, the model of which is human–computer fighting. Nevertheless, with the increasing popularity of the Internet and the emerging piracy, an ever-growing single-player game also begin to need the support of the Internet, the reasons of which include piracy prevention, download service for follow-up content and convenience for online multiplayer. Most single-player games include a multiplayer machine and "multiplayer" modes such as direct IP and LAN battle. With the advance of game culture, the single-player game also constantly strengthens multiplayer modes and network elements, the boundary between which is getting increasingly blurred, which explains cultural impacts classification, while classification promotes culture.

Here I will introduce a classic racing game—*Need for Speed* for everyone. *Need for Speed,* a famous racing game produced by Electronic Arts, is set to find balance in cool racing and vivid vehicle design, which is why the game is irreplaceable in the eyes of the world's car fans. There are 18 works of the company from 1995 to 2013.

Speaking of *Need for Speed*, it is hard to avoid mentioning a huge game—EA Games. The publisher of *Need for Speed* series is Electronic Arts (EA for short), a company founded in 1982 with its headquartered in Redwood City, California, which is the world's leading interactive entertainment software company that mainly engage in a variety of businesses including electronic games development, publishing, and sales. As of 2009, Electronic Arts has branches or subsidiaries in many countries and cities including another American cite, Canada, UK, Australia, China and Hong Kong, a total of over 7000 employees around the world.

"EA Games," the main brand of Electronic Arts, mainly possesses games including action, role-playing, racing and fighting in its brand. In addition to traditional boxed retail single-player games, EA Games also released a wealth of multiplayer online games. Its products have dozens of the type including Madden NFL, NHL, and FIFA series, the NBA Live series, Tiger Woods PGA Tour Series, The Sims series, Command, and Conquer series, Honor Medal series, Battlefield series and Need for Speed series. In the performance ranking in 2012 of cross-media rating website "Metacritic". EA Games won the title with its 37 unique works and 75.2 scores of average meta score.

The Legend of Sword and Fairy, another masterpiece of a classic single-player game, is a computer game released by Softstar Entertainment Inc. (Softstar Entertainment or Softstar for short). "Legend" stands for a human fairy, while "sword" is a swordsman representing the brave heart. The story of *The Legend of Sword and Fairy that* takes ancient Chinese fairy demon ghost tales as background, martial arts, and Xian Xia as its theme has published seven generations of single-player play games, a business simulation game, two online games and a social network game so far. Its first work, which was published in July 1995, won numerous game awards and was hailed as "an unparalleled masterpiece" by myriads of players. Its originals and the first three generations have also been adapted into a TV series in 2004 and 2008. *The Legend of Sword and Fairy,* together with *Xuanyuan Sword* of the same company, are recognized as two classic role-playing game series in the Chinese world. *The Legend of Sword and Fairy* succeeded in mixing game culture and Chinese traditional culture together, which can be described as the software leader.

Online Game

Network Game, also known as "online game", OL for short, refers to continuous individual multiplayer online games that take the Internet as a transmission media. The game operation business server, and the user computer are regarded as processing terminals. The game client software as the interactive information window aims to realize entertainment, leisure, communication, and virtual achievement. Judging by its definition, it can be seen that its form is the Internet multiplayer online, while its access to the game needs to use the client, which forms a contrast with those online games without a client. Once standards in software classification are identified, it is necessary to seize any difference to make careful distinctions.

World of Warcraft, the first online game produced by the famous game company Blizzard Entertainment, is a massively multiplayer online role-playing game. The game takes the plot in Warcraft, a real-time strategy game produced by the company, as its historical background, providing game players with a magnificent Warcraft World based on Warcraft's historical events and heroes.

World of Warcraft, which has been in public beta in 2004, released in the United States, New Zealand, Canada, Australia, and Mexico in November of the same year. In April 2005, the game conducted a full open beta in China. In January 2007, Blizzard announced that global users of *World of Warcraft* exceed 8 million people. In April 2008, *World of Warcraft* took up to 62% market share in MMORPG. By the end of 2008, the world's paying customers of *World of Warcraft* exceed 11.5 million, breaking the Guinness world record successfully.

Blizzard Entertainment is a world known computer game developer and publisher that was founded by Michael Molem, Alan Ed and Frank Pierce, three graduates of the University of California, on February 8th, 1991. Originally known as silicon & Synapse, the company is an affiliated company of American Blizzard and a holding subsidiary of French Wei Wangdi group that Headquarters in the Gulf of California.

Blizzard's products enjoy a high reputation in the electronic game industry. Although there are few produced games, most of them are very popular. Among them, games including Warcraft, StarCraft, Diablo, Furnace Stone Legend and World of Warcraft heroes sweet around the world and are highly praised by players. Also, they are listed as competition events by numerous electronic competitive events.

Browser Game
The browser game is also known as a Web game, sideless Web game, WG for short. It is an online multiplayer interactive game based on web browser. There is no need to download the client to enter the game after waiting some time by simply open the IE page. The importance of machine allocation in web game is not as prominent as that client game. It is most important for its convenience in closing or switch, which is suitable for office workers. Web game is the product of fast food culture and a new category of game software.

Although Web game market is a mixed bag, City of Heroes, a game operated by Tencent Company is remarkable both in public praise and efficiency. The game, developed by Suzhou City Snail Electronics Co., Ltd., is now run by Snail Electronics and Tencent Company. Readers will find words such as "war strategy," "role playing," "fire" and "puzzle adventure" in game classification when downloading games in application market, which is a good classification method to make the theme of the game understandable for players. However, the drawbacks of this classification are obvious. Many games have various themes. Take *City of Heroes*, which abounds in a lot of popular game elements including war strategy, role-playing and simulation of the operation, resulting in the difficulties in classification. Especially when computer hardware configuration is getting increasingly high, computer games develop in the direction of multi-elements, making it rather hard to adopt the classification of game themes. However, in embedded systems, the majority of games mainly provide a single element to ensure the smooth flow of game due to hardware limitations of mobile devices. Therefore, when explaining mobile game software classification in an embedded system, the book employs methods focusing on game themes.

3.3.1.3 Security Software

Security software can be divided into antivirus software, system tools, and anti-rogue software according to people's functional requirements. Security software can be used to protect the computer from all known program code harms to computer inflicted by malicious software and unauthorized intrusion, and can help people manage computer security. The quality of security software determines the quality of virus checking and killing and determines whether people can operate their personal account with ease and enjoy the convenience and high efficiency brought by network life at the same time.

Security software focuses on prevention and is integrated with prevention and treatment. The following describes the detailed division of security software, each of which is used to deal with a particular security threat.

Antivirus software

Antivirus software, also known as an antivirus program, can find known procedure codes such as computer viruses and Trojan that are harmful to the computer and then eradicate them. The earliest antivirus software should be McAfee launched in 1983 by a company that is the sole antivirus partner to Microsoft. KILL is the earliest domestic antivirus software developed by the Ministry of Public Security for Chinese. It was unveiled by the virus research group of Computer Management and Supervision Bureau Supervision Division in Ministry of Public Security in July 1989. The version 6.0 can be used to detecting and removing six viruses in China. Other mainstream antivirus software includes G data (Germany), Baidu Antivirus, 360 Antivirus, Kaspersky Internet Security, Avira, Rising Antivirus Software, Kingsoft, Microsoft Security Essentials, Norton, and so on.

As the important software to defend the system, the quality and performance of antivirus software draw the attention of users. That is why antivirus software has an important test, that is, the ability test. At present, authoritative ability tests are VB100, AV-C, AV-test, etc.

Auxiliary security software
The main functions of these sorts of software are clean up the garbage, bug fixing and Trojan's killing, such as Baidu guards, 360 security guards, Jinshan guards, rising security aides, Advanced SystemCare, etc.

Anti-rogue Software
This kind of software mainly focus on rogue software cleaning and system security protection, for example, Nawras PC Supervisor, BleachBit, IObit Malware Fighter, Super Rabbit, Windows Cleanup Assistant, etc.

Encryption software
It mainly encrypts data files to avoid leakage, so as to ensure the security of information assets. Encryption software can be divided into passive and active encryption by the implementation of the method. Currently, driven layer transparent encryption technology on the market has become the most reliable and the most secure encryption technology, representing that manufacturers are in possession of Guangdong South information security industry base. The world's first computer password can be traced back to around 1960, a time when the large CTSS Compatible Time-Sharing System was utilized by the Massachusetts Institute of Technology in its construction.

3.3.1.4 Multimedia Software

Multimedia files usually refer photo music, video and other media files that computer can handle. Every innovation of multimedia software will have an immeasurable impact on human life and culture.

The level of software development prompted multimedia applications to continue to expand. Multimedia is showing a distinct advantage in all aspects of culture, education, technical training, e-books, tourism, commercial, and family entertainment of our life. In some aspects of these areas, multimedia technology has become the core technology. Multimedia technology makes pictures, animations, video, music easy to be accepted vividly by the public in the most acceptable way. The multimedia software is the essential part to accomplish all of these.

Multimedia applications are mainly multimedia authoring tools or editing tools, including word processing software, graphics software, image processing software, animation software, sound editing software, and video software. This software, generally speaking, is belonging to multimedia playback software and multimedia authoring software.

Multimedia player software
Most users use the multimedia player software to listen and watch multimedia programs. Popular multimedia player software includes Windows XP system with its own Windows Media Player, Apple QuickTime Player and so on. Also, there are Real Player, Daum PotPlayer, KMPlayer, Storm, RealONE Player V2.0, ALPlayer, DAPlayer, etc.

Multimedia authoring software

Multimedia software including text editing software, image processing software, animation software, audio processing software, multimedia authoring software, and video processing software.

(a) The text editing software, such as Word, WPS, and so on.
(b) Image processing software, such as Photoshop processing of bitmap images, CorelDraw processing vector graphics.
(c) Animation software. The first type is animation drawing and editing software, such as Animator Pro (flat animation authoring software), 3D Studio MAX (three-dimensional animation modeling software), Cool 3D (three-dimensional character animation software), Poser (three-dimensional human animation software). The another type is the animation processing software, such as Animator Studio (animated processing software), Premiere (film images and animation software), GIF Construction Set (web animation software), After Effects (film Imaging and Animation post-synthesis software).
(d) Audio processing software. Audio processing software can be divided into three categories. The first class is digital sound conversion software, such as Easy CD-DA Extractor (the CD track is converted to digitized WAN format), Real Jukebox (recorded on the Internet, edit digital audio broadcast signal). The second class is sound editing software, such as Goldwave (digital recording, editing, compositing software), Cool Edit Pro (sound editing software). The third class is the voice compression software, such as L3Enc (compress WAN audio file format to MP3 format files), Windac 32 (convert and compress the CD sound rail into MP3 format files).
(e) Video processing software: its role is to organize video camera data, acquired film, and television recorders or direct design video, such as Movie Maker built-in Windows XP, Adobe's Premiere Pro, Ulead's VideoStudio, Pinnacle Studio, and so on.
(f) Multimedia authoring software: its role is to complete the acquisition and edition of multimedia material, and finally through the creation of a platform to integrate a variety of materials. Common multimedia authoring software is PowerPoint (presentation software), Authorware (creation software), etc.

3.3.2 Specialized Software

3.3.2.1 Education Software

Educational software, a branch of software, is the specific performance of software in education and teaching. Unlike other software, educational software not only includes all features of the software, but also includes learning and education functions. Educational software is a tool for learners to have education information intellectualized. Therefore, different users have different expectations and requirements for educational software.

Different demands lead to various kinds of educational software. However, educational software basically can be divided into several broad categories including education management software, teaching software, and auxiliary educational tool software according to users and the main function of the software.

Education management software is an auxiliary tool for school and education authority to conduct model management, information collection and exchange of information. It is necessary to possess functions such as school roll management, personnel management, teaching management, security management, property management, and so on.

The main applications of teaching software are in student learning, teachers teaching and parents counseling environment, including schools, training centers, and family. Its applicable people include teachers, students, and parents.

As a specific tool, auxiliary tool software mainly provides helps to teachers, students, parents, and education management personnel, such as campus network instant messaging system, auxiliary tools for teachers and students to communicate in the campus network, and course authoring tools that mainly offer teachers helps in making electronic courseware.

"Teaching and learning" is the core in education activity, while others all provide support for it. Therefore, with education culture penetrating deep into software culture, it plays an integral part in software culture. In this section, I will explain it alone. Educational software is usually divided into educational management software, teaching software, and educational auxiliary tool software. This is a classification method based on users and the main function of the software.

Education management software is an auxiliary tool for school and education authority to conduct information collection, management, and exchange. It is necessary to possess functions such as school roll management, personnel management, and teaching evaluation and so on. For example, the teaching quality assessment system, teaching resource management system, course arrangement system and academic system generally used by educational department belong to this category.

Teaching software is the software that used to student learning, teachers teaching and parents counseling environment, including schools, training centers, and family. Its applicable people include teachers, students and parents, for example, online examination system, foreign language learning software and electronic classroom system.

Auxiliary tools, a service software usually used in the education industry, is usually the custom software of general software in an education sector, such as special experimental simulation tools and campus instant communication tools.

3.3.2.2 Application Software for Other Industries

Application software for other industries includes financial application software, factory control, and so on.

Among this software, we will introduce financial software first. Financial software is an important example of the organic integration of social sciences and natural sciences. Currently, the international level of financial software is not high, and there is still great potential for its development.

Due to the characteristics of the financial industry, this software started early in the financial sector with rapid development and intense competition. In 2001, the financial application software market accounted for about half of the applications market. Currently, the industry application software consists of three major financial industries, namely banks and security software, securities trading management software, and open-mode fund system software.

As the demand for application software industry is on a steady upswing, application software for a specific industry is an important force in the development of Chinese software market. The development prospects of the financial industry application software market are broad.

Banks and security software
With the commencement of network services and banks continuing to introduce new services, banks and security software has also been widely used in a relatively short period. Now, there is the "Securities Link" in China, which is interconnected by Dapeng Securities and computer systems of banks. Through this, investors can trade by trading systems and complete liquidation of funds by the opened savings account of the bank. This business was launched by the China Construction Bank in April 1998.

Manufacturers of securities trading software in China are Hang Seng, gold card, the new Lee, SunGard, Apex software, etc.

There are Hundsun China, Aozun, Neusoft, etc., in Open-end fund business in China. Hang Seng company currently occupied almost half of the open-end fund business.

Factory controls software
Factory control software includes human–machine interface software (HMI), PC-based control software and production management software. Since the use of programmable controllers, factory control software has become an inseparable part of industrial automation. However, in practical, application control software is not isolated. It integrated with other software to play its role better. Generalized Factory control software should include data collection, HMI, process control, database, and data communications. It is now developing from simple control to the management of integration of plant information.

Through the use of binary code, assembly language, high-level language programming, to further the development of configuration software, the development of factory control software is accompanied by the emergence of computer technology for factory control. AutoCAD software is directly used on the screen to control the design process flow diagram and electrical schematic system diagram, and then automatically generate the program by a computer (engineering station). By AutoCAD, users can design and visualize virtually any concept with 3D free-form tools, and it will automatically create appropriate measurements based on the drawing context. The AutoCAD also boosts detailing and documentation work with tools designed to maximize productivity. Although much industrial automation software still uses text or dedicated graphics configuration mode, it is no doubt that the industrial use of AutoCAD software will become the mainstream of factory control software.

In the past we always thought Programmable Logic Controller (PLC) is suitable for logic control, Distributed Control System (DCS) is suitable for analog adjustment. However, developments of technology prove that PLC and DCS are interpenetrating and differences between them are becoming increasingly smaller. The functions of PLC, DCS and PC, are converging, what in the past can only be done by the PC such as advanced control strategies now can also be done on the PLC and DCS. Therefore, the integration of these three functions also promotes the development factory control software.

On the other hand, the majority of current factory control software is developed by the automation system equipment manufacturers in the environment of hardware, which is bundled with the automation systems and specialized equipment. There are various production processes and equipment in a factory, which requires selection of different automation systems equipment according to different objects, such as IPC, PLC, DCS, etc., even the same kind of automation systems have to be equipped differently as its industrial software is not the same. One person needs to simultaneously understand and master function of several software which are roughly the same. This situation causes great inconvenience to users and increases the consumption and investment of human resources.

This proposes engineers to think about that whether they can develop a hardware-independent factory control software in the familiar Windows operating system constraints for a wide range of automation system equipment. In this way, users can choose different automation systems equipment according to different objects, at the same time, software developers and maintainers only need to know one or a few factory control software. In this way, the ideas and products of soft PLC and soft DCS were born.

In the 90s, the HMI visualization software represented by InTouch of Wonderful us is the marketing pioneer who runs under Windows. Nowadays, it has grown to be able to provide a plant information system which has a hierarchy structure from bottom to top, beginning from the plant bottom operators.

To sum up, the characteristics of the development of factory control software are

(a) Organization of the sequence is controlling, analog adjustment and calculation functions.
(b) Full use of AutoCAD programming techniques.
(c) The combination with factory control software and informational factory.
(d) Generalizing of factory control software [31].

3.3.3 Embedded Software

Application software, the upper software in embedded system, defines the main functions and applications of the embedded devices and is responsible for interaction with users. Application software is the embodiment of the embedded system's function, such as flight control software, mobile phone software, MP3 software, electronic map software, and is oriented towards specific application fields. Some embedded application software requires a specific embedded operating system support due to the time and precision requirements of users in the course of using.

Application software in embedded system is the most active force, each of them owns specific application background. Small scale as it is, it is more professional. Let us appreciate the unique embedded application software by different functions to see whether you can find new fields.

3.3.3.1 Browser Software

As the mobile Internet has gradually become a hot topic, its importance should not be overlooked. In the PC terminal era of the Internet, the browser is clearly a monopoly of the entrance of the Internet. For a time, in the global market, IE, Firefox, Chrome compete; and in the Chinese market, Sogou, QQ, 360 and other browsers are taking the leading position. All these show the importance of browser on the Internet.

Like talk to the phone, due to the function of mobile applications is more and more powerful, the role as the entry of Internet of browsers is weakened. However, according to the data released by StatCounter Global Stats, the mobile browser is still an important Internet entrance for mobile.

In the data released by this company, the one occupies the top two global market shares are Android system build-in browser and Safari browser of Apple iOS. Opera browser is the third place, and domestic browser UC Browser takes the fourth place.

As a third-party browser, Opera browser and UC browser occupy a large market share. The home page interface of Opera browser is very simple and refreshing. The address box is on the upper left corner; search box is on the right, and the address for quick access is in the middle, below that is the browser navigation buttons and settings buttons. UC Browser has a new upgrade rendering capabilities. Its operation is very smooth.

3.3.3.2 Electronic Map Software

As time goes by, the appearance of cities is constantly changing. It is not easy to find the right direction when walking in the corner of an unfamiliar city.

Sometimes, even walking in the huge campus with the pines and cypresses also make a person disoriented. So the Electronic map software gradually becomes the essential application for smart phones.

The purpose of embedded application software is to meet the needs of users. When people are holding an old map without revision for years, only to find themselves struggling with the same location for a long time, an electronic map which can search interactively and navigate automatically is needed urgently.

Now the mainstream mobile phone map software is very powerful. As long as the user enters the destinations, the software will immediately automatically position it at the top of the map. They have much shorter update cycle and incalculable mass of information on the Internet than paper maps. There are all kinds of information including shopping, food, housing, transportation, entertainment, etc. Moreover, new information will be updated every day.

Mainstream mobile map software includes Google map, Amp, Baidu Maps, etc.

3.3.3.3 The Office Applications Software

Nowadays, we have increasing pressure with the ever-accelerating pace of life; there are always some documents even need to be handled on the way to work.

In the mobile Internet era, all kinds of powerful mobile terminals with fair prices can be found everywhere, particularly the smart phones and tablet computers. People need to use all kinds of mobile office productivity software in their daily work. Next, we will show you some commonly used office productivity software on Android platform to show how these essential office productivity software work. Of course, other embedded platforms also have excellent office productivity software; we will introduce Android platform as an example due to limited space.

We will list eight mainstream office productivity software, including Documents To Go, OfficeSuite5 Pro, WPS Office, Picsel Smart Office, ThinkFree Office, Quickoffice Pro, OliveOffice, and Polaris Office. They can be divided into software on iOS platform software, software on blackberry platform and software on Android platform by their compatible software platform.

The overall color of Documents To Go is blue-gray, which is consistent with the characteristics of the office productivity software business. Moreover, this color is softer, which does not give the feeling of glare. The initial list is the basic software interface form. Clicking on the different functions will take us into the secondary pages. In the subsequent pages, the toolbar will appear in a dynamic manner. As one of the few domestic software, WPS Office is more concise, only have the upper portion of the toolbar interface and its underlying composition editor browser window. Clicking on the toolbar function button, there will be a secondary tool button bar.

3.3.3.4 Mobile Gaming Software

When on a bus or a subway, if anything can take the time mostly, it is the mobile gaming software. In the Sect. 3.2.1, we divide the game into the console game, online game and browser game. In this section, according to the subjects, we will classify games into the following: role-playing games, action shooting games, flight simulation games, adventure and puzzle games. There are also sports games, casual puzzle games, strategy tower defense games, strategy management games, board and cards games, car racing games, music rhythm games and so on.

Dungeon Hunter is a game of Gameloft, in which players join the game by playing a certain role in the game, which is why it is classified as roles play the game. The game not only provides players with a single-player mode but also supports Player versus player (PvP) multiplayer mode. If according to the classification method in Sect. 3.2.1, it needs a detailed textual research to determine whether the game should belong to a single game or online games. However, the classification method in this section is much easier.

Gameloft is indeed the world's leading company to develop games on the mobile device. Shadow Guardian was also published by Gameloft. It is an adventure game which mixes the elements of action, adventure, puzzle, adventure, and third-person shooting. In the game, the player becomes ancient Egyptian to complete exciting missions. The classification of the game, if according to the classification in this section, cannot simply be defined as action shooting or puzzle adventure game. Nevertheless, it can be easily defined as a single-player game according to the classification method in Sect. 4.1.2.

Speaking of mobile games, whether it is role-playing game or action game, the group of players has limitations, but almost everyone who has a smart phone has ever played casual puzzle games. By the end of 2009, the first version of "angry bird" was published. In early 2010 the first version of "Fruit Ninja" was published. After constantly updating, these two games firmly grasped a large group of players.

More classic the game is, easier it is to spread. As a casual puzzle game, Tetris appears in major mobile application markets.

3.3.3.5 Mobile Social Software

On February 24, 2014, WhatsApp which was acquired by Facebook's by $19 billion announced it would open a voice call function, which will directly impact the mobile operator's business. WhatsApp Messenger is an instant messaging software, the software is very powerful, and cross-platform users can send messages through it.

In February 2014 WhatsApp had more than 450 million active users, nine months ago. WhatsApp has just announced that it has 200 million active users, which has caught up with Twitter, and only nine months later it exceeded 450 million users, which means that there are more than one million users to install WhatsApp and start chatting every day. What's more incredible was that the active users every day were 72% of the login users per month. In contract, the industry standard was only 10–20%.

In the past 150 years, the development of personal communications has developed from Pony Express, Telegraph, airmail to telephone and email. WhatsApp is following this trend, and become the standard-bearer of personal communication.

As the mention of WhatsApp, we cannot ignore WeChat which is the domestic leader of mobile social software. In China, almost everybody knows its name.

Before WeChat, BlackBerry Messenger was developed for BlackBerry platform. This application allows users to communicate with friends by words and expressions very easily. In this application, users can share pictures, music, video and other files with others. As this application is only designed for Blackberry platform, the Kik Messenger was born. Three months later, Talkbox, an application based on voice recording and voice transmission, taking dialogue and information push as core service received users' attention. In this context, WeChat was born. After several years of development, WeChat almost covers all the functions of the software.

The first WeChat client is released three days after the release of the Talkbox. At that time the WeChat can only chat, share photos and modify avatar. Even it cannot be thought as the replica of QQ as QQ has more powerful functions then it. At that time the mobile terminal software management program mostly regards WeChat on the "it" category awkwardly. Moreover, WeChat is just relied on the users of QQ. So this awkward position makes WeChat an underdog.

From January to April 2011, WeChat only accumulated less than 500 million users. In May 2011 after adding the WeChat voice intercom, the number of users had a significant growth. On 2011 National Day, WeChat released its 3.0 version, which joined the well-known "Shake Shake" function, which led to an explosion of user growth. At that time, WeChat has been a significant social element, and it is inappropriate to divided WeChat into the catalog of instant messenger. From that, WeChat appeared in the social applications category and started to carve out its way to a pinnacle future.

With the shift of positioning, Tencent has gradually expanded the scope of WeChat and found a new field, which opens the door to its progress. There are numerous embedded applications. At the end of October 2013, the applications in the iOS system application store—iTunes store, exceed 76,0000. Also, there are many embedded applications with customized function in the industrial field. The book will not mention it due to the confidentiality of the industry as well as the special nature of the software.

There are seas of application software; the book only describes some commonly used software. At the end of this chapter, let's look at the issues discussed at the beginning of Chap. 4: how do we look at software classification and software's culture? It is necessary to have a unified standard when it comes to classification. The location of the software should be specified to see each software standard. With the different time and functions, the location of software will change, which explains why there is a social culture of various stages in the classification of software.

The earliest instant messaging software of Tencent is QQ. As QQ game becomes more and more powerful, gradually, Tencent released the independent QQ game. QQ game has been gradually divided into QQ battle platform and QQ games hall. When some of the functions of software are becoming stronger and stronger, the features different from the main features of the software will appear, and the specific function will be separated from the software as a stand-alone software. This stand-alone software will be classified into a different classification. As the software comes into a new field, the software will encounter with other competitors, which encourages its development further and the software culture will be moved forward. In turn, the development of software culture is also promoting the advance of software and improving people's life.

3.4 Summary

This chapter presents the related content of the system software and application software, which have effectively improved the social productivity, promoted the development of society and culture, and even changed the way people working and thinking which also contributed to the formation of the culture styles of the people who develop and use the software. As the system which can control and coordinate the computer and peripheral equipment, system software supports the development and application of software, and it liberates computer operators from the underlying hardware of computer systems. Application software is the kind of software which arises from users' demand of different areas. It greatly expands the application areas of a computer system, extends the functions of the hardware. It also significantly meets the needs of customers and their using habits. As the human culture is used to depict the characteristics of a group, it was greatly affected by the software development. Due to the space limitation, this chapter only introduces the operating system, database system, drivers, developing tools, program compilation tools, general software, specialized software and embedded software which is only the tip of the iceberg to open the subject for discussion simply. If you want to learn other detailed contexts that are not covered in this book, please reference other literature. In the subsequent sections, we will further introduce the applications of the software.

References

1. Dangermond, J (1983). A classification of software components commonly used in geographic information systems. Design and implementation of computer-based geographic information systems, 70–91.
2. Grottke, M., & Trivedi, K. S (2005). A classification of software faults. Journal of Reliability Engineering Association of Japan, 27(7), 425–438.
3. Zuse, H (1991). Software complexity. NY, USA: Walter de Cruyter.

4. http://en.wikipedia.org/wiki/Category:Software.

5. Brünger, A. T., Adams, P. D., Clore, G. M, DeLano, W. L, Gros, P, Grosse-Kunstleve, R. W & Read, R. J (1998). Crystallography & NMR system: a new software suite for macromolecular structure determination. Acta Crystallographica Section D: Biological Crystallography, 54(5), 905–921.

6. Silberschatz, A, Galvin, P. B, Gagne, G, & Silberschatz, A (1998). Operating system concepts (Vol. 4). Reading: Addison-Wesley.

7. Tanenbaum, A. S., & Bos, H (2014). Modern operating systems. Prentice Hall Press.

8. https://en.wikipedia.org/wiki/DOS.

9. https://en.wikipedia.org/wiki/Microsoft_Windows.

10. Solomon, D. A, & Russinovich, M (2000). Inside Microsoft Windows 2000. Microsoft Press.

11. Page, R.D (2001). TreeView. Glasgow University, Glasgow, UK.

12. Campbell-Kelly M, Aspray W (1996). A History of the Information Machine. Notes, 30(1).

13. Myers, B. A (1998). A brief history of human-computer interaction technology. Interactions, 5(2), 44–54.

14. Bach, M. J (1986). The design of the UNIX operating system (Vol. 1). Englewood Cliffs, NJ: Prentice-Hall.

15. Nguyen, T. T. UNIX Operating System.

16. Narten, T., & Burgess, M (2003). Unix operating system.

17. Deitel, H.M (1984). An introduction to operating systems (Vol. 3). Reading, MA: Addison-Wesley.

18. Pan, G., & Bonk, C. J (2007). The emergence of open-source software in China. The International Review of Research in Open and Distributed Learning, 8(1).

19. Singh, A (2006). Mac OS X internals: a systems approach. Addison-Wesley Professional.

20. Jinn-Yuan, L. A. Y. (2015). U.S. Patent Application No. 14/593,880.

21. Gandhewar, N., & Sheikh, R (2010). Google Android: An emerging software platform for mobile devices. International Journal on Computer Science and Engineering, 1(1), 12–17.

22. Silberschatz, A., Korth, H. F., & Sudarshan, S (1997). Database system concepts (Vol. 4). New York: McGraw-Hill.

23. Bernstein, P. A., Hadzilacos, V., & Goodman, N. (1987). Rrency Control and Recovery in Database Systems. Addison-Wesley.

24. Garcia-Molina, H., Ullman, J. D., & Widom, J (2000). Database system implementation (Vol. 654). Upper Saddle River, NJ: Prentice Hall.

25. Codd, E. F(1970). A relational model of data for large shared data banks. Communications of the ACM, 13(6), 377–387.

26. Cattell, R (2011). ScalableSQL and NoSQL data stores. ACM Sigmod Record, 39(4), 12–27.

27. Dongarra, J. J (1993). Performance of various computers using standard linear equations software. University of Tennessee, Computer Science Department.

28. Powell, K. C., & Kalina, C. J (2009). Cognitive and social constructivism: Developing tools for an effective classroom. Education, 130(2), 241–251.

29. Luk, C. K., Cohn, R., Muth, R., Patil, H., Klauser, A., Lowney, G., … & Hazelwood, K (2005, June). Pin: building customized program analysis tools with dynamic instrumentation. In ACM sigplan notices (Vol. 40, No. 6, pp. 190–200). ACM.

30. Lattner, C., & Adve, V (2004, March). LLVM: A compilation framework for lifelong program analysis & transformation. In Proceedings of the international symposium on Code generation and optimization: feedback-directed and runtime optimization (p. 75). IEEE Computer Society.

31. Ma Hongyuan (2004) Industrial control software and factory information. In: National Workshop on Informatization of Factories, 2004.

Chapter 4
Software Applications and Software Culture

Abstract As civilization plunged into software and eventually grew coated over generations, society inevitably ran to the "every body" can use age. At that stage of development, software drew closer to mankind. Industries called for software applications to handle their data, leading to an elephantine production of database management systems in the 1970s. Later in the 80s, following the advancement in hardware, software amplified its scope into a network of disciplines such agriculture where it made possible outcome prediction and the medical sector, where software applications monitored medical equipment. Meanwhile software applications engulfed the entertainment market with virtual and augmented reality, the Internet and Mobile applications furnished completeness of services. As of emerging industries involving Space, Scientific Exploration, New energy, Internet of Things and Unmanned Aerial Vehicle areas, software applications provided ways of accelerated explorations and analysis, together with advanced data transformation and interpretation. Currently as we are writing this book, a lot of software simulation and exploration is taking place in the software industry. They are carried out in an attempt to visualize future opportunities. As mankind constantly receives threads from its environment and nature, it has been endlessly seeking for the next station. From these examples of software application, readers will have a better understanding of software culture. This chapter discusses the relationship between software applications and software culture from two aspects: software applications in traditional and emerging industries.

4.1 Relationship Between Software Applications and Software Culture

In Chap. 3, we show the readers a wonderful software world, but one chapter can never involve all areas of software. Software culture can be spotted from any aspect of in our life. In the highly developed information era, the applying of software is around us everywhere. Finished reading the classification of software in Chap. 3, we believe our readers must have a deep understanding about the multifunctional

© Springer Nature Singapore Pte Ltd. and Zhejiang University Press 2018
Z. Qin et al., *Fundamentals of Software Culture*,
https://doi.org/10.1007/978-981-13-0701-0_4

and tremendous diversities of the software. However, people must be feeling distanced when facing all those complicated software.

The application is usually defined as using something regarding its needs. *The Book of Song* said: "Device serves for needs, business, for wealth." [1] We can see that the application is the "device" here, and the meaning of "device" is even more plentiful, it refers to all kinds of instruments. The applying of software in different areas shows up as the instrument. Moreover, when talk about "applications", people will naturally think about the software. The "application" even consists of the meaning of "device". It is clearly that with the applying of software becoming more and more extensive, the software culture is blending in people's life and even in the ideology.

What effects does this software have on our life? What roles have they played in the promotion of the development of industry? Moreover, what contributions have the computer software made to the agriculture areas, the fundamental areas of human beings? This chapter will discuss the relationship between software applications and software culture from two aspects: applications in traditional industries and applications in emerging industries. It is aimed at providing a better understanding of the development of software culture for the readers, and meanwhile, help them look forward to the future development of the software.

In this chapter, we will present the software from different areas in serial, to let the readers feel that: software culture has an important effect on small things as well as the improvement of the nation and the society.

4.2 Applications in Traditional Industries

4.2.1 The Applying of Software in Industry

The applying of software in industry refers to that software played a significant role in the development and manufacturing of the industry, it even becomes a technical trend. Some of the industrial software is general software, other kinds of software such as industrial control software belong to industry application software. In this chapter, we will introduce the applying of software in architectural industry, civil engineering industry, hydropower industry, environmental industry, engineering industry and electronics industry.

4.2.1.1 The Applying of the Industrial Control Software

No matter in what industry, people will first think about the industrial process control software when talking about "industrial automation". Thanks to the applying and popularization of the Industrial PC (IPC), there comes the development of the industrial process control software. IPC refers to the personal computer used in the industry; it can also be used as the controller of the industry.

The fundamental characteristics and compatibility of the IPC are basically the same as the Business PC at the same level. However, IPC has more protective measures to deal with different situations, for instance, the control of the mass production line of beverage or automobiles; to operate stably under a harsh environment, such as dustproof, waterproof, or antistatic. We do not require IPC to reach the highest efficiency at present, only require that it can reach the standard of the system; match the requirements of reliability and stability in the industrial environment. Otherwise, if the IPC goes down during the production process, it will result in severe losses. Therefore, the standard value of the IPC should follow strictly by the regularity and scalability.

In the early 80s, the American AD Company had already brought out an initial stage of IPC called MAC-150. Then, IBM officially brought out the IPC called IBM7532 [2]. Due to the reliability of the function, variety of the software and low price, IPC became the leading role in the computer market and was applied in more and more areas. Nowadays, IPC has been widely used in communication, industrial automation, medical care, environmental protection, aviation and many other aspects of human life.

The large-scale application of the IPC makes the realization of a greater range of industrial automation possible. With the manufacturing industry transformation in developing countries as the leading part, the automated requirements of the enterprises become higher and higher; and with the great varieties of control equipments and widely applying of the process surveillance devices, the development of the industrial control software market would be pushed forward. Estimated by the ARC Advisory Group, the 65 hundred million Process Automation System is at the end of its life. However the demand of industrial control software market will still be increasing.

The Applying of SCADA

SCADA is short for Supervisory Control And Data Acquisition [3]. It is the major part of dispatch automation system; in the petroleum industry, it is called the tube "clairvoyant" of the electronic era.

In general, the SCADA system would include the following subsystems: HMI, for Human–Machine Interface, the HMI display system that makes it convenient for operators to monitor and control the program. The surveillance system can collect the data, and also submit and control the process of the surveillance program. The RTU, for Remote Terminal Unit [4], will use the sensor to collect data and make the D/A (digital to analog) transformation, and then send the result to the surveillance system. The PLC [4], for Programmable Logic Controller, is used as field device or the RTU system with special functions; the communicative network is used to provide surveillance system and the channel for exchanging the data between RTU (or PLC).

High-quality SCADA must be extraordinary in flexibility, reliability, and extensibility. In the meantime, it should also be capable of open data accessing, having convenient configuration and practical data analysis control.

The SCADA system is widely used in the industrial areas. Drainage pumping plant needs the water to be sent away in time. This act requires programs like dewatering, well cluster, preventing tide, waterlogging drainage and piloting water. It also needs realization of the auto-monitor of the equipment of pumping station to achieve the centralized dispatch and management. This is done so as to collect the data of water and workers in real time. For the purpose of remaining the unchanging structure of the drainage pumping plant, and also making sure the engineers can run the support center remotely which realizes the possibility of online diagnosis and online observation of the actual operating field, it requires the use of Remote Secure Communicative System of SCADA system.

This system realizes the function of data measuring, remote control, alerting, and video surveillance and restriction management. Meanwhile, this system can make any increase or decrease of the number of a pump station that being monitored, and reserve the communicative access to other systems. The drainage pumping stations control and transmission industry network system consists of devices like PLC (Programmable Logic Controller), the host computer, and frequency converter, well satisfies the requirement of the wholeness surveillance and intelligent of the drainage pumping station.

SCADA system is the important surveillance power in the process of automation of the energy industry. The petrochemical production has the characteristic of inflammable, explosive, poisonous and harmful. To ensure the long-term stable production and guarantee the national profits, as well as the health of the workers, mass adoption of the SCADA system as the control system in automation of the production process management, becomes a trend. In Guangzhou Petrochemical Co., the SCADA software in the host computer mainly uses the Intouch of Wonderware and WinCC of Siemens, while the subordinate computer uses all kinds of PLC control system from different major manufacturers. In this system, there are three major operating modes of the SCADA system: remote operation, local operation and automatic operation. Besides the petroleum industry, other kinds of energy industries also adopt SCADA system. The SDACA system of Shanghai Dazhong Gas Co. is provided by Rockwell International Corporation; the surveillance range covers three storage and distribution stations, 23 data collecting sites. The surveillance traffic is about 8 MB data usage per minute, which requires the forming of a complete and independent remote real-time surveillance network.

In the traditional metal and nonmetallic mining, the SCADA system is also indispensable. The Argyle diamond mine is the biggest diamond mining around the world. The yield of diamond there accounts for 70% of the whole world per year. The Argyle diamond mine began to use SCADA system in 1992, the system is on the platform of Windows; the surveillance range covered 30,000 analog quantities, 16,000 switching quantities, 20,000 alerts, 40,000 historical tendencies and 10,000 display screens; which needed 50 operating sites, the average updating time is 1.7 s. The development of SCADA can be divided into three phases: monomer, distributed mode, and network phase. During the first level of SCADA system, the concept of the network was not clear, for which the calculations were processed by mainframe computers. The researchers who developed the SCADA system did not consider it to connect with other systems. Therefore, the SCADA system is an independent system without the ability to connect with other systems. With the time passing by, SCADA system becomes more sophisticated. However, its popularization and investment from the enterprises still need to be increased. According to a report issued by Deloitte Touche Tohmatsu Limited, the mining industries around the world should take more advantage of the IT strength. The company believes that although many mining companies show their intention to be innovative, they are not successful in using back-end technology like data analysis method or build different technology platforms after mergers and acquisitions. To lower the cost as well as improve the management, they should rethink the IT strategies; consider the PLC, SCADA, MES(Manufacturing Execution System), Business Intelligence System, Data Analysis Method and Advanced Manufacturing Systems. This shows that having been through a long-term of development, the SCADA system still has a space for development in the future.

The most obvious deficiency of SCADA system is the security issue. The threats for SCADA system is from two aspects: the unauthorized access of the control software and the datagram from the Internet aiming to attack the host computer. SCADA is the core operating system of the power supply industry, so its security and confirmation issues are well considered while designing. However, it remained the vulnerability. On Oct. 1999, a hacker from the US claimed that he was about to make a report public; in the report, there would be specific methods to invade the inner network of the enterprises and to shut down the electric networks of more than 30 power supply companies in the US. If there was only one hacker, it could be seen as the alarmist; however later, a federal investigative organization also issued the alarms, it believed that "With the access of only a computer, a modem, and a telephone wire, anyone from anywhere in the world can cause the power failure in a large area". In Jun 2010, the security company VirusBlokAda from Belorussia discovered a worm virus attacking the Siemens' WinCC/PCS7 system run by the Windows platform. That is the first case of computer worm virus attacking the SCADA system.

The general supervisory control and data acquisition
The common software under this branch is RSView32 and Honeywell Plantscape. RSView32 is the software used by the Rockwell Company in the US on their standard PC program [5]. It is an MMI (Man Machine Interface) datagram operated under Microsoft Windows 9X and Windows NT environment using the MFC (Microsoft Foundation Classes) and COM (Component Object Model) as the basic technology. It is a structured program based on the VBA (Visual Basic for Applications) script program; therefore it can exchange the data with other Windows applications and databases. Also, the user program of VBA can make the special control functions in RSView 32 possible. Furthermore, RSView 32 can take advantage of ActiveX control which has hundreds and thousands of standard

program interfaces; it has powerful extending capacity, and in the meantime supports the OLE (Object Linking and Embedding), which is compatible with products like Microsoft Office and Back Office.

During the operation, this program adopts the graphical tools based on the MS Windows standard, which can establish, edit and display the images. The program also develops the function of drag-drop, sharing, copying and animating based on the objective-oriented graphics library, providing a great convenience for users to drawing and configuring.

Honeywell International develops Honeywell Plantscape software series; this company is a diversified advanced manufacturing enterprise [6]. Its business covers aircraft industry, architecture industry, automobile industry, engineering industry, material industry and some other areas around the world. Its industrial control technic is also on the cutting-edge in a word.

Honeywell Plantscape is the representative product of this company. Same as RSView 32, Plantscape also bases on Windows NT 4.0 system and uses the objective-oriented technology, supporting ActiveX control and OLE. Plantscape configuration mode is very flexible with a simple interface and easy to operate. It is unique in communication function and security.

4.2.1.2   The Applying of Digital Virtual Manufacturing Software

Due to the economic globalization, increasing manufacturing cost and many other reasons, manufacture industry invests more money on the new high technology, to reduce the growing pressure on labor cost. The development of information technology brings out the virtual reality technology. This technology allows people using their instinct to create the virtual environment for the 3D simulation model of the computer. In another word, it is a computer system that can create and experience the virtual world. Out of the question, the applying of this technology in the manufacturing industry will cause a revolution in industrial software. Therefore, the virtual manufacturing software is developed.

Virtual manufacturing can realize the simulation in reality without consuming actual sources or energy. In the simulation, it can comprehensively emulate the five essential factors of the manufacturing system (human, organizational management, logistics, information flow and energy flow). There are lots of software can be called the virtual manufacturing software, such as 3DS MAX, Unigraphics, Pro/Engineer, I-DEAS, ANSYS, CATIA, SolidEdge, SolidWorks, ROBCAD, etc.

ROBCAD is the famous robot simulation software in the world [7]. Since first introduced to the world in 1986 by Tecnomatic Company in Israel, it has been applied in many different areas of manufacturing production and has become one of the most popular robot simulation software around the world. Many automobile companies such as Ford, Volkswagen, Fiat, and also the Lockheed Martin Space Systems Company are using the ROBCAD to process the layout designing of producing line, industrial simulation, and offline programming. In 2004, the UGS made the merger with Tecnomatix Company. Moreover, in 2007, Siemens Company made the merger with UGS.

ROBCAD plays the role as a concept and structure designing in the early stage of the product life circle. Its major characteristics are the perfect integration with mainstream CAD (Computer-Aided Design) software (e.g., NX, CATIA, IDEAS); make the visualization of the equipments and tools, robots and operators possible; manufacture units, tests, and programming simulation.

ROBCAD is the powerful software that consists of the testing simulation program of 3D modeling, industry layout and resource management; the analysis of assembly line balance and the function of human factors engineering analysis; it can also export offline programming that can be accessible for robots from different companies (ABB, NACHI, etc.). It helps to reduce the workload of layout planning by finding out the mistakes in advance, thus increases the rate of success and reliability of the layout planning and production. Furthermore, it helps to reduce the production cost, optimize the investment and shorten the time for the market of the products.

The virtual manufacturing software is widely used in automobile industry.

Besides, 3DS MAX has been introduced in the previous chapter. ROBCAD plays the role as a concept and structure designed in the early stage, while Unigraphics (UG) focusing on the whole process of the product development: from the designing concept to the process of product modeling, analyzing and manufacturing. It provides its users a flexible hybrid-modeling module. Unigraphics is a powerful CAD/CAM software produced by Unigraphics Solutions Company; we will call it UG in the rest of the book. As the first-class product, UG provides a whole series of instruments, including art instruments for CAID (Computer-Aided Industrial Design); and has close integration with the solutions of powerful CAD/CAM/CAE. UG has the unique function of KDA, in this way UG integrates the knowledge of the products and process.

The engineering components are characterized as complex in structure and complicate in the parameter. Especially when designing the chemical equipment, the technical stuff has to read lots of handbooks and figures, conducting the drawing by theories and experience. It would consume lots of time and energy without the guarantee of the accuracy of the drawing. UG fixes this problem, makes the designing of chemical components much easier and the manpower are released. UG has become the most advanced software in the world for computer designing, analyzing and manufacturing. It covers many industrial areas such as aircraft, aviation, automobile, shipbuilding, general machinery and electronic.

ANSYS is the large finite element analyzing software that consists of powerful functions like structure, heat, electromagnetism and fluid analysis [8]. This software adopts the APDL, which can realize the sharing and exchange data with much CAD software such as AutoCAD, UG, SolidWorks, I-DEAS, PRO/Engineer. This software is produced by ANSYS Company, one of the biggest large finite element analyzing software companies. It is also one of the high-rank CAE instruments of the modern product designs. Up to the beginning of 2013, ANSYS was still the only analyzing and designing software that qualified by ISO9001 in the world.

ANSYS includes three parts: preprocessor, solution part, and postprocessor. The preprocessor has the function of solid modeling, loading, and the dividing of the grid; solution part has the function of structural analysis, fluid dynamic analysis, magnetic field analysis, sound field analysis and piezoelectric analysis; postprocessor consists of the general postprocessor which presents the results and the time history response postprocessor.

Now, let us see the applying of ANSYS in the aluminum industry and aircraft industry. Numerical simulation is the inevitable methods to the process of material designing, heat treatment, casting, rolling down and impact modeling. In aluminum industry, numerical simulation has great effect on the electrolysis and processing of the aluminum. The good arranging of the three parts of ANSYS makes ANSYS become the researching analysis instrument throughout the processing of the aluminum.

During the electrolysis of the aluminum, ANSYS helps the engineers to design the new type of energy conservative aluminum cell and the stable electric field model. During the casting, ANSYS is mostly used for analyzing the stability of the products, transient temperature and stress field. During the rolling down process, ANSYS is mainly used for analyzing the three connected fields: temperature field, fluid field, and stress field.

The applying of ANSYS in the aircraft industry is even more outstanding. Raetech Company used ANSYS Workbench to make FEA analysis on the complicated bearing structure at the rivet connection part of T-34, which had already been forbidden to fly by Federal Aviation Administration in December 2004. The evaluation shows that T-34 has not reached its end and could get back flying.

Besides those examples, ANSYS can also make dynamic response analysis, whole airplane analysis, simulated fault analysis, simulated bird-incident analysis, airfoil's designing analysis, and senior fluid dynamic analysis.

ANSYS also applies in many other industries such as engineering and chemical equipment industry, automobile industry, shipbuilding industry and intelligent robot industry; we will not finish them all in this chapter due to the lack of space.

4.2.1.3 The Applying of New Technology Software in the Industry

After knowing something about the applying of the industrial configuration software and the digital visual manufacturing software, we are going to cover the cutting-edge technology in the industrial areas. We will focus on the fast developing 3D printing in the industry.

3D printing is a kind of technology that bases on the digital model files, using an adhesive material such as powder metal or plastic, to build the object by multi-layer printing [9].

Since the later period of the 1980s, 3D printing is widely used in industrial designing, architecture industry, automobile industry, aviation and aircraft industry and medical services, which has made a tremendous incredible breakthrough. In Nov. 2013, Defense Distributed Organization, an organization focused on 3D research, used 3D printing to make the first 3D printing metal gun. This organization claimed that the gun had been tested to shoot 50 bullets. 3D printing technology will be used in devices that have open source and back-up facilities that support other scientific researches; even to make organs in bioengineering area.

An engineer called Anjan Contractor designed a 3D food printer; the guarantee time of the food (powder) that could be used in the printer is 30 years, which was long enough for astronauts to go on long-term traveling; and he got supports from NASA.

3D printing is mainly used for rapid prototyping and manufacturing in the industrial areas; it aims at simplify the process of producing products in the industry and lower the manufacture cost. The 3D design engineers would first design the 3D model by using the 3D modeling instruments such as Rhino, 3DS MAX, and MAYA. Then they use the 3D printer to print the model layer by layer.

Similar to the 3DS MAX in the previous sections, softwares like Rhino and MAYA are both very powerful at building 3D models. Besides, there are other similar Softwares: XSI, LightWave, Softimage and Houdini. Rhino does not require the high standard as the old modeling software MAYA, and itself is less than a hundred megabytes in size; compare to other software it can be seen as tiny.

The 2013 World 3D Printing Technology Industry Conference is held for three days from May 29, 2013, in Beijing, China. Graham Tromans, the president of British Additive Manufacturing, believed that 3D printing would be more powerful in the applying of industry in the future. Although 3D printing was widely used in the industry, it still could not get rid of the traditional processing or make the large-scale of independent manufacturing possible. For example, 3D metal components printing still needs to combine with the heating process. Moreover, organ printing and food printing are still the dream of human being.

4.2.1.4   Software and Industry 4.0

The 3rd Session of 12th NPC (National People's Congress) was held on Mar 5th, 2015. Premier Li Keqiang proposed "Made in China 2025" on the Report of Work of The Government. "Made in China 2025" focuses on industries and policies; it is the Chinese version of "Industry 4.0". This initiative was approved and signed by the Premier Li Keqiang, and issued by the State Council on May 8th, 2015. However, there is a little difference between the two initiatives. "Industry 4.0" focuses more on technology and modes, yet the aim of intelligent manufacturing is the same.

"Industry 4.0" puts building the intelligent factory in the first place, by installing a large amount of sensors in the production facility and make it becomes the intelligent producing instrument. In this way, people can realize the intelligence monitoring and operating. In the future intelligent factories, the components of the products will bring information by themselves; they will communicate with the production system and facilities directly according to their needs; also they can send out the operating instructions during the producing period until the production facilities finish producing them. Meanwhile, during the manufacturing, the processing will be more flexible through the dynamic allocation of the productive resources. Therefore, the manufacturing process will be more efficient; the allocation of the resources will be more reasonable; and the production circle of the products will be shortened and show more creative.

"Made in China 2025" emphasized on intelligent manufacturing. It is the same goal as the "Industry 4.0" issued by Germany.

"Industry 4.0" wants to realize "intelligent factory" through "Cyber-Physical System". It means that conducting real-time sensation through implanting different sensors of Internet of Things; controlling precisely of the whole process through the broadband network and data, which are both on the production facility level. On the production management level, it requires the realization of the information sensation, Internet communication, accurate controlling and remote collaboration of the physical facility through series of Internet service consists of technology, such as Internet technology, cloud computing, big data, broadband network, industrial software, and management software. Therefore, the BITKOM and Fraunhofer described the involving technology in the Germany "Industry 4.0" by a picture in their research report.

Through automated facility, intelligent robot, and virtual reality technology to realize the intelligence of the factory, through Internet of Things, sensors, and implanted system to realize the Cyber-Physical blending of hardware and software. These are based on collecting and excavating the big data under cloud computing; the robustness network of the mobile communication and mobile device; the network security and the information security of the industrial control system.

Thus, the development of automated facility, sensors, intelligent robot, industrial control system and industrial big data and another aspect of "Industry 4.0" will bring out the new revolution of the applying of the software in the industry. That is what we should continue tracking and doing researches on.

The new generation of information technology and manufacturing are deeply integrated, and this integration is now influencing the profound industrial transformation, forming new production pattern, industry type, commercial mode and economic growth point. Every country in the world is now putting more and more efforts on the innovation of the technology, achieving a new breakthrough in areas like the 3D printing, mobile Internet, cloud computing, big data, bioengineering, new energy, and materials. The intelligent device intelligent factories and other kinds of intelligent manufacturing are now leading the transformation of the manufacturing mode. Based on cyber-physical system which includes the network pack, collaborative design, large-scale of customization, precise management of the supply chain, products lifecycle management and e-commerce are now reshaping the industrial value chain system. The wearable intelligent products, intelligence appliances, intelligent automobile and other intelligent terminal products keep expanding the new areas for manufacturing. Those transformation and innovation in those areas intertwine with each other when they play the supporting role as the software of the thinking abilities. Therefore, the transforming and updating of the Chinese manufacturing industry, with the development and innovation in that area;

and the innovation and revolution under the new technology are facing both challenges and opportunities.

4.2.2 The Applying of Software in Agriculture

Agriculture is the industry that cultivates animal and plant production of food and industrial raw material [10]. Agriculture is the primary industry; the science study on agriculture is called agronomy. The objects of labor in agriculture are living animals and plants; the output is the animals and plants themselves. Agriculture involves growth and development laws of animals and plants, and departments gain products from artificial cultivation. Agriculture provides the fundamental products that can support the construction and development of the national economy.

China has a long history of agriculture. Agriculture began from the ancient age where there was no written record; it grew from the ancient gathering and hunting economy. In Chinese ancient legend, there was a man called "Sheng Nong". It is said that before the existence of Sheng Nong, what people ate were cattle, reptiles, vegetables and shells. With the growing population of human beings, there came the shortage of food, and the needs for new food resources were of great urgency. Thus, Sheng Nong tasted all the herbs he could find; he was poisoned many times and found out the antidote at the end; it was a tough journey. Finally, he discovered the grain that was edible for a human. Then he observed the timing and place; built tools and teach people how to use them to grow grains. Therefore, the agriculture and medicine appeared. In the meantime, people had the command on skills like ceramics, spinning, and weaving. This legend is the history influence left since the beginning of the agriculture.

As one of the seven miracles in the world, the Hanging Gardens of Babylon presented the most prosperous period of the development of the civilization of the ancient Babylon. The circumference of the Hanging Gardens is about 500 m, built on a high platform using the 3D gardening methods. The artificial mountain was piled up with stone pillars and broad layer by layer, up the right to the sky. When looking at it from a distance, the Hanging Garden looked like in the air. There are three parts of the artificial mountain: upper, middle, and lower part. Every part is supported by the huge stone pillars with palaces. In order to prevent the water from getting in, each floor is covered with willows sunk in the tar. On the top of that, there are another two layer of bricks covered in lead. Finally, on the top of the lead, people plant many beautiful flowers and grasses around the world with well-designed irrigation. In the record of Babylon, the Hanging Gardens remained a mystery; not even one paragraph talked about it.

Nowadays, the information technology leading by the computer software is spreading the world; human beings are in the transformation from industrial society into information society, from products economy into the knowledge economy, from modern agriculture into information agriculture. Moreover, people are also under the huge revolution of thinking pattern, producing pattern and living pattern.

The rapid growing industry of software has widely applied in all aspects of the development of agriculture, which also forms a complete functional system in the applying of agriculture. In the following paragraphs, we are using China as an example to introduce the integration of the software and agriculture and the software culture involved in agriculture.

4.2.2.1 The Development of Agricultural Informatization in China

The widely applied information technology in Chinese agriculture is influencing the agricultural management, production, marketing, technology, and education with great changes. It also showed the prosperous prospect of this area, bringing unprecedented opportunities for agricultural industry, pushing forward the modernization of the agriculture greatly. Moreover, in the meantime, it brings challenges for the science and technology agricultural workers to face the revolution of agricultural information technology.

Since 1980s, with the developing of the computer technology, the applying of computer technology in the agriculture has become a popular trend. It is widely used in areas like grain production, animal husbandry production, agricultural machinery, agriculture products processing, the surveillance and control of the agricultural environment, crop-yield forecasting, agricultural pests forecasting and agricultural information service. The computer technology not only brings high efficiency, high profits and high quality to agricultural management, production, and scientific research, but also gradually forms a special branch in the agricultural science and technology areas by itself. Nowadays, Chinese agricultural informatization has shipped the applying focus from scientific computing, mathematical programming and statistical techniques to areas like the process of natural resources data in agriculture, the information management and service generalization of the agriculture. It has also covered the planning and policy-making on the agriculture, the practical process, and control during the producing period. The computer technology has been applied to every agricultural subject. China has already built up the ARICMS, Agricultural Literature Database of China, the Agricultural Science and Technology Achievement of China, The Database of Agricultural Research Projects in China and Agricultural Practical Technology Database. Meanwhile, China takes part in some major agricultural database around the world, such as AGRIS (Agricultural Information System), AGRICOLA and CABI (Center for Agriculture and Bioscience International), and is now building the National Network for Agricultural Science and Technology. The Network Center of Chinese Academy of Agricultural Sciences has been built up connecting with Ministry of Agriculture, State Science and Technology Commission and International Information Center. These acts have improved greatly on the development of Chinese agricultural science and technology as well as the generalization services. Through the computer technology, it makes it possible for the leaders of all levels and agricultural science and technology workers to know more about the technology news, level, and tendency. This in turn enables them to have a good command of the settings and development of the scientific research, learn more about the generalization and applying of the agricultural scientific and technology achievements. It also provides effective methods for the proposal and cooperation of the research programs, which makes it easier for farmers to gain access to the technology information. With the development of network and the construction of intelligent expertise on the network, farmers can consult expertise from homes; this can advance the transformation of the agricultural science and technology achievements.

4.2.2.2 The Applying of the Computer Information Technology in the Production of Chinese Agriculture

The first time the Ministry of Agriculture put the applying of agriculture research in the national program was when the "7th five-year" plan was issued. It concluded the huge development of different kind of dedicated systems that applied greatly in the areas of agricultural production and management like mathematical model design and programming, research on crop production model and study on models of cultivation techniques. Building up different types of the database is the main content of the computer applying in recent decades; this matched with the development of the computer applying cause in China. China set up hundreds of rural information network point and established a supporting system of county level economic resources information and management policies. At present, some of the function of the database has already reached the advanced standard in the world. The operation and service of these databases have achieved the social and economic benefits to some extent.

The main application of information technology in China is in four aspects: grain production simulation model, expertise system, the real-time control of the agricultural output and grain yield estimation by remote sensing. The grain production simulation model uses the professional knowledge and mathematical models to solve all kinds of difficulties and uncertainties through analyzing and emulate the growing of grains by computer. China has already developed RESODS, CPMSS/CGSM, DSSWPM, ACRIS, APCS and simulation model of grain storage and drying. The expertise system is the computer system that can solve the real problems in specific areas of human expertise on the base of knowledge. The agricultural production real-time control system is mainly used in irrigation operations, fruit harvest, automated control of animal husbandry production and agriculture products processing, and the industrialization of the agriculture production. The automated control of livestock production can optimize the feed formula and adjust the producing environment. The industrialization of the agriculture production, such as greenhouse cultivation, mixed up the biotechnology and information technology, which would shorten the life circle of the grains and save the land. China also uses the technology of remote sensing and geographic information system to develop the cultivated land changes monitoring system and remote sensing investigation system of the cotton growing area. These achievements have improved the modernization and informatization of the agricultural production management in China greatly.

4.2.2.3   The Prospect of Computer Information Technology in Agricultural Production in China

The modern agriculture is developing towards a more accurate way in the information era, by using sensors to gain the data of the soil-plant, then using the remote technology to provide the information of growing environment and status. Next is using the GPS technology in the coordination of the geographical data management function of the geographic information system, and controlling the intelligent farm machinery such as the planter, the fertilizer distributor, insecticide sprayer, reaping machine and the intelligent robot through the decision and commands made by the expertise system. They are all based on the development and applying of the computer information technology. The whole system operates automatically without supervision every day. The accuracy aims at the kinds of soil, not the land; therefore, we can apply fertilizer and insecticide regarding the growth status, soil fertility and pest-problem of grains. In this way, we can achieve the goals of reducing the fertilizing amount, the sowing quantity, and the pesticide amount; and increasing the output and its quality. This can solve the long-term negative influence on environment pollution and low efficiency and low quantity caused by the pesticide. With the establishment of the Chinese market, the information of agro-production factors, such as natural resource information, law, and regulation information, market information and real-time technique information are very important to the leaders as well as all the farmers. The essential foundation of management is the timely, accurate, reliable and comprehensive information. No matter the leaders or the farmers, they can both make some wrong decisions with the lack of the right information, which can usually be seen in actual production. Thus, it is necessary to establish the agricultural macro decisional information system and application of information technologies service system. In the period of "9th five-year" plan, the Golden Farming Project that focused on the application of information technologies of the rural economic is now make the agriculture information highway compatible gradually with the CNII (China National Information Infrastructure).

2013 is the crucial phase of the "13th five-year" plan for it would begin a new phase in the future of agriculture. The application of information technologies of the agriculture is an important part of the information technology services. The "12th five-year" plan proposed to "speed up the modern agriculture". It also mentioned to "develop the agricultural information technology, meanwhile increase the ability on the application of information technologies in the producing management of the agriculture". One of the main points was also to "ensure the smooth progress in determining, registering, and certifying contracted rural land-use rights; make sure the farmers have the legal right to use and gain the benefit from the land they contract with". In 2003, "Number One" document proposes that the government should use five years to cover determining, registering, and certifying contracted rural land-use rights; and in the meantime, solve the problems of the contracted rural land-use rights for the farmers properly. This document speeds up the development in the application of information technologies of the agriculture. On May 27, 2015, President Xi Jinping pointed out, on the Main Party Members of Seven Province in East China, ten goals of the "13th five-year" plan including "speeding up the modernization of the agriculture". On November 3, 2015, "Recommendations For the 13th Five-year Plan for the Economic and Social Development" pointed out that China should push forward the application of information technologies and standards in agriculture.

From above, we can see that the modernization of agriculture will be the main subject of the "13th five-year" plan and it requests the comprehensive integration of agriculture and application of information technologies. The application of information technologies in agriculture will be the main goal in the "13th five-year" plan of information technology services. To realize that, we should use application of information technologies to help the innovative development in agriculture.

4.2.2.4   The Problems and Solutions for the Applying of Information Technology in Agriculture in China

The problems

Although the achievements of information technology in Chinese agriculture are on a quite advanced level, the technology is not compatible with each other; many types of research are focusing only on one subjects and cannot be applied in other aspects. Many technologies are comprehensive studies of all the subjects. We are in lack of products that is the integration of multiple information technologies, multifunction, intelligence and networked. We are also in lack of the secondary development in the information instrument of an agricultural system that suits the agricultural condition in China; the agricultural information software are usually providing the thoughts rather than providing practical methods for farmers. On the one hand, the reason can be interpreted as the lack of quantity and quality in established agricultural information database that cannot form the information industry, since the absence of the data standard, many databases can only be provided by the department solely. On the other hand, due to the great differences from place to place, many provinces, cities, and counties have not established the database that devoted to the local agriculture. So the construction of information resources cannot meet the need of the agriculture. Therefore, compare with the developed counties, China has not invested enough money in the information technology aspect; also the application of the information technology is restrained because of the short of talents in the development of advanced information technology.

Solutions

Currently, the information technology is developing towards a more comprehensive, intelligent and generalized form. We should focus on the secondary development in the information technology that aims at the agricultural situation in China. We use and develop the technology at the same time. We concentrate more on the applying of the practical information technology, which includes enhancing the remote technology, the geological information system, the development and application of GPS in the agriculture, also improving the integration of the agricultural information technology, organizing research among different subjects. Forming the expertise system consisting of a different function of expertise in the economy, agriculture and other areas, reinforcing the research agricultural software in the internet, multimedia, and visualization. In this way, we can realize the remote education of the agricultural information technology. The government should take the responsibility to be the guiding role for the application of information technologies in agriculture; meanwhile, it should also develop the application of information technologies in agriculture by advocating the social organizations, farmers, and other social forces. As for the strategy, the government needs to popularize the computer and knowledge about computer, develop the agricultural information market and information industry. Therefore, we can improve the information system and provide a good environment for the application of information technology in agriculture. China should enhance the regulation and guidance for the development of agricultural information resources, gradually perfect the information resources from each level and establish the updating system for standards and data, and reinforce the researching and use of the updating data skills. Furthermore, China needs to have strict regulations and laws for information market, avoiding the repeat of the database construction, increasing the connective standard of the database to strengthen the sharing of the data. Also, the agricultural database in provinces, cities, and counties needs to be well developed to improve the developing of the agricultural information construction, building the regional network to connect with the domestic main network and the Internet to let the agricultural technical staff, managing personnel and farmer get in the network. The last thing is to develop special talents in advanced agricultural information technology areas. In this way, China can increase the quality of researches and development in agricultural information technology and then lead the technology to the positive direction of the practical phase of "application-experiment-generalization".

All in all, we can see that with the development of the computer information technology and the arrival of the information society, the application of the software would promote the revolutionary change in the agricultural production and management in China, and bring wonderful opportunities for agriculture in China, too. Those changes will increase the contributions made by the technology; change the increasing mode of agricultural benefit; and increase the resource utilization and labor productivity. Thus, the agriculture in China can start its new path on the high and steady production with high efficiency and low energy consumption. This path can also be described as a harmonious relationship between human, resource, environment and relations of production. That is sustainable development.

4.2.3   The Applying of Software in Medical Area

Medicine is the science that dealing with the relevant problems of the human body under the healthy condition [11]. It aims at curing and preventing the disease and increase the health of human beings. The medicine can be divided into modern medicine (Western medicine) and traditional medicine (Chinese medicine) and many other types of medicine. Different regions and nations have their medicine system; the aims and purposes will also be different as well. Medicine is divided into Chinese medicine and Western medicine, they both developed under the influence of their history.

In second A.D, two giant in the history of east and west, Zhang Zhongjing and Claudius Galenus, learned different academic thoughts, built completely different medicine modes, developed and perfected different theories, which led Western medicine and Chinese medicine into different developments. Before Zhang Zhongjing wrote "Treatise on Cold Pathogenic and Miscellaneous Diseases", there had already been classic medical books such as "the Internal Canon of Medicine" [12], "Classic on Medical Problems" and "Herbal Classic". Zhang summarized the medicine achievements before Han Dynasty, learned the basic theories and abundant medicine knowledge. Combining with his own experience, he wrote the "Treatise on Cold Pathogenic and Miscellaneous Diseases". This book established the unique theory system of treatment based on syndrome differentiation.

For the western part, Galenus lived under the ruling of the Antony and his father in Ancient Rome. The prosperous of Roman Empire at that time provided the reliable guarantees on politics, economics, science and technology and culture for the achievement made by Galenus and the prosperity of the western medicine. Galenus inherited the theory of Hippocratic and wrote more than 200 books. In the existent 83 books, it involved contents about anatomy, physiology, pathology, hygiene, medicine, research on "Hippocrates Corpus", philosophy, linguistic, logic, math, history, and laws. He advocated the evidence-based medicine, and his scientific methodology characterized in experiment focusing, the partial orientation of the disease, formal logic, and deductive methods, which influenced the development of the western medicine greatly.

4.2.3.1   Medical Information System

In the modern society, the wide gap between Chinese medicine and Western medicine has been filled by the existence of the computer. The Hospital Information System (HIS) refers to an information system that is using modern methods such as the computer hardware technology and the network communicating technology to manage the staff, goods, and financial part in all kinds of the department of the hospital. Therefore, the system can provide comprehensive and automated management and services in getting information from collecting, storing, operating, picking up, transforming, gathering, and processing of the different phase of the running of the medical activity. Using this system, doctors can choose a more appropriate curing for the patients between Chinese medicine and Western medicine.

In the early 1960s, America, Japan, and some countries in Europe had already built up the HIS. In the 1970s, there were many large-scaled HIS had been established. For instance, Stockholm, the capital of Sweden, established the central information system called MIDAS, which connected all the hospitals in the city. The developing trend for HIS is to connect the medical devices online and build the network to connect around the whole country. The key problem is that this requires the standardization of the medical record registration, testing and diagnostic criteria from different systems. The higher level of HIS will widely use the medical expertise system, establish the medical quality supervision and control system to increase the level for medical and healthcare.

In HIS, the information system that has a direct connection with the medical activity is called medical system. The medical system includes medical expertise system, auxiliary diagnosis system, assistant teaching system, critical patient care system, drug counseling and monitoring system, and some other special systems such as CT (Computed Tomography), ultrasonography, automatic ECG (electro-cardiogram) analysis, blood corpuscle, and automatic biochemical analysis. These systems are relatively independent and form the specialized system controlled solely by computers. They mainly accomplish the first step collecting and analyzing works. The result can be checked or used by doctors through files and database offered by the connecting network.

4.2.3.2 Computer-Aided Diagnosis System

Computer-aided Diagnosis System (CADS) refers to the physical or biological methods such as iconography and medical image processing technology, combined with the analyzing and calculating of the computer to help the radiologist to find the problems and therefore increase the accuracy of the treatment [13]. The CAD is mainly pointing to the iconography of the CADS. Moreover, we should distinguish the difference between CADS and CAD. The focus of CAD is to point out the abnormal parts and provide general imaging processing technology without the diagnosis. The CADS is the extension and final goal of the CAD, CAD is the necessary and basic part of CADS. People called the CAD "the third eye" of the doctor. Using CAD will improve the sensitivity and specificity of the doctors' diagnosis.

With the development of the modern technology, the use of the modern high-definition imaging equipment such as DR (Digital Radiography), CT, MRI (Magnetic Resonance Imaging) and PET (Positron Emission Computed Tomography) provides a great help to the diagnosis of the clinical disease. However, although the functional imaging such as PET provides a great help to the diagnosis, due to the limits of the condition, most doctors will use this device as the assistance and make the diagnosis according to the clinical experience of their own.

Due to the personal difficulties of the patients and the deficiency of the doctor control of the imaging system, there may be mistakes from time to time. According to the information provided by the modern imaging, we should use the visual of the "intelligent robot" to correct or diminish the mistakes. Moreover, this leads to the concept of CAD.

In the 1990s, with the development of the computer technology and the artificial neural network, the research of the CAD has become the focus of the modern medical imaging research and showed its clinical value. Nowadays, CAD research is more sophisticated in pathology on mammary gland and lungs. Moreover, the researches of the virtual endoscopy, diagnosis of liver diseases, brain tumor, cerebral perfusion and Chinese medicine are still at the primary stage; many types of research are still in process. Usually, in the medicine imaging, CAD can be divided into three steps: the first step is to extract the problems from the normal structure; the second step is the quantization of the characteristic of the image; the third step is to get to the conclusion by processing the data. Because the computer can make accurate analysis to the image, therefore the results will be positive and reliable. It makes the diagnosis more accurate. With the development of the modern technology, CAD will be combined with the technologies such as image processing and FACS; it will be easier to operate and be more accurate. Furthermore, it will expand the ranges in the clinical use.

4.2.4   The Applying of the Software in the Entertainment Area

Entertainment can be seen as an inspiring activity that brings the joy to the recipients through the skills to express one's emotions or other people's emotions. Obviously, this definition is very general. It includes comedy and tragedy plays, all kinds of competitions and games, music and dancing performances.

In Chinese ancient times, there are six entertainments for a gentleman: rituals, music, archery, driving, calligraphy, and mathematic. Also in "Historical Books: Ji Lian Lin biography": "The King of Zhao heard that the king of Qin is good at playing a Qin instrument, and he presents the instrument to the king of Qin and asks him to play it for entertainment". In Chap. 51 of "Annals of the Kingdoms in the East Zhou Dynasty": "You have such a beautiful place to live in. Why don't you bringing some pretty girls and ask the teachers to teach how to dance and sing for the preparation of the performances? That thought would be fantastic." Once Confucius heard a piece of music and could feel the taste of meat for three months. He was good at an instrument and learned from a music teacher called Shi Xiang. Moreover, Li Shimin, the king of the Tang dynasty, prepared music that can inspire the army when they are in a war. In the west, the music appeared along with the Greek mythology, Zeus, the most powerful god of The Alps, who was also very fond of those. Therefore, he began the famous Olympic Games. There was a story that the king of Elis was looking for a husband, who is good at fighting and art, for his daughter. There were 13 men that died by the hitting of the spear until the grandson of Zeus won in the test. Pelops and the princess get married before the temple of Zeus. On the wedding, there was a competition of the war cars, wrestle. Moreover, that was the primary image of the Olympic Games.

In the modern society, there are more forms of entertainment: we can go and see a competition, dancing performances concert in live. Also, we can see live shows on the television and TV series. Entering the computer era, we have more ways to enjoy our life.

4.2.4.1 Computer Games

Personal computer games, also called as Computer games or PC games, refer to the games that run on the computers [14]. This is a kind of computer software that has an entertaining function. The computer industry relates closely to the computer hardware, computer software and the development of the Internet. Computer games provide the participants with a virtual space and let them play different roles in another world; it can make people get rid of the real world to some extent. Meanwhile, with the development of the computer media, games offer people lots of great experience and joy.

The appearance of computer games had a great connection with the entering of computers in the American universities in 1960. At that time, a great many of programming experts had raised under that environment. In 1962, a university student called Steve Russell was famous for his programs in a game "Space War" presented on the PDP-1 computer by the DEC. That was the first interactive computer game in the world. Usually, we believe that he was the inventor of computer games. In the 1970s, with the development of the computer technology, the cost was lower and lower. In 1971, Nolan Bushnell invented the first commercial video game device in the world. Then he established the first video game company in the world—ATARI. Willy Higginbotham and Ralph Baer can be called the real "Father of video games", but Nolan Bushnell brought this kind of entertainment to the public. In the 1970s, with the born of the Apple computer, the computer games had begun its commercialization. At that time, the image effects of the computer games are very simple, but different types of games had shown.

Since the 1980s, PC appeared in our life, and multimedia technology was more mature. Computer games have become the pioneer of those technologies, especially when the 3D display cards provided by 3Dfx Company brought the world the imaging revolution.

Since the 1990s, the development of computer hardware and the use of Internet brought great energy to the computer games. In the twenty-first century, Internet games lead the computer games into another area.

Due to the tremendous variety of the computer games, we will only introduce real-time strategy and fighting games (FTG) in the following passage.

Real-time strategy
We can hardly identify the predecessor of the real-time strategy because its forms have changed a lot from time to time. In Britain, the first real-time strategy was "Stonkers" and "Nether Earth", which were invented by John Gibson. Both of the games were played on the ZX Spectrum personal computer. In America, "The Ancient Art of War" was the forefather of the modern real-time strategy, as well as its series "The Ancient Art of War at Sea, in 1987". Besides, some data indicates that the "Utopia" played on the Intellivision device was the first real-time strategy, but it used the half turn system. Those games above cannot be called the real real-time strategy because they were a lack of base building and the "real" resource collecting. However, they have the fundamental element: conquer.

In 1989, the "Herzog Zwei" published on Sega Genesis device and the "Battle Master" published on Amiga and Atari ST device were the first two games that contained all the elements of a real-time strategy needed. The fundamental game of real-time strategy was the "Dune II: The Building of a Dynasty" published by Westwood Studios in 1992 (Westwood Studios also published a real-time strategy called Battletech: The Crescent Hawk's Revenge). Since then, the real-time strategy has stepped into the golden age.

The success of Dune II affected the Blizzard Entertainment and formed a competitive relationship with Westwood, which began at in 1994 when "Warcraft" was published. "Warcraft" is basically the simulation of Dune II. In 1995, "Warcraft II: Tides of Darkness" gained great success. Moreover, Westwood Studios also published "Command & Conquer" in the same year. These two video games both enhanced the interface and the operability, and the competition burst out. "Command & Conquer" allowed players to play against each other through Internet because both of the disks can run separately. It replaced the "Red Alert" and became the most popular battle game.

In 1997, "Total Annihilation" brought 3D and the concept of the unit into the game, emphasizing the macro operation. In the same year, "Age of Empire" also appeared and characteristic in the combination of low-pace and the era of civilization.

In 1998, the Blizzard Entertainment published "Star Craft" and gained a great success.

In July 2002, the Blizzard Entertainment published "Warcraft III" and made the players focus on the "fighting control unit" rather than "fighting produce unit". Compare with "StarCraft", this game requires players to concentrate more on the small-scale battles.

In 2006, Relic Entertainment published the "Company of Heroes", which changed the operating mode of the real-time strategy and the methods to collect the resources in the game. Therefore, it created a more strategic, grouping working and grander fighting scene for the player. Metacritic, the famous site, gave the game 93% in the overall rating according to the evaluation provided by other games sites. Moreover, this is the highest score ever.

In September 2007, UBISOFT published the "World in Conflict" based on the Cold War. This game did not provide fundamental construction and resources collecting; players needed to buy the unit in the reinforce point that had certain quantity in advance. It gained many high evaluations and many awards.

In March 2007, the Electronic Arts published "Command & Conquer III", and this was one of the Tiberium series. Moreover, also, it was the second game of this series that allowed the players to update the army freely.

The real-time strategy manly focus on the use of strategy and tactics, it is just like playing the chess. The units and the buildings are in a more reasonable way; when the real-time strategy becomes a kind of competition performance (1998, StarCraft became the international competition), the pace of the game became super-fast to attract the audience.

The real-time strategy transformed from 2D to 3D fast. In 1997, "Total Annihilation" is in 3D form, but it was in the overlook version. Therefore there wasn't much difference compared with the 2D form. Although the geography part of the 3D had not improved from many years; the "Warzone 2100" and the "Homeworld" published in 1999 has changed the situation. During that period, many ground real-time strategy players believed the 3D version might affect the visual range, however, using the adjustable perspective will affect the maneuverability and the pace of the game, and these are series problems in network champion mode. It was not until 2002 that the "Warcraft III" and "Command & Conquer: Generals" provided the long distance perspective, which solved part of this problem.

Fighting game

The fighting game refers to games that the players choose the character they want to be and fight with the computer or the other players [15]. Like the shooting games, it often appears on the arcade game. The setting of the system is very different from the sports game that related to the sports.

2D fighting games usually use drawings by hand or the vivid digital imaging and can be moving to the left and right, dodge and jump. However, in most of the games, the setting does not allow the side moving and moving towards the screen. The game uses the fixed perspective but can be moved to the left or right in 2D. The game setting is the air hike, jumps and leaps, special skills (clutch shot, including magic attack, aircraft, super nature) and "up, middle, down" attacking, stand and crouch defense system. 2D fighting game characters are usually capable of symmetry ability.

"King of Fighters" is the representative of the 2D fighting game published by the Japanese company called SNK in 1994 [16], and the company published other versions of this games every year since then and named after the years since then. In 2002, SNK went broke with PLAYMORE got all the knowledge property of SNK and continued the publishing of the game. It officially changed the company name to SNK PLAYMORE in 2003. In 2004, SNK PLAYMORE announced the new series of "King of Fighters" would no longer be named after the years.

"King of Fighters 96" is the most classic games of this series, which was published by SNK in 1996. In the system settings, "King of Fighters 96" abandoned the mature settings of the former games and changed the "avoid sideways" into "emergency avoiding". The former one can be used in certain characters. Moreover, the super time was shortened, and the MAX function is added into the game.

"King of Fighters 96" was more aggressive in the system; it added the emergency avoiding and small, middle jumping. Since then, the "avoid sideways" changed into "emergency avoiding"; and later in "King of Fighter 97" and "King of Fighter 98", it showed that this transformation was necessary. When the player used the Max, there would be a blue light in sight, which was very unique at that time. With the large changes in the system, the fast speed games will bring more joyful experience for the players.

In 3D games, the characters and stages are formed by the poly bump on the 3D models. There's no fixed perspective for the game, and the characters can move to every direction as the player want. Since the limitation of the 3D technology in the early times, the jumping function has been decreased. There were not many aircraft in the game. Usually, there would be "up, middle, down" attacking, stand and crouch defense system. However, whether it is a 3D fighting game is not judged by the existence of the stand and crouch defense system.

Technically speaking, the 3D fighting games familiar to the public is not the 3D fighting games; they are just 2D fighting games in 3D rendering. There would be no influence on the game if we cut the 3D effect. It is because of the promotion of the operators that people tend to think that fighting games with 3D effect can also be called as the 3D fighting games.

The first real 3D fighting game is "Tekken II". Since then, the character Kazuya Mishima can make the lateral movement and avoid many attacks. In "Tekken III", all the characters were using this movement, and this movement was improved in "Tekken IV". Meanwhile, the beam attack appeared at the same time as the horizontal movement system. When the opponents make the lateral movement, this attack can make them stop. In the later works, there were more clear indications for the tracking of the attack effectively; therefore, this is also the main difference between the 3D fighting game and the 2D fighting game.

At the same time, the "SoulCalibur" was also published; this was a game focusing on 3D space, and the characters can make the lateral movements. Meanwhile, the players can use A to track the opponent and to prevent the opponent to make the lateral movements, therefore form a psychological warfare or calculation, which is very different from the 2D fighting games.

4.2.4.2 The Management System of KTV

KTV is the short term for Karaoke Television. Karaoke is a Japanese name. "Kara" means "empty" in Japanese. The narrow sense of KTV is the place providing people with the Karaoke media system and singing areas. In general sense, it means the entertainment places that provide people with drinks and mostly at night such as Karaoke, slow-rolling, HI room and background music [17]. KTV became popular in the 1990s in Japan. The consuming parties are usually the white collar, family unions, and company parties. The price was reasonable; usually, the business would provide the Karaoke without the playing of high or disco music. The Karaoke works 24 h a day, there's no minimum charge for the consumers, and the rooms are charged by hours. The drinks and food can be bought self-service. KTV can make the consumers relaxed and is a place to outlet their troubles.

The KTV management software runs the management of the KTV. KTV song request software (search by the names, search by strokes, search by the number of words, search by the groups…) is the system that chooses the songs for the consumers according to their favors. Furthermore, consumers can learn the introduction of the singers; play the music; control the music and order the drinks order services. This system includes many different interfaces, which is initiated in China. The system uses the multi-module cross-use function, when the consumers are ordering drinks or the demand service, they can still control and operate on the performances that are on demand. With the KTV managing system, the management of the KTV become much easier and makes the users have a better experience.

The components of KTV managing system
KTV managing system includes the following parts:

The background system: it consists of much software, and they are all called the system. They are specifically for the management of the KTV.

The reception and consultant: this is used for the control and management of the rooms, such as inquiry, booking, purchasing, getting a room, changing the room, combining the room and close the room.

The drinks software: the consumers can order drinks through the computer in the room, and asking for the price.

The cashier system: it is used for the checkout of the consumers. The entertainment places set the fee standards and forms according to the nature of business.

The market cashier system: it is used for wholesale kind of KTV.

The music editing system: it is used to manage the music in the music system, such as adding, editing, making, deleting, and changing. This system can be divided into hardware editing and software editing.

The manager query system: it is the operator of the entertainment places to check the operating conditions, finance costs, and expenses inquiry.

The service response system: this is used for both the consumers and the operators. The consumers' requirements can be divided into "asking for waiters" or "asking for DJ", this service information will be sent to the service response system, and it will be arranged according to the needs of the consumers. The operator can use this system to send texts, ads, congratulating words and search notice.

The financial management system: it helps the accounting departments of the entertainment places to do the financial management, such as income, expenses, book keeping, sales status, financial statements, and staff management.

The storehouse managing system: this system is to manage the storage products in a stocking, selling and storing. All the function of the software and usage can be found in the manual book. If users have special needs, the manufacturer can revise the software.

The song requests software

The song request software is the most important part of the KTV managing system; the quality of the software will affect the experience of the users directly. If a song request software can find the songs wanted by the consumers, or find the songs by the information provided by the consumers, then the consumers will have a good experience. If they cannot find what they want by this software, or the song they want is not in the software, this will influence the consumers' impression on the KTV.

The song request software consists of several parts: the song request software, song request managing software, music editing software and music automated distribution software.

The song request software: it consists of the advantages of all the software in the market. There are three versions (single interface, multi-interface, and flash dynamic interface). The multi interface that can be chose by the users, multi interface in the single-interface version, multi-background pictures, and multi-languages song request function.

The song request managing software: it can manage the song request software effectively. It is responsible for setting the parameters and the functions on the interface. It makes the song request software alive. No matter you are a user or an agent; you can put your thoughts into the software.

The music editing software: it can come up with different plans of music according to the hardware capacity, the number of the servers and the copy song scheme. It suits perfectly to the agents who use their servers.

The music automated distribution software: it can arrange the songs to form a new database through the arrangement of the ranking list. According to the new database, one can rearrange the songs anytime; update the new version of the music on the hardware automatically; download the database into the local hardware automatically.

4.2.5 The Applying of Software in the Internet

The Internet started in America in 1969; it is a global network that transfers public information [18]. It is convenient, widespread, and the most popular media in the world. This media is faster than any other media in the world. The Internet consists of WAN (Wide Area Network), LAN (Local Area Network) and a single machine that forms an international computer network according to some communication protocol. These network protocols are the crucial part of the Internet.

4.2.5.1 The Network Protocols

Protocols are the terminology that used to describe the process of the exchanging of the information and data [19]. In the computer network, two communicative objects that are in the same place will have to exchange the information, so that they can coordinate to reach the sync. Moreover, the rules on how to exchange the information should be set before the process.

The network protocol is the set of the rules, standards, and protocols on the exchanging of the information [20]. For example, a microcomputer operator connects a macro-computer operator on the network, due to the different character set used on the data terminals, the operator cannot meet the demand of each other. To make the connection, all the character set should be transformed into the standard character set before they are sent. Of course, for the incompatible terminals, besides to change the character set, other characteristics such as display format, the length of lines, the number of lines and screen rolling mode should also be changed.

The network protocols consist of three elements

(a) Semantics. Semantics will explain the meaning of every part of the control information. It regulates the control information that needs to be sent, and what response will be present and what action should be finished.
(b) Grammar. Grammar means the structure and the format of the user data, the control information and the order of the data.
(c) Time sequence. The time sequence is to indicate the events in time order.

People describe these three elements in this way: semantics indicates what to do; grammar indicates how to do; time sequence indicates the order to do the things.

In order to make the communication between the different computers made by different manufacturers possible, and make the computer network in a larger range, the ISO issued the Open System Interconnection/Reference Model in 1978. It divided the communication protocols into seven levels; they are Physics Layer, Data Link Layer, Network Layer, Transport Layer, Session Layer, Presentation Layer and Application Layer.

The fourth layer is responsible for transmitting the data; the first three layers are user-oriented. To each layer, there are at least two standards: the service definition and the protocols regulation. The former one shows the exact definition provided by the service, the latter describes clearly the motion and all kinds of regulation of the protocol, to make sure the services.

TCP/IP is definitely the most important one in the three protocols. As the basic protocol of the Internet, one cannot access the Internet without this protocol. Any operations involving Internet cannot leave the TCP/IP. However, TCP/IP is also the most complex one in the three protocols. If you want to access the Internet through LAN, you have to set the parameters such as IP, gateway, subnet mask and DNS (Domain Name System).

Although TCP/IP is the most popular network protocol, its communication efficiency in LAN is not satisfying. Therefore, when it browses the computer though the "On-line neighbor", there will usually be troubles during the process. Then installing the NetBEUI will solve the problem.

NetBEUI refers to NetBios Enhanced User Interface; it is the advanced version of the NetBIOS and has been used by many operating systems such as Windows for

Workgroup, Win 9x and Windows NT. NetBEUI can be useful under many circumstances; it is the default protocol for the operating systems before the Windows s98. NetBEUI is a small but useful and powerful broadcasting protocol. There's no need to configure the settings after installing, and it suits the transmitting of data in the "On-line neighbor". Thus, the computer should be installed the TCP/IP as well as the NetBEUI for computers in LAN. Another thing is that if a Windows S98 with TCP/IP would like to join the WINNT, it should also install the NetBEUI.

IPX/SPX is the protocol that designed specifically for the NetWare by NetWare, but most of the connected computer games can also use the IPX/SPX, such as "StarCraft", "Counter-Strike". Though these games can use TCP/IP to get connected to the Internet, using IPX/SPX is more convenient for there's no need to configure the settings. Besides, IPX/SPX is not very useful under non-LAN conditions. This protocol is unnecessary if one is certain that he will not play games inside the LAN.

How do computers exchange information on the Internet? Just like we are using certain language to speak, computers have certain language to communicate with each other. That is called the network protocols. Different computers must use the same network protocols to communicate with each other.

Network Protocols are the set of communicative rules for all the devices (network servers, computers, and switches, routers, and firewalls) on the Internet. Most computers will use a layered structure; every layer is built on the layer below that, and offering service to the layer on the top of it, shielding the course of how to provide the service to the upper layer. The N layer of one device if want to communicate with another device of the same layer, they have to use the N layer protocol. In the layer of the network, there are many protocols; the receiver and sender must use the protocol on the same layer, otherwise they cannot communicate.

Of course, there are many kinds of network protocols; we have to decide which one to choose according to the circumstances.

The reason ARPANET can gain the success is that it used the TCP/IP. TCP/IP is a standard network protocol of the Internet; it was issued by the ARPA(Domain Name System) from 1977 to 1979. With the development of the Internet, TCP/IP receives further application and development and has become the "common language" of the Internet.

4.2.5.2 The Internet Software in Common Use

The twenty-first century is the Internet era; people cannot live without the Internet. The Internet influence our lives greatly, besides, we can learn a many things through Internet. People can do online shopping without going out, and the Internet games also bring us much joy. Furthermore, the Internet can enhance the communication between people and allow us to make more friends. The Internet also affects our spare times and makes our life more joyful.

QQ

QQ is an IM (Instant Messaging) software developed by Tencent Company [21]. QQ supports functions such as online chatting, video chatting, sending the files point to point, sharing the files, network hardware, personal interface and QQ mails; it can be used in many kinds of communicative mobile e terminals.

In Feb 1999, Tencent issued the first real-time communicative software—"OICQ" (mentioned in Chap. 3), later it changed its name into QQ. The online users developed from two people (Ma Huang & Zhang Zhidong) to more than a hundred million users until now. It is one of the most popular chatting software in China.

QQ gained a great success for its reasonable design, well application, powerful function, and stable and efficient system. The former QQ emulated the ICQ (an international chatting system). ICQ means "I seek you"; OICQ plus an O in front of the ICQ, which means "opening I seek you". However, it was charged for violating the property of ICQ, so the boss of Tencent changed OICQ into QQ. Despite the change of the name, there's no change in the logo, the penguin. Girls love the lovely penguin; it can be called as cute, which share the same sound of Q. Therefore, using the penguin to represent QQ is a good idea.

In 2000, OICQ accounted for nearly 100% of the real-time chatting market in China. It is basically the big boss of the real-time chatting software in China. It is not just only the real-time chatting software; it connected with many telephone stations and mobile communicative company, to realize the connection with the radio-paging network and the text communication of the GSM. It i is the most popular real-time chatting software in China. In the meantime, QQ can connect with the communicative mobile terminals, IP telephone network, and radio page; it makes QQ more than just an Internet visual device; it is more like a convenient, practical and efficient real-time communicative tool. QQ may be the most used communicative tool in China. The status of the QQ is: online, Q me, leave, busy, do not disturb, invisible and offline.

Whether the winter of Internet will come, the penguin has changed greatly. With more and more users of the QQ, people do not see QQ as the "children's toy". In this platform, there are lots of potential clients, which mean they can bring a tremendous amount of fortune.

Weibo

Weibo is short for Microblogs, which means "one sentence blog". It is a platform that is providing the information sharing, spreading and acquiring based on the connection of the users [22]. Users can establish the personal community through WEB and WAP; and realize the real-time sharing in updating information in less than 140 words, expressions, and pictures.

Weibo is a broadcasting, social network platform that people can share the brief instant information through the following system. There are five aspects of this system

(a) The following system: can be either in one-way or double-way;
(b) Brief content: less than 140 words (including punctuation mark);

(c) Real-time information: the newest information;
(d) Broadcasting: the information goes public, all people get access to the information you share;
(e) Social network platform: Weibo is a kind of social network.

With the development of Weibo, there also appeared a tool called the long Weibo, which allow the users to send information more than 140 words. Weibo provides people a platform where they can be either the audience or the publisher. You can choose to be the one to skim the information you are interested in or the person who send the information. The contents of the information are usually short with the instant thoughts or emotions. People can also share pictures and videos. The biggest characteristic of Weibo is that it posts out the information really fast, and the spreading speed is also fast. For instance, if you have 2000 thousand fans, the information you send will be sent to 2000 thousand people immediately.

The earliest software like this is called Twitter in America. Twitter is a website that provides service for social network and microblogs. It is one of the top 10 visiting websites on the global Internet. It uses a wireless network, wired Network, and communicative technology to realize the real-time communicating, which is the typical application of the microblogs. It allows the users to post their status on the phones or personal websites through text forms, not only just send to one person.

In Aug 2009, Sina issued the private version of Weibo in China. It becomes the first website that provides the users the experience of Weibo and Weibo begins to be popular. With the development of the Weibo, many hot words also become popular on the Internet, the effect of Weibo begins to show. In the first half of 2013, the registered Weibo users reached 5,360 hundred million; in the third season of 2012, the registered users reached 5,070 hundred million. Weibo has become the most popular activity for Chinese.

The social network site
We should differentiate the difference between the social network site and other kinds of sites. Social networking refers to the network of personal relationships; this idea is used in the SNS (Social Networking Services) [23]; it aims at helping people to establish the Internet application service under the social network. It also refers to the matured information carrier, such as SMS. Technically speaking, the SNS in China does not serve for the social network service; it is more like the social network site. Such as RenRen site and KaiXin site in China and the Facebook in America.

In early times, the Internet provides many services for the users to get connected, such as BBS and news group. Moreover, at that time, the social network was showed in an online form. The users will chat in the chat room. With the appearing of more and more new communicative network tools, users can build the personal website and share the information they like. Between 2002 and 2004, the three most famous social network services websites are Friendster, MySpace, and Bebo. In

2005, MySpace became the largest social network service website in the world; it was said the visiting rate surpass Google at that time. In 2006, Facebook became the most popular website in the world based on the using of the API. Since then, many websites emulated Facebook to build their API. Now we use Facebook as the example to show you the development and future of the social network.

Facebook is the most famous social network in the world; the name of if came from the traditional paper "registered names". Usually the American universities hand out the "registered names" to the freshman or the new staff to help them know the school better.

The initiator of the Facebook is Mark Elliot Zuckerberg; he was the student of Harvard University and graduated from Ardsley high school. At first, the register of the websites is limited inside the Harvard. In two weeks, the register spread to schools in Boston, such as Boston College, Boston University, MIT, Tufts and Rochester, Stanford, NYU, Northwestern University and all the schools of Ivy League. In the second year, many other schools joined in the Facebook. Finally, the students who have an email suffix as .edu, .ac, .uk could get an account. Later on, the Facebook supported the establishment of the high school and the companies. According to the data in Jul 2007, students in colleges and universities are the majority of the Facebook: 34 million active users, including the people who were not students. From Sep 2006 to 2007, the position of this website went up from the 60th to the 7th. Meanwhile, Facebook is the website where people share their pictures mostly; every day there are 85 hundred thousand pictures uploaded. In 2010, Facebook surpassed the Microsoft and got the first position in the 500 world's brand.

In Jan 2010, according to the research of the Compete Company, the independent IP visiting rate of Facebook was 1.34 hundred million, Yahoo was 1.32 hundred million. Facebook had surpassed the second largest website in America, and just under the first place of Google. Yahoo was once the flag of the Internet; in Feb 2008, Google surpassed it; and now, it lost its second position. The success of Facebook indicates the strong power and bright future of the social network.

On 18th May 2012, Facebook opening at 42.05 dollars, which is higher than the issue price of 38 dollars, increased by 10.66%. If calculate according to the opening price, the market value of Facebook is around 115.2 billion dollars, just lower than the 11 large technology companies below. The Apple Company (market value: 495 billion dollars), Microsoft (market value: 249 billion dollars), IBM (market value: 228 billion dollars), China Mobile (market value: 221 billion dollars), Google (market value: 203 billion dollars), AT&T (market value: 195 billion dollars), Intel (market value: 131 billion dollars), Oracle (market value: 130 billion dollars), Vodafone (market value: 129 billion), Verizon (market value: 117 billion). In the future, the prospect of Facebook is still bright, based on the huge user quantity, it will move towards to the first-class Internet enterprises.

4.2.6 The Applying of Software in the Mobile Industry

People are familiar with the Mobile device; it can satisfy the needs of the users anytime and anywhere. The development of the mobile device needs the controls. The developer may encounter the problems on the interface phase; the controls can solve the problem. Compared with the traditional device, the mobile device supports operating by hands; therefore the controls of the mobile device focus more on the design of touch screens.

The traditional controls such as buttons, text box, and dates have increased the support for the mobile device platforms. However, with the mobile device platform become more and more complex, the demands of people get higher; they require a prettier interface, more convenient and simple operating and the controls. Therefore the Android operating system was developed, and become the mainstream of the mobile device operating system.

4.2.6.1 Android

We have introduced the Android in the previous part of the passage. Here, we will talk about the structure of Android and its application in the mobile industry.

The original meaning of Android is "robot", it is also the name of Linux platform cellphone's operating system developed by Google on 5th Nov. 2007. This platform consists of operating system, middleware, user interface, and the application software.

Android first appeared in the fiction book "L'ève future" by French writer Auguste Villiers de l'Isle-Adam in 1886. In the book, he called the machine that looked like a man "Android".

The Logo of Android was designed by Ascender in 2010. The design was inspired by the logo of the man and woman outside of the bathroom in public. Therefore, the company drawn a simple robot, its body was like a can with two aerials on the top of its head; there came the logo of the Android. The font it used was designed by the Ascender special for it called "Droid". Android is a green robot and green is also the symbol of Android. The drawing of the color adopted PMS 376C and the #A4C639 in hexadecimal. Sometimes, it will also use the pure text of the logo.

In Jul 2012, Business Insider, the technology blog website elected the most important electronic device in the twenty-first century, Android and iPhone were on the list.

The system structure of Android is just like the other operating system using the layered structure.

We can see that in Fig. 4.1, Android is divided into four layers, from top to bottom are: Application, Application Framework, Libraries and Android Runtime and the Linux Kernel.

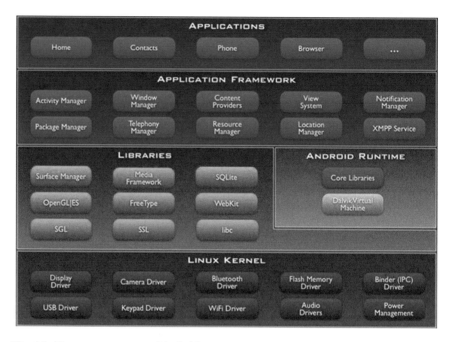

Fig. 4.1 The system structure of Android

The advantages of the Android platform

(a) Opening:

The most important advantage of Android is its opening. The opening platform allows all kinds of mobile terminal manufacturers to join in Android. The obvious open source attracts more developers. Therefore with more and more users and applications in Android, a new platform will also walk into the mature status.

Android can increase its reputation by its opening, which is from including consumers and manufacturers. To the consumers, the benefits are the software resource. The opening platform will also attract more competition; therefore, the consumers can buy their favored cellphones at a lower price.

(b) No limits:

In a very long time, especially in European and American areas, the use of the cellphones' applications was limited by the operator. One should use what kind of function to access into what network was limited by the operators. Since iPhone was on the market on 2007, the users can access the Internet much easier with the limits from the operator decreased. With transformation and improvement of the 2G and 3G mobile network such as EDGE (Enhanced Data Rate for GSM Evolution) and HSDPA (High-Speed Downlink Packet Access), the free access to the Internet has been realized.

(c) Plentiful hardware:

This is connected with the opening of the Android. Due to the opening of the Android, many manufacturers developed many different kinds of products. The differences and the characteristics of the function will not affect the data sync and the compatible of the software. For instance, someone who used the Nokia Symbian phone changed his phone to an iPhone; he can still bring the excellent software from the Nokia to the iPhone as well as the contacts on his old one.

(d) Easy to develop:

Android provides the third party a broad and free environment without limits. Many new kinds of application can be developed. However, there's also a disadvantage to this point. How to control the bloody, violence, sexual applications and games is one of the problems for Android.

(e) The application of Google:

Google has been on the Internet for ten years, from the search giant to the Internet, the services of Google such as maps, mails, searching engine have become the important belt between the users and the Internet, and Android phone combines perfectly with the Google service.

Because of the advantages above, Android rises from many operating systems and becomes the most widely used and the most plentiful operating system.

4.2.6.2 The Applying of Software on Mobile Phones—WeChat

WeChat, is the most popular communicating method in China. No matter how old you are, or what kind of phones you are using, almost all the people are using WeChat. "Shake it" becomes the most popular way to greet each other. Then, let's see how the WeChat becomes so success and changes our life.

WeChat is developed on January 21, 2011 to provide the mobile phones a free application with real-time communication service. WeChat supports different operators and different platforms with only a little network flow. People can send free voice messages, videos, pictures and texts through the Internet. Meanwhile, people can use the files in the shared streaming media content and also services such as "shake it", "message bottle", "moments", "official accounts" and "audio note".

The WeChat was started by the Tencent Technology (Shenzhen) Li in Oct 2010, and developed by the group of researches in Guangzhou. Zhang Xiaolong, the manager of the group who had successfully developed the Foxmail and QQ mails. Ma Huateng, the CEO of the Tencent Company, chose this product and called it "WeChat".

In March 2012, the number of WeChat users exceeded a hundred million, which only took 433 days.

On September 17, 2012, the number of WeChat users exceeded 200 million, which only took less than 6 months.

On January 15, 2013, the number of WeChat users exceeded 300 million.

On August 5, 2013, the WeChat 5.0 was online.

On January 28, 2014, the WeChat 5.2 was online, which changed a lot from the past.

Until December 2015, the WeChat 6.3 had widely spread in public.

As the most popular social information platform and also the access of the mobile device, it has changed into a large commercial trading platform. The changes brought by the marketing industry have been more obvious recently. The development of the WeChat Mall is thriving. The WeChat Mall is a social electronic commercial system based on the development of the WeChat. Consumers can realize the products' inquiry, selection, experience, interaction, booking and paying online through the WeChat platform.

WeChat is one of the representatives in the mobile client software; the software culture involved in it is changing our life and also the world.

4.3   Applications in Emerging Industries

I believe we all have seen two famous movies, "The Terminator" and "Matrix." The Terminator introduced an artificial intelligence defense network known as Skynet which will become self-aware and initiate a nuclear holocaust. In this movie, two beings from the year 2029 arrive in Los Angeles: one is a Terminator, a cyborg assassin programmed to kill a young woman named Sarah Connor; the other is Kyle Reese, a soldier sent to protect her from the T-800. After the Terminator kills a gang member, a gun-shop manager, two other women named "Sarah Connor" listed in the telephone directory, Sarah's roommate Ginger, and her partner, it tracks its target to a nightclub. Kyle arrives and saves Sarah from the Terminator. The two steal a car and escape, while the Terminator steals a police car and pursues them. Kyle explains to Sarah that shortly, an artificial intelligence defense network known as Skynet will become self-aware and initiate a nuclear holocaust. He mentions that Sarah's yet-to-be-conceived son John will rally the survivors and lead a resistance movement against Skynet and its army of machines. With the Resistance on the verge of victory, Skynet has sent a Terminator back in time to kill Sarah before John is born, as a last-ditch effort to avert the formation of the Resistance. From then on, the story begins developing. Moreover, in "The Matrix," the world is a computer program—"Matrix," it controls humans and obtains energy from humans for their use. However, human does not know they are controlled by a computer program until a hacker investigates a mysterious incident and he discovers the truth. These two movies both indicate that in the future, the computing capacity of supercomputers will surpass human. However, the computer will be so evil as described in science fiction movies? Of course not! The computer is just a tool, like a double-edged sword, as long as we use it properly, it can be of very good service for a human.

4.3.1 Applications on the Space

4.3.1.1 A Brief History of Space Exploration

For thousands of years, there are everlasting legends concerning "space exploration" among Chinese people. Apart from the well-known myth stories including Legend of the Moon, Wangjia of the Eastern Jin Dynasty recorded in the 4th century AD that "in the 30th year of Yao emperor's ascendance to the throne, there emerged a colossal ship floating in the West Sea. Whenever the night fell, it would give out soft light kept flickering, resembling something from stars and the moon. The ship floated around the four seas all the year round, circling the world endlessly for 12-year time. Hence, it was called as Guan Yucha, also known as Hang Xing Cha. It is rumored that there are fairies live on the ship who can prompt the world dark and the sun and the moon lightness by spraying the dew in their mouths after rinsing. In the late Yu and Xia periods, there was no record of the ship. Nevertheless, her mysterious story is widely known among people traveling everywhere.

Natural History by Zhang Hua of the Western Jin Dynasty also recorded that there were men who traveled to the Milky Way by the ship. Also, according to Record of Cavern Heaven, in the ninth-century AD of Tang Xiong period, there existed a fairy Cha that was over 50-feet long with a sound similar to that of copper and iron, and an indestructible body, almost resembling today's spaceship.

In the Ming Dynasty, Wan Hu became the world's first pioneers in space exploration with historical records. The brave Wan Hu sit calmly in the chair tied with 47 rockets to do flight experiment, which was failed later, prompting his heroic sacrifice. His flight experiment has the same theory with the most advanced launch vehicle in modern life. International Astronomical Federation named one of the ringed mountains on the moon as "Wan Hu Mountain" in honor of his immortal feats.

People's Republic of China's aerospace industry started in the late 1950s. Since April 24, 1970, China successfully launched the first artificial satellite Dongfanghong, to the beginning of 2005, China has successfully launched more than forty satellites. By the end of 2003, "Shenzhou V" spacecraft sent China's first astronaut Yang Liwei into space. This marked that China became the third country to send a man into space.

As the capability to explore the space shows the comprehensive strength of a country, in recent years, the pace of space exploration program has been greatly accelerated. With the joint of a supercomputer, human's understanding of space has been further deepened.

4.3.1.2 Supercomputer Simulations of Supernova Explosion

Argonne National Laboratory physicist had used IBM "Blue Gene" supercomputer simulated physical processes in supernova explosion.

Argonne National Laboratory's supercomputer supernova clearly presented the process of supermassive star brief violent deaths. Different colors and transparencies specify different energy information. By adjusting the color and transparency selectively, scientists will be able to strip the outer layer of supernova by computer simulation and observe what happened inside.

4.3.1.3 Extremely Large Cosmological Simulation Made on Lenovo DeepComp 7000

How did the universe begin from a hot, dense uniform phase and evolve into what we observed today with plentiful structures composed of stars, galaxies, clusters of galaxies, super-clusters, voids and filaments? It is the main question in modern cosmology. An extremely large numerical experiment has been made on Lenovo DeepComp 7000 supercomputer installed in Computer Network Information Center of CAS. The experiment is part of the "Pangu Project" led by the Computational Cosmology Consortium of China (C4)—a group of young astronomers from Purple Mountain Observatory, Shanghai Astronomical Observatory, National Astronomical Observatories and Supercomputer Center of CAS [24].

The "Pangu Project" aims to run a series of extremely large simulations to resolve the structure formation in the universe dominated by dark matter and dark energy using China-made supercomputers. This simulation uses nearly 30 billion particles to track the evolution of the matter distribution in a cubic region of the universe of 4.5 billion light-years on each side. The series of simulations will help us to understand the complex physics underlying in the formation and evolution of galaxies, central supermassive black holes. Moreover, they will enable Chinese astrophysicists to make a comprehensive comparison with the wide field galaxy survey by the ALMOST telescopes, also provide useful mock catalogs for the Antarctic astronomy at Dome A, Antarctica.

4.3.1.4 Wireless Network

Wireless network involved in all aspects of life. Covering the world with a wireless network is a good and a U.S. technology company plans to turn it into reality. The company expects to send hundreds of miniature satellites into orbit, and these satellites continuously release wireless signal to the world. In this way, any electronic terminals can be connected to the wireless networks.

The ambitious company is American media development Investment Fund Company, whose project is called "Outernet." The company is contacting with NASA in the hope of getting help to conduct signal release test in the international space station. It also needs NASA to send hundreds of Mini satellites "CubeSats" into designated orbit in later periods. According to the plan, satellites entering into the pre-selected orbit can receive network data released from the ground station. Satellites have to analyze these data and then release them to the earth after converting them into a wireless network.

4.3.2 Applications in Scientific Exploration

In Marxism, science and technology is a permeating element in productive force system." Also, Deng Xiaoping had pointed that "Science and Technology are the first productive force." As computer software is mankind's most advanced production tools, how to use the computer software in scientific exploration to find scientific truth is an important problem.

4.3.2.1 Living Earth Simulator

Living Earth Simulator is a simulator that can replicate everything happening on Earth, which is created by an international group of scientists. This project aims to advance the scientific understanding of what is taking place on the planet, encapsulating the human actions that shape societies and the environmental forces that define the physical world. If it can be created successfully, people will be able to understand the global weather patterns, the spread of diseases, international financial transactions, and so on.

The original idea
Many problems we have today—including social and economic instabilities, wars, disease spreading—are related to human behavior, but there is apparently a serious lack of understanding regarding how society and the economy work. The purpose of Living Earth Simulator is to improve human's cognitive level of things happening on earth and summarize the impacts of human behaviors on society and environment.

Technical principle
For a start it would need a framework, to use the collected data to cover the entire activities on the planet. As these traditional social science researchers have done some works for many years and they have some useful data, the only way to achieve the simulator is to make social scientists, computer scientists and engineers work together to make joint operation rules of the simulator.

The technology needs to be developed step by step. Maybe we have to wait for ten years for "live earth simulator" technology to be mature, that is, human will have to wait until the "semantic web technology" is maturity.

If there are any massive social and economic data, it is necessary to establish supercomputer center to compress the data and simulate the earth.

How to run

Firstly, the data about the activities in the earth should be inputted into the simulator.

Then, an uncompleted supercomputer is needed to evaluate these huge data. Although hardware has not been built, many data have been produced.

After these, integration a large number of data from financial markets to the medical records can finally start the Live Earth Simulator.

Application

If the Live Earth Simulator is developed successfully, people will be able to predict infectious disease and other major events, to find ways to address climate change, even to find clues before the outbreak of a financial crisis.

Also, regardless of the type of climate, the spread of disease, or international financial transactions, even the application of Keynesianism can be copied to the simulator.

Despite that the Living Earth Simulator project is facing many challenges, its will be able to help people better understand the global socioeconomic trends in the future. For example, in the past few years, it is clear that we need better indicators to determine the social development degree rather than relying solely on the gross national product.

Live Earth Simulator project will be able to develop better methods for detecting the state of society to address health, education and environmental issues. These are all about people's well-being.

4.3.2.2   The Human Genome Project

"Human genome project", first proposed by American scientists in 1985, was officially launched in 1990. Scientists in the United States, the United Kingdom, France, Germany, Japan and China have participated jointly in the "human genome project" worth up to $3 billion budget. According to the plan, it is set to unlock passwords of about 100 thousand genes in the human body at around 2015, and draw human gene map at the same time. In other words, it is to uncover the secrets of 3 billion base pairs constituting 40,000 genes in the human body. "Human genome project," together with "Manhattan atomic bomb project" and "Appollo plan" are known as the three major scientific projects, and are hailed as the "Life Sciences" moon landing program." It is known that the human genome project has declared its completion and has currently entered into post-genomics research and proteomics research.

The "human genome project" is a large-scale and interdisciplinary scientific exploration project who aims at testing nucleotide sequence composed by the 30 billion base pairs in human chromosome (haploid). The goal of the test is to draw human genome map and identify the carried gene and its sequence, so as to achieve the ultimate goal of deciphering human genetic information. The genome project, an important step for human beings to explore their secrets, is another great project in the history of human science following the "Manhattan plan" and "Appollo moon project. By the end of 2005, the sequencing of human genome project has been basically completed (93%). The publication of 2001 human genome working draft (completed by public funded international human genome project and private enterprise Celera Corporation on their own and published independently) is thought to be a milestone in the success of the "human genome project."

Why choose human genome to study? The reason lies in that human are the most advanced creature in the process of "evolution," studying them can help them to recognize themselves, grasp the law of birth, aging, sickness and death, disease diagnosis and treatment, understand life's origin and even make people live forever.

By detecting the sequence of 3 billion base pairs of human genome DNA, we can find all human genes and then find out their position in the chromosome to decipher all human genetic information.

In the "human genome project", there are researches towards five biological genomes, including Escherichia coil, nematodes, fruit flies and mice, which are known as the five "model organisms" of a human.

The purpose of HGP is to decode life, understand life origin and life growth and development rules, know the differences between species and individuals, know biological phenomena of disease mechanisms and longevity and aging, so as to provide a scientific basis for the diagnosis and treatment of disease.

As the workload is very large, scientists use supercomputers as the computing tools. The Human Genome Project have created perhaps the most powerful and the most seductive database—the human genome. However, the analysis of these data is a huge mathematical problem, and this is the real progress to reveal secrets hidden in our DNA.

Computers can be used very effectively to indicate the location of genes and of regions that control the expression of genes and to discover relationships between each new sequence and other known sequences from many different organisms. This process is referred to as "sequence annotation." Annotation is the essential prerequisite before the genome sequence data can become useful, and the quality with which annotation is done will directly affect the value of the sequence. In addition to considerable organizational issues, significant computational challenges must be addressed if DNA sequences that are produced can be successfully annotated. It is clear that new computational methods and a workable process must be implemented for effective and timely analysis and management of these data.

Therefore, the scientists developed calculation algorithms related to the Human Genome Project. This algorithm can help scientists to visit genomic data much faster—the waiting time shortened from 447 years to one month. Such software is installed on the world's second-fastest computer. The powerful computation ability will help researchers to research the potential genes relations of complex diseases. Screening of large amounts of genetic data, so as to find out the cause of the potential gene combination form is difficult. This powerful tool will help researchers find the key relationships between genes.

This new computer will be able to perform 7.5 trillion calculations per second. To be exact, this machine is composed by 1250 computers whose disk storage is 2.5 gigabits and has 50 billion online disk storage.

For scientists, this machine will be a huge driving force in the development of Human Genome Project. The power of computer software makes the Human Genome Project completed much earlier than expected.

4.3.3   Applications in New Energy

New energy is also known as unconventional energy. It refers to a variety of energy sources other than traditional energy sources. It refers to the energies those are at the beginning of exploitation, such as solar energy, geothermal energy, wind energy, ocean energy, biomass and nuclear fusion energy, and so on.

Conventional energy Refers to the energy whose technology is relatively mature and has been used on a large scale. New energy, often referred to the energy has not been as large-scale use and is in research. Therefore, coal, oil, natural gas and large and medium-sized hydropower are considered as conventional energies. Solar energy, wind energy, modern biomass energy, geothermal energy, ocean energy and hydrogen are regarded as new energies. With the progress of technology and the establishment of the sustainable development concept, organic industrial and life wastes have been considered to be reused. Therefore, waste recycling use can also be regarded as a form of new energy technologies.

Modern renewable energy technology development is very rapid. In 2010, it surpassed natural gas and became the second energy which follows the coal power fuel. The cost of renewable energy is becoming cheaper as relatively technologies are becoming more mature.

As we all known, new energy will occupy a great market in the future and the computer software gives much help in the development of new energy.

4.3.3.1   Simulation of Nuclear Fusion

In nuclear physics, nuclear fusion is a nuclear reaction in which two or more atomic nuclei come very close and then collide at a very high speed and join to form a new nucleus. During this process, matter is not conserved because some of the matter of the fusing nuclei is converted energy. Fusion is the process that powers active or "main sequence" stars [25]. Nuclear fusion energy is 100 times of nuclear fission. However, now nuclear fusion is not under control. Controlled nuclear fusion only exists in labs. As the experiment needs large space and high costs, to simulate nuclear fusion by software is a reliable way to reduce the cost of experiments.

At present, the "inertial confinement fusion" is the challenge in the world. Aim to control nuclear fusion energy and use the ultimate energy peacefully, the United States, Japan, Russia, and the EU are positive to invest in the researches.

Half century ago, scientists discovered that when deuterium and tritium atoms fused into a helium nucleus and a neutron, it will release enormous energy. Due to its energy release mechanism is the same as the sun, the project was commonly known as "man-made sun." The fusion energy contained in the three bottles of mineral water is enough for the power supply of a family of four for a year. Also, this kind of energy is low radiation, no emissions and can be used for human billions of years. However, nuclear fusion reaction condition is extremely harsh, and it is difficult to control the process. Currently, it can only be used in the manufacture of nuclear weapons—the hydrogen bomb.

The process of inertial confinement fusion reaction is very complex, involving the high temperature and high density which are much higher than the matter we know. Also, the physical contents are in quantity, the time and space scale also varies widely, the reaction process is very fast. The pressure in the reaction process is equivalent to 1 trillion standard atmospheric pressure, deuterium, and tritium can be compressed to one over one thousand of the liquid volume with the same quality and the reaction time is most the only 10,000,000,000th of a second.

It is difficult to go deep into the inside measurement fusion fuel for such extreme reactions by the existing experimental detection means. While, simulation with supercomputer, we can simulate the process step by step to study the physics details, which is greatly conducive to experiment design and analysis of experimental results. Therefore, computer software has great help in the research of nuclear energy in the future.

4.3.3.2 Construction of Nuclear Power Plant

In October 2004, a large pressurized water reactor nuclear power plant instrumentation and control equipment system (Qinshan Phase II computer monitoring system) was awarded the Ministry of Information Industry Science and Technology Progress Award. The project is the key project of Chinese 95 plan. This project includes two main parts of the nuclear power plant computer monitoring system (KIT/KPS) and the conventional island control system (CIC).

In the aspect of the logical structure of hardware, the system can be divided into three level including data acquisition and control, central data processing and human–machine interfaces. Central data processing part communicates with the human interfaces through high-speed Ethernet. Data acquisition and control part communicates with the central data processing part through token bus network.

4.3.4 Applications in the Internet of Things

4.3.4.1 Introduction to the Internet of Things

"Internet of things" is a network concept to extend and expand its user side for information exchange and communication between any items based on the Internet. It is defined as follows: According to the agreement, a network concept that connects anything to the Internet for information exchange and communication to realize intelligent recognition, positioning, tracking, monitoring and management by information sensing equipment such as radio frequency identification (RFID), infrared sensors, global positioning system and laser scanner [26].

It is universally recognized that the phrase "Internet of things" was first put forward by Professor Ashton of MIT Auto-ID Center during his research RFID in 1999. The same year when China gained an understanding of "Internet of things," which was known as "sensor network" at that time. In the corresponding report released by the International Telecommunication Union (ITU) in 2005, the definition and, scope of "Internet of things" has changed, with a great expansion of coverage rather than merely being the Internet of things based on RFID technology.

The ITU Internet report released by the International Telecommunication Union made a normative definition for "Internet of things." According to the agreement, a network that connects anything to the Internet for information exchange and communication to realize intelligent recognition, positioning, tracking, monitoring and management by information sensing equipment such as two-dimension code read device, radio frequency identification (RFID), infrared sensors, global positioning system and laser scanner.

According to the definition by the International Telecommunication Union, "Internet of things" mainly concerns the interconnection between thing to thing (T2T), human to the thing (H2T) and human to human (H2H). However, unlike traditional Internet, H2T refers to employing the connection between general devices and objects to make the connection between things simplified, whereas H2H refers to the interconnection between people and people without relying on PC. Since the Internet does not consider problems concerning any item connection, we adopt the Internet of things to this problem in the traditional sense. "Internet of things," just as its name implies, is the network that connects goods. Many scholars, when discussing the "Internet of things," will often introduce the concept of M2M, which can be interpreted as Man to Man, Man to Machine and Machine to Machine. In essence, most of the interaction between human and machine, machine and machine are to realize information interaction between man and man [27].

"Internet of things" means to make real-time collection towards any objects needs to be monitored, connected and interacted, or process information through various information sensing devices, forming a huge network together with the Internet. It aims at realizing the connection between objects and objects, objects and people, all objects and network, so as to make it easier for identification, management, and control. In 2011, the "Internet of things" industry scale exceeded 260 billion yuan, with five levels constituting the industry of "Internet of things." This include support layer, perception layer, transport layer, platform layer and application layer, accounting for 2.7%, 22.0%, 33.1%, 37.5% and 4.7% of the "Internet of things" industry scale respectively. Among the above, the perception layer and transport layer of the Internet of things had numerous manufacturers, making the two the most competitive industry fields.

4.3.4.2 Application Areas of Internet of Things

"Internet of things" has a very extensive use. This includes intelligent transportation, and environmental protection. In the same thinking, we could mention government work, public security, safe home furnishing, intelligent fire control, industrial monitoring, and environmental monitoring. It also encompasses street lighting control, landscape lighting control, building lighting control, Plaza lighting control, the elderly care, and personal health. Last but not least, it equally applies to flower culture, water monitoring, food traceability, enemy investigation and intelligence gathering.

The International Telecommunication Union portrayed the scene of the "Internet of things" era in its 2005 report: the car will give an automatic alarm when the driver makes operational errors; briefcase will remind the owner if he forgot something; clothes will tell washing machine the color and temperature requirements and so on. Application of "Internet of things" in logistics field is as follows. A logistics company uses truck equipped with "Internet of things" system, which will remind you once you are overload and tell you the exact overload amount and the remaining room. Then it tells you how to match light and heavy goods. When handling personnel unloads goods, one good may emit sound saying "throwing hurts me". It may also say things like "dear, please you do dot be too brutal, will you?". In case the driver and others are chatting, the truck will play the alarm and sound "man, time to go!".

"Internet of things" fully applies the new generation of IT technology to all walks of life. To be exact, it embeds and equips sensors into various objects, including power grids, railways, bridges, tunnels, highways, buildings, water supply system, dams and oil and gas pipelines. Moreover, then integrates the "Internet of things" with the existing Internet to realize the integration of human society and physical system. In the integration of network, there exists super powerful central computer group that can integrate the personnel, machinery, equipment and infrastructure within the network to realize real-time management and control. Based on this, human beings can manage the production and life in a more precise and dynamic way to achieve the "intelligent" state, boost resource utilization and productivity level and improve the relationship between human and nature.

4.3.4.3 Application of Internet of Things—Smart City

"Smart city", which fully applies a new generation of information technology to all walks of life in the city, is an advanced form of urban information based on the next generation of innovation knowledge society (innovation 2.0). From the perspective of technology development, smart city construction requires realizing comprehensive perception, general interconnection, pervasive computing and fusion application through a new generation information technology application such as networking and cloud computing represented by mobile technology. From the perspective of social development, "smart city" also requires achieving sustainable innovation in the knowledge of the society environment. This environment is characterized by user innovation, open innovation, mass innovation and collaborative innovation. We need to understand this is achieved through the use of tools and methods including wikis, social networking, Fab Lab (micro fabrication laboratory), Living Lab and comprehensive integration method. In this process, emphasize on value creation to realize a comprehensive sustainable development of the economy, society, and environment that is people-oriented [28].

"Smart city" often mixed with regional development concepts including digital city, perceptive city, wireless city, smart city, ecological city and low-carbon city, or even with industry informatization concepts such as electronic government affairs, intelligent transportation, and smart grid. The interpretations of the concept of "smart city" are often divided. Some reckon that "smart city" focuses on technology application, others believe in network construction. Still others argue in the participation of people and the remaining emphasize wisdom effect, while the informatization constructions in some leading cities focus on people-oriented and sustainable innovation. In a word, wisdom is not just smart. "Smart city" is not just another name of the smart city or the intelligent application of information technology. It also includes connotations such as the participation of people wisdom, people-oriented and sustainable development. By summarizing the development origin of the ideology and regional informatization practice around the world, the book "Smart City": from the Perspective of Innovation 2.0 makes an analysis of "smart city" from the innovation in technology development and social-economic development, emphasizing that "smart city" is not only the application of information technologies in new generation such as the Internet of things and cloud computing. More importantly, it is the methodology of social innovation 2.0 oriented towards knowledge.

With the rise of the Empire Network, mobile technology integration development and innovation democratization process, the "smart city" supported by knowledge and social environment is the advanced form of city informatization development after digital city.

Smart city in the world

In November 2008, IBM proposed the idea of the "wisdom earth" at a Foreign Relations Council held in New York, prompting a wave of "smart city" construction.

In 2006, the EU launched the European Living Lab organization that uses new tools, methods, advanced information and communication technologies to mobilize of "collective wisdom and creativity" from all aspects to provide opportunities for social problem solving. The organization also launched the European "smart city" network. Living lab is completely user-oriented. By creation, it opens innovation space and helps people to use information technology and mobile application services to enhance the quality of life, so as to make their needs obtain the maximum respect and satisfaction.

Based on the network, South Korea creates an ecological and smart city that is green, digital and has a seamless mobile connection. With the integrated public communication platform as well as ubiquitous network access, it is not only convenient for consumers to conduct remote education, health care, and tax management but also enable them to achieve intelligent control over home building energy consumption.

In 2006, Singapore launched the "Wisdom Country in 2015" plan, in the hope of building Singapore into an international city with world-class economic and social development through the positive application of new generation information technology such as "Internet of things." Singapore gains remarkable achievements in electronic government, people's livelihood and general Internet, in which "intelligent transportation system" provide real-time and appropriate travel information to the public through a variety of sensing data, operational information, and rich user interaction experience.

Fab Lab (micro-fabrication laboratory), launched by the Bits and Atoms Research Center of Massachusetts Institute of Technology, attempts to build user innovative manufacturing environment that is user-centered and application-oriented on the basis of social technology development network ranging from personal communications, personal calculations to personal making, which enables people to design and manufacture products that they imagine at will even in their homes. However, the practice from Fab Lab to Fab City in cities such as Barcelona interprets people-centered sustainable innovation of "smart city" from another perspective.

Smart city in China

With the accelerated process of urbanization, the city has been endowed with unprecedented economic, political and technological rights, which inevitably pushes the city into being the center of the world stage to play a leading role. At the same time, the city is also faced with challenges including environmental pollution, traffic jam, and energy shortage, housing shortage, unemployment, and disease. In the new environment, it becomes an important proposition for city planning and construction as to how to solve various problems brought by city development and realize sustainable development. Under this background, "smart city" has not only become a feasible way to solve city problems but is also the trend of future urban development. The acceleration of "smart city" construction will greatly boost the rapid development of local economy, and also promote the rapid development of industries such as satellite navigation, Internet of Things, intelligent traffic, intelligent power grid, cloud computing and software services industry, offering new development opportunities for related industries. The development of "smart city" in China has entered into the scale promotion stage. So far, there are 154 cities proposed "smart city" construction. With the total investment expected to reach 1.1 trillion yuan, a new round of industry opportunities is around the corner.

In 2012, the industry market size of China's Internet of things reached 365 billion yuan, an increase of 38.6% over the previous year. As an emerging industry with high expectations develops from intelligent security to smart grid, from two-dimensional code popularity to "smart city" completion, "Internet of things" is thriving everywhere, influencing people's lives quietly. Some experts point out that, along with the improvement of technology progress and related ancillary facilities, technology and standard localization, operation and management systematization and industry generalization as well will become the three major trends in the development of China's "Internet of things" in the next few years.

On April 10, 2013, "smart city" Specification Training Session organized by urban construction energy saving and science and technology division in the Ministry of Housing and Urban-Rural Development was held in Beijing. Information from the session indicates that after over 80 billion yuan of investment and financing by the China Development Bank, two commercial banks made a commitment that they would provide more credit line than the China Development Bank to support the building of "smart city." Other investment institutions also signed investment amount of 200 billion yuan. It is roughly estimated that relevant investment will exceed 440 billion yuan.

China encourages carrying out application model innovation to promote "smart city" construction. Multiple Chinese cities including Shenzhen, Kunming, and Ningbo have signed strategic cooperation agreements with IBM, marching the first step toward creating "smart city." Beijing expects to release Wisdom Beijing Executive Summary after completing "digital Beijing" goal, while Shanghai involves "smart city" construction into its "12th Five-Year" development plan. Also, cities such as Foshan, Wuhan, Chongqing, and Chengdu have launched "smart city" strategy and unveiled related plans, projects, and activities successively. China's domestic excellent "wisdom industry" enterprises given an ever-growing emphasis on "smart city" research. It is precisely because of this that a large number of domestic outstanding "wisdom industry" enterprises emerge rapidly, becoming the bellwether in the construction of "smart city."

4.3.5 Applications in Unmanned Aerial Vehicle

The unmanned aerial vehicle, "drone" for short (English abbreviation is "UAV"). This is an unmanned aircraft using radio remote control apparatus and self-contained program to control device operation. The operation can be divided as follows from a technical perspective. An unmanned helicopter, unmanned fixed-wing aircraft, unmanned multi-rotor aircraft, unmanned airship and unmanned wing machine. Drone first appeared in the 1920s, a time when it was used as a training target, and it was a term used by numerous countries to describe a new generation drone. The term can be used to describe a cruise missile developed from a kite, a radio remote control aircraft to V-1 missile. However, terms of the military are only limited to reusable aircraft heavier than air.

Before the late twentieth century, "drone" was a little bit smaller than remote control aircraft with full size. The U.S. Military has an ever-growing interest in this type of aircraft in that it can provide war machines with a low cost and highly task flexibility. These war machines can be used without causing crew death risks.

In the 1990s, "drone" began to develop rapidly and was widely used after the Gulf War. The US troops have bought and made Vanguard "drones" on their own to serve as a reliable system in the second and third Gulf War towards Iraq.

After the 1920s, western countries were acutely aware of the role played by "drones" in the war. They therefore vied to apply high technology and software technology to the research and development of "drone". New airfoils and light material greatly increased the cruise duration of "drone". Advanced signal processing and communication technology improved the speed in image transmission and digital transmission of "drone". Advanced autopilot enabled "drones" to fly to circle point, change height and destination according to procedure rather than ground-based pilot TV screens.

4.3.5.1 Present Status of Drone

"Drone" in abroad
Modern war is the basic driving force to promote the development of "drone." The world's first "drone" was created in 1917, whereas it was during the Vietnam War that "drone" was first put into combat to serve as battle reconnaissance. Later, "drone" frequently appeared and made repeated battle achievements in local wars including the Middle East War, the Gulf War, the Kosovo war, the Afghanistan war and the Iraq War (the Second Gulf War). In particular in Afghanistan battlefield, where "drone" was well-deserved as the hero for its successful implementation of multiple "decapitation operations."

America's "drone" lead the world. The United States first started to develop "drone" in 1939 and has developed "Firebee" series and "chukar" series successively. the Since the 1950s to 1960s, the United States succeeded in developing tactical or strategic drones such as "Firebee," "Pioneer," "Hunter," "Predator" and "Global Hawk." The improved drone–the "Predator" was put into use in the Vietnam War, the Gulf War, the Kosovo war and the military operations in Afghanistan.

On February 26, 2015, the American *Huffington post* took a "festival" title–the Open of Toys "R" Us. Along was a picture in which a "drone" was attacked by a "Predator" as its headline. This content of which was that the United States opened the sale of its armed "drone" to its allies. It is reported that the U.S. State Department announced new regulations in selling "drone" to its allies, which include the specific approval process, time and approaches. It is the first time that America gives the "green light" in exporting offensive "drone", the first of which expected to be sold is MQ-9 "Harvest," the "drone" will be sold first to the British.

Japan, who has bought RQ-4 "Global Hawk" reconnaissance "drone", is likely to purchase offensive "drone" from America. The military analyst of observer network reckons that China "drone" is dominating markets in Asia and Africa and Latin America countries at a quick speed.

After the United States opened the "Pandora's box," no doubt there will emerge unexpected buyers including China Taiwan, Japan and the Philippines, even India and Vietnam are likely to buy American "drone". With such a huge business market, it is possible that American industry finds it hard to keep the "bottom line." It will not be long before the U.S. offensive "drone" appears around China.

"Drone" in China
On February 10, 2015, two "drones" of "Gui Fei" succeeded in their experiment at a base in the northwest. The experiment task is related to the promotion and implementation of "Gui Fei" drone base strategic positioning, and is also the basis for the transformed development of "Gui Fei."

At 9:07 am, July 3, 2015, a 6.5 magnitude earthquake occurred in Pishan county, Hetian, Xinjiang. Air Force Command and Air force troops stationed in Xinjiang strengthened their ties with local government to understand disaster relief needs timely and sent a "drone" to the earthquake region at 11:10 am to reconnoiter disaster. The "drone" of the air force that reconnoiters disaster flew over earthquake region for 100 min to conduct real-time reconnaissance and send ground disaster situation, providing a scientific foundation for timely and accurate judgments of the disaster. This is the first time that air force "drone" carries out a reconnaissance task in earthquake relief.

On the afternoon of August 6, 2015, over 20 "drone" drivers in Shenzhen obtained their "driver's license" for a drone after passing the AOPA (Aircraft in China have and Drivers Association) certification exam, becoming the first batch to have obtained "driver's license" for the drone in Shenzhen.

4.3.5.2 Application Fields of Drone

"Drone" enjoys an extensive use in industries including police, urban management, agriculture, geology, meteorology, electric power, emergency rescue and disaster relief and video recording. At the same time, "drone" succeeds in the battlefield, making it an integral part in the modern military war.

(a) Electric Power Inspection: "drones" that equipped with high-definition digital video camera, camera, and GPS positioning system can make autonomous cruise positioning and real-time image transmission along power grid, enabling monitoring personnel to watch and control on the computer at the same time. "Drone" has realized electronic, informational and intelligent inspection. This improved power line inspection work efficiency, emergency rescue level, and power supply reliability.

(b) Agricultural Insurance: having "drones" equipped with a high-definition digital camera, spectrum analyzer and thermal infrared sensor flow over farmland can calculate the accurate cultivated area. Moreover, the data collected can be used to assess crop risks, insurance premium rate and can have damage assessment for affected farmland, also, the drone inspection has also realized crops monitoring.

(c) Environmental Protection: the application of "drone" in environmental protection field can be roughly divided into three types. Firstly, environmental monitoring: to observe air, soil, vegetation, and water quality to realize real-time tracking and monitoring the development of sudden environmental pollution incidents. Second, environmental law enforcement: Environment supervision departments employs "drones" equipped with collection and analysis devices to cruise in specific areas, so as to monitor the exhaust gas and waste water emissions in factories and enterprises and find pollution sources. Thirdly, environmental governance: using soft wing "drones" that are equipped with a catalyst and meteorological detection to spray in the air. Its working principle is similar to that of "drone" spraying pesticides, i.e., to eliminate smog in a certain region.

(d) Film and TV Drama shooting: "drones" equipped with a high-definition camera can, according to the needs of the program, shoot in the air under wireless remote control. There are numerous successful cases of show business using "drone". For instance *The Continent* the debut of the new director Han Han, or the hugely popular reality show–*Dad, Where Are We Going?*, or the blockbusters such as *Harry Porter Series, Skyfall,* and *Transformers 4.* "drone" is omnipresent behind the scenes. Also, "drone" has made undeniable contributions in the major incidents reports including Sochi Winter Olympics and Qiantang River Tide in CCTV.

(e) Ownership Issues: "drone" is capable of aerial photography from bilateral territorial dispute to rural land ownership. Recommended reason: take the Diaoyu Islands. "Drone" is flexible enough to record conspiratorial tricks of Japan around China's Diaoyu Islands without a single soldier. In fact, boundary right of some countries also involves different races. Therefore, it can effectively avoid potential social conflict by sending "drone" to collect boundary data.

(f) Streetscape: use "drone" with the photographing device to carry out large-scale aerial photography to realize aerial implementation effect. The streetscape pictures shot by "drone" not only are a bird's-eye view of the world perspective, but also carry with them a touch of art. Mind you, "drones" have to charge up in areas where there are perennial clouds and fog and severe smog and where the remote sensing satellite is not agile enough.

(g) Express: "drone" can deliver goods that are smaller than shoebox packaging. It will fly to the destination once you enter the recipient's GPS address into the system. It is far from being a fantasy in that both Amazon of the United States and China's SF Express are in excitedly busy testing this sort of business. Moreover, Domino's pizza shop in the United States has succeeded in carrying out its first pizza delivery in the UK by air. It is reported that Amazon claimed that "drone" can deliver goods to customers who are within 1.6 km within 30 min. The reason why China's SF Express research and develop "drone" to deliver goods is to solve the difficulty in remote areas delivery.

(h) Rescue after Disaster: use "drones" equipped with a high-definition photographing device to carry out aerial photography in disaster-affected areas to provide the latest images there. "Drones" are quick in speed. It takes only 7 minutes in their takeoff and landing to complete aerial photography of 100,000 km^2, which is of extraordinary significance for post-disaster relief work that wastes no time. What's more, "drone" can guarantee the safety of rescue work through aerial photography, which can avoid the collapse-prone dangerous zone to provide a valuable reference for rational rescue forces allocation, relief key areas determination, safe rescue routes selection and disaster reconstruction site selection. Also, "drone" can implement real-time monitoring of the disaster-affected areas' situation in all dimensions, so as to prevent the occurrence of secondary disasters.

(i) Remote Sensing Mapping: remote sensing refers to perception from far away. In a broad sense, it means to use remote control technology to investigate local situation without going to the target area on your own. In a narrow sense, it refers to satellite images and aerial pictures. Remote sensing mapping is the act of using remote sensing technology to make the calculation in computer and realize surveying and mapping purpose. "Drone" has a place in the application of remote sensing mapping, enjoying the limitless prospect.

In a word, "drone" enjoys extensive use, low cost, and good cost-effectiveness. When applied in military, it can reduce casualties risk with its strong survival ability and good mobility. Also, it is easy to use, playing an imperative role in modern war. When used in reconnaissance design, it can effectively accomplish battlefield reconnaissance, surveillance, orientation and emendation, damage assessment and electronic warfare. When in civilian use, such as border patrol, nuclear radiation detection, aerial photography, aerial prospecting, disaster monitoring, traffic patrol and security monitoring, it can also serve as the target for gun and missile.

4.3.5.3 Future Application Prospects of Drone

Microsoft Company has released an analysis report entitled *Human Nature: Human-Computer Interaction in 2020*, claiming that physical boundaries between human and computer will completely disappear in 10 years, a time when human will rely more on technology and conventional media for daily use such as mouse, keyboard and display will become more visual ones, for example, touch screen input system and voice recognition systems. So, by 2020, to what degree will the computer be developed? Moreover, to what degree will software be innovated? Is it true that the physiological boundary between man and machine will disappear?

According to Qiu Bo, a Chinese scholar in Japan with multiple computer inventions, the future development of the computer can be summarized into the following three directions:

(a) "Higher" performance and faster speed. The main manifestation is an increasingly higher computer main frequency.
(b) Parallel processing development. Device speed can improve several orders of magnitude through the invention of new devices, such as quantum devices, and the use of technologies including nano-technology and system on a chip. It is another important approach to enhance computer system performance through the innovation and progress of large-scale architecture marked by large-scale parallel.
(c) "Deep" development, namely, to the development of intelligence information.

With the computer information technology penetrating into all areas of economic and social life, the world is gradually entering into anew economic era that is information industry oriented. The development of the Internet, mobile phones, and satellite networks exert a huge influence on human economy and society.

Shi Zhongzhi, vice chairman of Chinese Artificial Intelligence Association pointed out that, "Computer can solve many problems unable to be solved by human brain itself, such as the use of" social computing "to study social problems. Moreover, for example, as for Wenchuan earthquake, the computer is capable of analyzing the impact of the earthquake on community and even every family, etc. By 2020, computer will possess a variety of basic sensory functions, including listening, speaking, watch, smell, and touch, which is the direction that we are currently exploring." the prospects of the development and application of computer that takes software as its thought can be mainly represented as the following:

(a) Physical boundaries between man and machine will disappear

In early 2008, Bill Gates predicted in an interview with the British Broadcasting Company that computer keyboard and mouse will be upgraded into more natural, more intuitive technology means and that interfaces with touch, vision, and voice will enjoy extensive use. For now, this prophecy has fulfilled.

When human–machine interaction devices develop from "mouse and keyboard time" into "T-touch, "voice interface" or "visual type, physical boundaries between human and machine will disappear gradually, and even disappear completely. By that time, a human can control and communicate with machine directly through language. Alternatively, it will only take a look or a gesture for the computer to be able to respond quickly and act as the occasion demands. Also, in the future, some super micro computer systems will be implanted into the human body to act as people's sense and physical organs, becoming an integration of computer and human with the disappearance of boundaries. The realization of these ideas cannot do without the support of powerful intelligent software.

(b) More intuitive media

With the popularization of computer technology, in the early 1990s, there emerged a new human–computer interaction technology—"touch screen" input technology, which can operate its host computer once the finger touches on the computer screen icons or text, making it all the easier for human–computer interaction. Therefore, the "touch screen" technology has currently become the most popular input device. Whether you are shopping in the mall or the midst of bank deposit and withdrawal, the touch-type automatic server can provide you with a quick service.

"Touch screen" technology is a very promising interactive input technology. With the input of R&D strength, new types of touch screen are constantly emerging. For example, today's extensive use of pointing information query systems, such as electronic bulletin board that enjoys high brightness, clear images, and easy interaction has produced the notable effect. With the development of technology, "touch screen" development will show a tendency with profession, multimedia, three-dimension and large screen, along with the greatly improved identification and display accuracy of future touch screen.

At present, intuitive media similar to that of "touch screen" have gained popularity in daily life and there are signs of their future development prospects. Nevertheless, the future development prospects for voice control system are gloomy.

(c) Speech recognition

Voice recognition system is the most natural way of communication between people and machines. However, the research in this field remains a world problem. Different voice recognition needs specific and long-term training, which we now can only achieve specific speech recognition with limited thinking, a specific vocabulary, and special groups. By 2020, it is difficult to predict how far the speech recognition technology will be developed. In the future, it will mainly focus on searches of command control, information retrieval, response and huge volumes of multimedia documents in speech recognition, and it is a very important direction to adopt voice technology to help to learn a foreign language.

(d) Wearable devices

In fact, wearable machine refers to a new generation of personal mobile computer systems and digital products, which is very convenient to carry and use. With their many unique features, it is especially suitable for the outdoor and mobile application. Today's "wearable machine" can be able to exist inside clothes, that is, the computer attaches to human body just like clothes. Some "wearable machines" are be made into small portable accessories such as watches, bags, rings, and cards. People who wear these small accessories can have an accurate determination of angle and strength in playing billiards, while those who cannot dance know how to dance by wearing them. Some people also tried to compress "wearable machine" into pieces to implant computer chip under the skin of human body, but they gave up later due to installment inconvenience. Nevertheless, it is likely to become a reality in the future.

At present, it is not the right time to put "wearable computer" completely into daily life. "Wearable machine" requires small size, light weight and long-time endurance. However, today's "wearable machine" weighs approximately 5 kg. Regarding radio communication, it demands that "wearable computer" enjoys a long distance diffraction that can enable waves to bypass, and that it has a high speed and wide band at the same time, which is contradictory. Regarding software, "wearable computer" must develop its embedded operating system, while numerous operating systems suitable for PC is a bit larger for it. As for the current problems, the future research direction should focus on developing "wearable computers" that are more portable and have longer time endurance.

(e) Free Office

The report *Human Nature: Human-Computer Interaction in 2020* also points out that, "An interconnected digital medium means that human can get in touch with the entire world from anywhere. The difference between being in working place and home will no longer exist and the difference between private time and work time will disappear with it".

However, as for the popularity of "the difference between being in working place and home will no longer exist and the difference between private time and work time will disappear," some scholars have different opinions. Nowadays, our free office equipment and communications facilities need to be completed, office personnel qualities remain to be improved, office systems (range from government to company) require to form a complete set, all of which are the problems exist in China's "free office" popularity and remain to be solved. For now, "free office" that only be achieved in some occupational areas is unable to be fully realized in society as a whole.

4.4 Summary

To provide a better understanding of the applications of software and development of software culture for the readers, this chapter discusses the relationship between software applications and software culture in both traditional industries and emerging industries. Traditional industries involved in this chapter are industry, agriculture, medicine, entertainment, the Internet and mobile industry. Emerging industries include the space exploration, scientific exploration, new energy, Internet of things and unmanned aerial vehicle.

With the development of human society, the computer is now getting into our lives; it is everywhere. We can say that without the computer, all the industry that human beings rely on will be paralyzed; mankind will step into a dark age. After reading this chapter, we hope that the readers can have a general understanding of the computer applications. With the time passing by, human beings will be more civilized. Therefore, the computer will be more advanced, and there will be more and more applications, and even bring human civilization to a new level.

In the future, the computer will develop toward a more portable, subtler, more convenient and more intelligent direction. Moreover, the development of "quantum computer" and "bio-computer" will make a new stage in the development of the computer.

New requirements bring new ideas, and new ideas inspire innovation and invention. Software and computer complement each other to create more material and spiritual wealth for a human.

References

1. Waley, A (1937) The book of songs. Houghton Mifflin Co.
2. Compgroups (2004) IBM 7532 Industrial Computer project. http://compgroups.net/comp.sys.ibm.ps2.hardware/ibm-7532-industrial-computer-projec/2181874. Accessed 21 Feb 2004.
3. GE MDS, Supervisory Control and Data Acquisition (2013). http://www.gemds.com.cn/news/news934.html. Accessed 3 Nov 2013.
4. FORCECON, Oil and gas SCADA software eForceConV2.1. http://www.sunwayland.com/Home/article/index/category/91/id/279.html.
5. Rockwellautomation, Rockwellsoftware. http://www.rockwellautomation.com/rockwellsoftware/products/rsview32.page.
6. Oil and Gas Online, PlantScape System. https://www.oilandgasonline.com/doc/plantscape-system-0001.
7. SIEMENS, Robcad. https://www.plm.automation.siemens.com/zh/products/tecnomatix/manufacturing-simulation/robotics/robcad.shtml.
8. Ansys Software (2015) CHN Baidu, zhliu. http://baike.baidu.com/link?url=MYyffDQyoT44M1Bt_AGUySTwcFSXNhtcJr_FDcnC6-aG1C0OvBjAZZ-T5246zIA6TXb6BJU__QVY4IXkuwj1eq2HOEZi0E4jD7zSvfRtk3W. Accessed 29 Jun 2015.
9. 3D Print (2016) CHN Baidu, fhb340. http://baike.baidu.com/link?url=Rojd0vWKxyB3sbvXAVt_MfZq5q3y2k_WGf0PoR3TtcT5ESpSVYw2qACjM_J1ZF8WRYEICxFNqFvgg_79s6c1m_GBHvqDIgw83-ZwQ1913Wa. Accessed 14 Aug 2016.
10. Agriculture (2017) CHN Baidu, Water cloud deep waves. http://baike.baidu.com/link?url=0G1C_DTG0PHG1I4v5jVBrFlrY6A89dubC64bivndLeVKNFYxGqV3vGCFopfmpJXpmtVtRVTFt82QElDnCYFKvx3xqlt96C-SEjNhIuoh29O#reference-[1]-16684-wrap. 17 Aug 2017.
11. Fu YiDong. On the Development of Medical Science in 19th Century [J]. Divine, 2014 (14):223–223.
12. Investigation of Theories Base on The Internal Canon of Medicine about Brain and Encephalopathy (2015), CHN CNKI, Xu Feng. http://en.cnki.com.cn/Article_en/CJFDTotal-GMZY201502004.htm. Accessed Feb 2015.
13. Li Wei. Design and Realization of CAD System Based on Multi-period Liver CT Image [D]. Shanghai JiaoTong University, 2011.
14. Liu YanSong. Research and Practice of 2D Game Development Technology Based on Java [D]. Beijing Industry University, 2011.
15. GameRes (2015) Detailed description of the fighting game numerical analysis. http://www.gameres.com/468370.html. Accessed 6 Nov 2015.
16. King of Fighters (2017) CHN Sogou. http://baike.sogou.com/v60299.htm. Accessed 24 Aug 2017.

17. KTV (2017) CHN Baidu, atreylemon. http://baike.baidu.com/link?url=mXn5b5tl9fws Wyv1NUI8Yt3dv8VShw24-jVq14wfmdNq2I9vc8zjJCN4vwx8E02UFZ7KP7a5sw8a-NxTI V1Nka. Accessed 31 May 2017.
18. Yjbys (2014) Internet and Social Science Research. http://www.yjbys.com/news/296664.html. Accessed 30 Dec 2014.
19. Jiang Yuanxiang. Research on the Application of Network Protocol and Its Performance [J]. Computer programming skills and maintenance, 2011(4):59–60.
20. Network protocol (2015) CHN Baidu, lztzr. http://baike.baidu.com/link?url=fUc9iFwi2oh–dh_1TQD-gTXWWJ4QlOMLFFHyyCrhsGEVBSM9YmvUyiB0NIFfm153dSFsB87Kp6eLd dFpYsqLX3VPe1_UhPgLHcvdWEnBAnZpqFgdR9IFZUl86UUgdZG. Accessed 29 Nov 2015.
21. QQ (2017) CHN Baidu. http://baike.baidu.com/link?url=Jsqqh64G6jkyx3005t1f4ppjLD4nJ_ 7EZNrVf3akJSnPJsCkz6c3uU_Yum4vqpyaoRt3DFANtQO1xM4e7qFVxElvialhrDGjmbgy 1vzTV-FaQCHZ3iEIZbdoRyTNHepcoqMhxWd1egJrlozpW4f8Ya. Accessed 19 Aug 2017.
22. Weibo(2017) CHN Baidu, KortLou. http://baike.baidu.com/link?url=VMwpEY0gfHWGEr VNkUjkChYRYGFQnvRqJOUNhyIDn0_9vbFgR_LSD0a-cpbOs05JTxTb8x989xG1xbXt3x kz_wJQQxRqmkFUxcc3_8KTfTm. Accessed 15 Jul 2017.
23. Social Network Site (2017) CHN Baidu, dino love. http://baike.baidu.com/link?url=BVh ElRAPMc9t7nKaXWBdPkYFBhoMMhxesCzdXrwSrFL3ULaW1P9FbJ7hlH4fc7k2tywzW MuUxYuOO75_39B4Gzuw8_8aWp1okmgISapoIexzzoROe_NuUgmG5lG_mvbg. Accessed 30 Au 2017.
24. China's astronomers in the domestic super computer to achieve ultra-large-scale simulation of the universe (2010). http://www.pmo.ac.cn/xwzx/twkx/201011/t20101115_3010917.html.
25. https://en.wikipedia.org/wiki/Nuclear_fusion.
26. Harvard Business Review (2014) Internet of Things: Science Fiction or Business Fact? https://hbr.org/resources/pdfs/comm/verizon/18980_HBR_Verizon_IoT_Nov_14.pdf. Accessed 23 Oct 2016.
27. International Telecommunication Union (2015) Internet of Things Global Standards Initiative. http://www.itu.int/en/ITU-T/gsi/iot/Pages/default.aspx. Accessed 26 June 2015.
28. Komninos, Nicos (2013) What makes cities intelligent? In: Smart Cities: Governing, Modelling and Analysing the Transition. Deakin, Mark, p 77.

Printed in the United States
By Bookmasters